THE CRITIC AGONISTES

THE CRITIC AGONISTES

PSYCHOLOGY, MYTH, AND THE ART OF FICTION

By DANIEL WEISS

*Edited by Eric Solomon
and Stephen Arkin*

UNIVERSITY OF WASHINGTON PRESS
Seattle and London

The illustrations in this book all come from woodblock prints by Daniel Weiss.

Copyright © 1985 by the University of Washington Press
Printed in the United States of America

Library of Congress Cataloging in Publication Data

Weiss, Daniel, 1918–1976.
  The critic agonistes.

  Bibliography: p.
  Includes index.
  1. Psychoanalysis and literature—Addresses, essays,
lectures.   2. Fiction—History and criticism—Addresses,
essays, lectures.   I. Solomon, Eric.   II. Arkin, Stephen.
III. Title.
PN98.P75W4   1985   809.3'9353   84-21953
ISBN 0-295-96161-9

**This book was published with the assistance of
a grant from the Andrew W. Mellon Foundation.**

~

Foreword

Although psychoanalytic criticism has been with us since Freud offered some comments on *Hamlet* in 1900, its practitioners have often disappointed expectations by dwelling upon the way the mind seethes rather than upon how it constructs. The relation between psychic problems and formal structure remains problematic. Are we to read works of literature as failed or successful attempts to encompass or transform or overcome the writer's difficulties? How a writer, prompted by urges which he is unlikely to understand or even to recognize, knows which area of language will best suit his (unknown) purposes, which rhythmical and syntactical devices will embody them, and at what moment the embodiment will be ready for others to read, remain perplexing. A tendency to reduce such problems to false if manageable proportions is to be seen in most applications of psychoanalysis to literature.

Daniel Weiss stands out among such critics because he saw, when quite young and flexible, to what extent Freudian principles might be useful to him, to what extent not. His criticism therefore alternated between penetrating analysis of authors' minds and brilliant close readings of their texts. His book on D. H. Lawrence, *Oedipus in Nottingham* (Seattle: University of Washington Press, 1962), owes its strength to his skill in both modes.

In this new collection of his essays, the same powers are at work. Weiss is aware of the demonic unconscious that subsumes creation and is beyond the conscious options of the creator; yet he can also detect and mark out the ironic distance which a writer affords himself, often (in recent literature) with some sense of its absurdity, to claim disengagement from his own brainchild. Daniel Weiss's opening essays address themselves to the question of how the artist at once expresses and combats his neurotic impulses, so as to render his mind with unredeemed complexity, and yet always by reference to a normality to which he clings though it may itself be only a last fantasy. In following essays Weiss shows how writers as varied as Stephen Crane, Ernest Hemingway, Sherwood Anderson, Thomas Mann, and Saul Bellow manage to use their weaknesses as counters in their artistic productions. He is alive to the ways in which writers of the most different stamp—say Crane and Shakespeare—can be said to fantasize the worlds in which their characters live as well as the characters themselves.

Daniel Weiss points to the ways in which writers born into the age of Freud can no longer pretend to innocence of Freudian patterns of mental life, and how instead they can explore further reaches of that life. For readers there is the advantage that they can see, beneath the archaic surfaces of older works, the vivid and familiar signs of our common psychic inheritance. As Coleridge and Wordsworth relied upon the Harleyan psychology of their day, modern writers and critics can make conscious use of the vastly improved psychology which Freud offered them.

Beyond Weiss's excursions into theory and practice of criticism, his essays offer the self-portrait of a wise, witty man, flamboyant yet modest, ready to take risks yet doing so with the greatest delicacy. As he advances over unknown terrain he recognizes the pitfalls and circumvents them. He is a Freudian whose allegiance to the master is never so great as to check his delight in the pungency of literary expression, both his own and that of the writers with whom he deals.

Richard Ellmann

Contents

Editors' Preface

During the many decades he taught literature at New York University, the University of Washington, and San Francisco State University, Daniel Weiss came to be regarded as a great resource by other literary scholars. As his colleagues, office-mates, friends, and, indeed, disciples, we listened to some of the most learned, brilliant, intense, and witty literary discussion we have ever encountered. That Weiss's superb insights were shared with only a few colleagues and a relatively small group of students always bothered us, but he was a shy and proud man who rarely ventured into print. When he did decide to share some of his critical perceptions that derived from his Freudian-mythic readings of fiction—in the cases of his classic essays on Stephen Crane and Saul Bellow and his remarkable book on D. H. Lawrence—the responses of readers, reviewers, and editors of anthologies were immediate and enthusiastic. Yet he wrote articles for memorial volumes that never appeared, for journals that disappeared, and for talks and lectures that went unrecorded. Nowhere in print appeared the lovely expositions we heard about British and American fiction, critiques that combined psychoanalytic depth, literary breadth, clarity, scholarship, and humor.

When we opened Daniel Weiss's desk files after his death in 1976 at the age of fifty-eight, we began with hope and trepidation; we discovered with delight the subtle and incisive pages of critical writing that seemed to exist in a special realm of original achievement. This man who was above all an artist (he created paintings, prints, woodcuts, sculptures, and carvings) and an athlete (wrestler, runner, swimmer, judo champion) and a humorist (he wrote and illustrated three children's books) combined these aspects in his literary criticism: his writing is creative, strong, and humorous.

These papers were in three forms: published material, essays prepared for publication, and a series of notebooks (bluebooks, actually) in which he wrote what he used as lectures but what we discovered to be carefully constructed articles. We read some thousand pages of manuscript and selected those included in this volume based on three criteria: sheer excellence of literary criticism; a finished contribution to the general theme of mythic, philosophical, and psychoanalytic literary theory; and a concentration on the art of the novel. Reluctantly, we omitted some excellent writing on Kafka, Fitzgerald, James, Mansfield, Shakespeare, Yeats, and Joyce.

Our editorial hands were not heavy. Previously published essays are reprinted here with no changes, except for minor modifications for the sake of typographical consistency. The unpublished essays have only a few corrections of spelling from the original manuscript. Notes citing sources and page numbers for quoted material have been added throughout the essays wherever appropriate. "The Critic Agonistes" and "The Black Art of Psychoanalytic Criticism of Literature," both in typescript, now include some changes for the sake of grammar and consistency and a few omissions to avoid redundancy. The first of these theoretical essays Weiss prepared for a memorial volume in honor of Fritz Schmidl, while the second was a public lecture, as was "Ernest Hemingway: The Stylist of Stoicism." As for "Shedding His Sickness in Books: Sherwood Anderson's Literary Case History," which appeared typed in a notebook, we cut some Anderson quotations that seemed excessive. We are grateful for the appropriate permissions to print the following essays: "The Red Badge of Courage," *The Psychoanalytic Review*, vol. 52, nos. 2, 3 (Summer and Fall 1965); "William

Faulkner and the Runaway Slave," *Northwest Review*, vol. 6, no. 3 (Summer 1963); "Caliban on Prospero: A Psychoanalytic Study on the Novel *Seize the Day* by Saul Bellow," *The American Imago*, vol. 19, no. 3 (Fall 1962); "Freudian Criticism: Frank O'Connor as Paradigm," *Northwest Review*, vol. 2, no. 2 (Spring 1959); and "D. H. Lawrence: The Forms of Sexual Hunger," which was published as part of chapter 4 in *Oedipus in Nottingham* (Seattle: University of Washington Press, 1962).

Weiss admired Sigmund Freud's reading of Sophocles' *Oedipus Rex* in part because the struggle to elucidate the meaning of a text gives way to the more important struggle to elucidate the meaning of human experience. In Freud's response to Sophocles, reader and writer are bound up in an activity that mimics the artist's own struggle to objectify and give meaning to the observed voices from the cellar of consciousness. Daniel Weiss was drawn to writers who wrestled with the psyche, who tried either to illuminate its workings or to win from it one true tale. His allegiance was first and most powerfully to Freud—and to Freud's own sources in the classics of Greek and Shakespearean drama as well as in the nineteenth-century philosophical giants. Freud's break with biological renderings of the mind and his exploration of the much darker realms of the psyche fascinated Weiss. And he in turn read literature not through the template of received Freudian opinion but in the headier, more adventurous spirit of relishing the play between obstreperous material and formal ordering strategies. He also read, and wrote, as an authentic ironist, whose quiet wit, specially cultivated sense of the ridiculous, and admiration for the comic in literature from Aristophanes to Benchley let him laugh both at heavy texts and at heavy interpretations of texts, and, best of all, at himself when his writing threatened to become solemn or pretentious.

In these essays, and particularly in the first two, Weiss's interest in Freud manifestly encompasses an interest in the nineteenth-century climate of ideas, a fascination with how "the high octanes of the mind, Kant's moral categories and Hegel's absolute mind . . . give way to crude diesels of Schopenhauer's and Nietzsche's and Freud's Will." How *mind* in its loftiest consideration becomes *will* in its somewhat battered form is the intellectual problem that Daniel Weiss confronted. If he does not seem to show signs in these pages of being overly involved in contemporary debates about psychoanalytic procedure or criticism, if he seems indifferent to object theory, French tailoring of Freud, and the various structures (*tristes* and not *tristes*) the clever interpreter can deconstruct down to, it is because Weiss was classical by temperament and, having staked out a problem area that fascinated him, stayed within it. He was a genuinely learned man, and he brought to his text his rich, scholarly memory of English literature, European history and philosophy, Greek art and drama, psychology, folklore, and anthropology.

If he was not as wide-ranging a reader of modern works as he might have been, Daniel Weiss became a great literary critic when he found in a contemporary writer such as Saul Bellow a significant encounter with materials Weiss knew intimately. He is, in the best sense, a deep reader of those authors, ancient or modern, who show signs of having won from the clash of psychic forces the kind of poised response, however troublesome or difficult, however beautiful or serene, that we call art.

Daniel Weiss was a scholar for all seasons, at once profound and responsive. *The Critic Agonistes* is a distillation of the best of Weiss and, therefore, of the best of Freudian-*cum*-historical literary criticism. As Theodore Roethke, one of Weiss's favorite poets and best friends, put it: "In a dark time, the eye begins to see . . . a steady storm of correspondence." Weiss was a good man for dark times or bright moments; his essays reflect the shadows and lights of what he discovered in great fiction, in the inner lives of authors and characters.

S. A. & E. S.

THE CRITIC AGONISTES

1 ~

ON FREUDIANISM
AND THE CRITIC

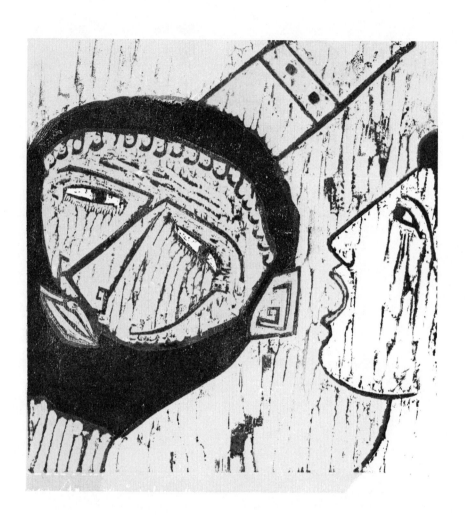

1.

The Critic Agonistes

I

For a long time I have allowed the techniques of psychoanalysis to take the first fruits of my attention in the critical reading and interpretation of literature. In the beginning I conceived of Freudian criticism, despite its limited acceptance as a method, as being, in a phrase from Thomas Mann, "highly questionable." I practiced it with self-indulgent irony as a compulsion of character rather than as a conviction of intellect. This was, originally, a very bad arrangement, with too many built-in disloyalties, like being a Roman *augur* or *flamen* moonlighting with Christians in the catacombs. Also my own modern sense of pluralism made me distrustful of a system that had failed to meet with any general acceptance. From psychoanalysis I had learned that any coherent system of ordering reality operates like a mystery religion whose rituals culminate in an epiphany or theophany in which all its communicants see the *same* thing without any assurance that it is the *real* thing.

But the years have made me nervier, not because Time is regularly the bearer of acceptances, but because these particular Times, whether lax or adventurous, seem to encourage one to transgress freely beyond the statutes of morality and esthetics. "Civic mediocrity"—the phrase is Nietzsche's, and it is entirely possible that I am writing in his spirit—has made us libertines of our own wills and encouraged us to think and write loosely, and if necessary, confessionally about our relations with learned matters. The high octanes of the mind, Kant's moral categories and Hegel's Absolute Mind, seem now to have given way to the crude diesels of Schopenhauer's and Nietzsche's and Freud's Will. There are moments, and this seems to be one of them, when civilization loses control of its history, if it ever had control, and history stops being a record of decisions and the lives of great men and becomes a galvanism of the will mumbled over by ideologues, demagogues, and gog magogs, and the world sings, as Joyce might put it, "It's a long way to Temporary."

Psychoanalysis, so far as the modern personality is concerned, has come to serve as a practical nexus for every shading of voluntaristic thought. Applied psychoanalysis, extended beyond therapy and even a coherent, defensible body of theory —popularized, simplified, and practiced—has seeped into that fecund stratum of human awareness where all sense competes for our scientific, moral, and aesthetic attention.

On the practical level, somewhere below the precise horizon of intellect, hull down, so to speak, with a tip of mainmast showing to prove that I have feeling and beliefs—in, as Beckett says in *Molloy*, "the brain and heart and other caverns where thought and feeling dance their sabbath"—I look upon psychoanalysis not just as a new set of data toyed with by the acquisitive artist or systematically used by the critic, but as descriptive of the conditions that have formed the consciousness of both. Under certain circumstances the artist cannot escape exhibiting these conditions, and by the same token the critic should not, if he has his insight before him, opt out of bringing the exhibition to the reader's attention. The silence of discretion and aesthetic selectivity is no longer a negative adjunct to criticism.

What this means so far as my professional relation to art is concerned involves the expanded consideration of what it means so far as my whole relation to experience is concerned.

It means, first of all, that at this specific historical moment in the flood-tide of its ambiguous material and spiritual evolution I am aware of energies rising about me which I can only imperfectly understand. I recognize them as collectively supra-human, as destructive of their agents as they are of those who follow them. Even allowing for the deep intoxications of the Church, I think that most of mankind in the past were stolidly pragmatic about their physical and moral conditions. I think that we moderns are becoming at an accelerated rate the restless children of pure thought, of disembodied energy. I must acknowledge these energies; whether I respect them or not is no matter, any more than a volcano would solicit my understanding, tolerance, or admiration. To detest them is to invoke egoistic privilege without being sure whether my ego is a citadel or a snag in the stream of things. To fear the energies is more excusable; it is an intrinsic part of the experience. I think sometimes that our national exuberance, the joy of excess, is in itself an antidote to the fears that attend our equivocal decade.

This acceptance means, on a more sober note of response, an enlightened self-awareness, an educated clarity of introspection, not too remote from the spiritual exercises of the religious mystic, but "perfumed," as the Tibetans would describe it, with all the desires and activities that ordinarily clutter one's life.

Such a position means, also, an unpreventably morbid and obsessive self-consciousness that can make of self-knowledge an instrument of torture. We have come to realize that nothing can betray a person with as much cruelty and finesse as one's own body and mind, that our compulsions and hysterias are moral and biological fictions in the service of psychological realities. It means that out of this heightened self-awareness we are incapable of attaching unitary values to our actions, that all the margins of moral choice and impulsive preference tend to blur into one another. It means that we try to be in the highest degree responsible for our actions and hold in equal respect (or distrust) the complexities of other minds. And this in turn means that we are morbidly responsible and push the terms of our own victimizings to the point of self-sacrifice, and nag each other to despair with understanding. It means pursuing integrity of intention to the Kafkaesque length of not being able to take yes for an answer.

This state of mind means, finally, that we are committed to an ongoing *hubris* in which we find more transcendence in the shallows of our own pleasures and griefs than in the culturally induced profundities that history has arranged for us. We conceive our moralities, our relations, and our arts in the light of their felt authenticity. We cultivate the most difficult and dangerous of capabilities: the ability to move about freely inside our own skins. We are always on the verge of personal mythologies.

Here is where the artist comes in. In the ambience of the psychoanalytic viewpoint, he has emerged with even greater confirmation as the great empiric of psychology, but at the cost of certain time-honored prerogatives that have traditionally been his. Nietzsche, writing about philosophers in *Beyond Good and Evil*, could as easily have been writing about the artist: "Gradually it has become clear to me what every great philosophy so far has been: namely, the personal confession of the author and a kind of involuntary and unconscious memoir." [1] If there is an art to art, I would maintain, then, that it lies exclusively in the capability for objectifying the "involuntary and unconscious memoir." I would argue that rather than dichotomizing between the psychoanalytic drift toward mental determinism and the brilliant options of the artist, one could better combine the two and describe the artist's work in terms of its brilliant inevitabilities, determinism rendered as necessity. At the height of his mimetic function the artist exhibits the disconcerting, almost stupid literalness of the mirror whose sinister capacity it is to reconcile our right hand with our left in the process of reflecting us to ourselves. Stendhal's mirror ("dawdling down a lane") is a trick mirror after all.

Yet I cannot simply maintain that a work of art is merely equatable with an interesting case history, that Flaubert's Emma Bovary is on the same footing with Freud's Dora. I think it is quite likely that sustained flights of creative activity can normally be catastrophic to the psychic life reserved for personal relations. In practice creativity becomes for the artist a complex matter of calculated risk and sacrifice that is comparable to the chances a soldier must take in excess of his ordinary prudence. Artists live, I imagine, with their eyes glued to one opening in themselves, like obsessed madmen. This obsession accounts for their extraordinary powers coupled with equally extraordinary limitations so that with all their cunning they can be caught in the flimsiest of nets. Most of us are happy to live all over our bodies, and in so doing sacrifice the sharp satisfaction of one single separate talent. Freud was after all spared Dora's soul-shattering misery; Flaubert subjected himself to Emma's (*"Mme. Bovary, c'est moi"*). The artist is the athlete of the Will; his mind is too libertine for sustained rationality. That is why he is often desperate in his own life and why his work sometimes intimidates us into "correct" aesthetic attitudes, in spite of our sense of deeper urgencies.

It may be that by some strange dispensation there remains a portion of the artist's mind forever undeeded to the standard causalities, as if the unconscious itself were educable (which it is) and emerged manifest in the work of art with an advanced degree in psychology without the artist's having to bother much about how and where he got his clues.

Freud's sense of the vivid fantasy-life of the infantile psyche, that period which Erik Erikson assigns to the birthplace of manmade cosmologies and world religions as well as schizophrenic disorders, may apply in an amplified form to the infancies of men of genius. In childhood, when the vegetative self literally crawls behind the mind, it is conceivable that an infant might *normally* be shaken by a nervous intelligence too vast for him to command through acts of conceptualization or cognition.[2] His maturity as artist would then preserve unchanged the dark core of sounds and shapes and inchoate recognitions as the normal and not the aggravated and traumatic baggage of his mind. Metaphor, seeking always to restore the unity of the differentiated world, seems to reflect the preverbal, oceanic mood of infancy. Metaphor is averse to the precise distinctions of language, which it subverts at every opportunity, and is, in effect, the nirvana of language. Certainly, this would seem to be the testimony borne out in the relation of the first few pages of Joyce's *A Portrait of the Artist as a Young Man* to the subsequent unfolding of the novel.

Nietzsche observes in *The Birth of Tragedy*, speaking of the Greek philosophers and poets, that

> . . . their heroes speak, as it were, more superficially than they act; the myth does not at all obtain adequate objectification in the spoken word. The structure of the scenes and the intuitively created images reveal a deeper wisdom than the poet himself can put into words and concepts: the same is also observable in Shakespeare, whose Hamlet, for instance, similarly talks more superficially than he acts. So that the previously mentioned lesson of Hamlet is to be deduced, not from his words, but from a profound contemplation and survey of the whole.[3]

It is not difficult from such suggestions for me to conceive that behind every drama there is a dream-opera or pantomime, full of histrionics and perhaps of questionable merit; and behind every novel, poem, or articulate form, there is some level of intelligibility where the work may be apprehended as a sound, or a sense of physical agitation, alternations of rest and movement, categories of infantile experience much broader and more benign than the Freudian concepts of primal scene, birth trauma, and the like.

These observations are not in themselves meant to be conclusive; they represent two heuristic assumptions, based on the premises of psychoanalytic theory and the admittedly shaky evidence of introspection. The first of these is my perhaps exaggerated belief that between the artist and his work there is a metamorphic identity, that the luxury traditionally his—the ironic distance between himself and his art—is reducible under psychoanalytic scrutiny to zero. And secondly, that there is, finally, within the nexus of the work of art a unity of artist, art, and audience, which is not only possible but necessary to aesthetic pleasure. The artist becomes, for the audience (that hypothetically ideal auditor) its alter ego, alter id, alter superego, and all the interstices between. Psychoanalysis suggests, if it does not always fulfill, this possibility.

II

Simply stated, Freudian criticism begins with the assumption that the creative process involves always a *demonic unconscious* whose contributions to the work of art are beyond the options of the artistic consciousness, and indeed often seem to represent all that is antithetical to the artist's avowed intentions. The contents of the demonic unconscious consist of wishes, impulses, instinctual aims, and objects that the ego has abandoned in the interests of its own safety, "the daily cares and convenient cowardices of men." The unconscious includes also, as I have suggested, certain precognitive forms of experience, which, while they are exempted from the tariffs of repression and the smuggler's ruse, have nothing to declare except their own innocent and enigmatic manifestations.

The conscious mind, assailed by ideas that are unacceptable to it, represses them, pursues a course of actions designed to ward off anxieties and conflicts or the merely irrational. But the consciousness never succeeds completely in resisting the dark undertow of instinctual demands. These make their appearance as more or less socially acceptable forms of action, or—at their most oppressive, as hysterias, obsessions, or as vicarious and perverse forms of gratification—in short, as any of the numberless vices and many of the virtues that mankind has contrived for control of these demands. At their best, these instinctual urgings can culminate in the highest productions of a culture: myth, religion, philosophy, government, and art. Psychoanalytic criticism transfers these unconsciously determined structures to works of literature, and assumes that these same conflicts and resolutions are just as normally generated in the fictitious world of art, assumes in fact that when a work of literature depicts (as is most often the case) a splendid ego in trouble, one source of its difficulty must inevitably be its own divided consciousness.

I can render this approach to the work of art graphically by dividing it into three concentric circles of interest. In the outer circle is the work of literature as a social phenomenon, morally and aesthetically acceptable, deliberately created and analyzable as a poetic communication. In the middle circle is the work of literature as a personal phenomenon, newly born in the artist's consciousness, a product of autobiography and craft, revisions and calculations, and smuggled contraband intentions. There lies the frontier between the Greeks and the Cimmerians, between clarity and obscurity. In the inner circle the work of literature exists, if it exists at all, as an inchoate, almost a biological phenomenon, a horde of urgencies in search of an outlet, levels below personality where the artist becomes *genus neurosis*, a mythical, or a psychological essence. This is the involitional level at which the uncalculated passionate interest of the artist communicates itself to the uncalculated interest and response of the audience.

The outermost circle of the work bears the same relation to the inner circles that a reliquary of silver and gold and precious stones might bear to the skull it encloses: a fact of existence is transfigured, one might say more accurately, denied by the other, to the intensification of both. If the outer circle is an aesthetic elaboration, it is from the inner circle that the elaboration issues. In the tensions among these circles the work of art subsists, and one may formulate this tension as between the aesthetic emotion (conceived as an emotion bent wholly so far as the artist is concerned on the production of a formal objectification of a sensual idea) and the welter of impulses clamoring for inclusion, between static enjoyment and active desire. The Freudian critic proposes that the work of art, both as product and process, performs the serviceable function of counteracting

instinctual excitement, specifically sexual excitement, in both
the artist and his audience, by binding it into forms which do
not in themselves possess any direct erotic appeal, but which
nevertheless transmit the allowably eroticized account of experiences that are the permanently increasing subject matter of
art. Life and death, relations human and divine, are invariably
treated in terms of the erotic polarities of love and hate and their
spiritual abstracts, good and evil, mortality and life eternal—
but never on a strict commodity basis, unless to show by
omission how essential the passions are to us.

There are two examples in modern fiction of the deliberate
use of these circles as a part of the work itself. Joyce's *A Portrait
of the Artist as a Young Man* and Thomas Mann's *Death in Venice*
are twin expressions of the dialogue between art and instinct;
what makes them particularly interesting when one considers
them together is that they go in opposite directions. In Joyce's
novel Stephen Dedalus constructs his aesthetic out of the not-
so-delicate smells and temperatures of urine, experiences of
infantile fears, fantasies, and inchoate sexual discriminations,
which ascend in increasingly expanding circles of consciousness, to emerge finally as a set of aesthetic axioms, in which the
original sexual objects still figure as disingenuously selected examples. In Mann's *Death in Venice*, the artist, Aschenbach,
whose *hamartia*, in Mann's eyes, has been his overdevelopment
of the aesthetic circle, is driven, in ever-narrowing circles,
down to the nonaesthetic, specific sexual excitement of his
latent, narcissistic, homosexual attraction to the juvenile embodiment of his idealized self. It is an excitement against which
he has defended himself all the days of his years.

For both artists these tensions were crucially intrinsic to their
art. Mann, the last flower, perhaps, of German Romanticism,
deliberately fashioned himself into the median man between
the Titanism of unchecked freedoms, political or personal, and
the Olympian sterility of control. And Joyce, inspired by
Nietzsche's creative materialism and Ibsen's mythical naturalism, repelled and attracted by the fleshless doctrines of the-

osophy, and imprisoned by Catholic dogma, conceived of art as discarnate life.

This discussion and my invocation of James Joyce and Thomas Mann lead inevitably by links too broad to be avoided to two of the most basic contributions that Freud, not to mention his predecessors, has made to the psychoanalytic study of literature: the libido theory of sexuality and the concept of disease, privation, and trauma in relation to creativity, as set forth in such essays as "The Poet and Daydreaming," *Beyond the Pleasure Principle*, "Three Contributions to a Theory of Sexuality," *Leonardo da Vinci*, and many more of equal importance. All of these make of art the cathartic method of choice for the artist— as opposed to the neurotic or psychotic personality, or that archaic Victorian type, "the Doer"—by which libidinal drives are reduced or gratified.

Let me consider libido theory for a moment within the narrow context of my claim to egoistic privilege. Sexuality, as a concept in psychoanalytic theory, is summed up in Freud's cryptic, almost Eleusinian statement that "originally we knew only sexual things." To this I make my *credo* (to which the cynical might add . . . *quia absurdum*) as much on the basis of empirical acceptance as on the basis of Freud's abundant ramification of that axiom. Let us say then that sexuality so far as one can conceptualize it as an overriding energetic force must remain forever a collaborative arrangement between oneself and the psychologist (or physiologist, or theologian) of one's choice: in my case, Freud.[4]

Sexuality, then, becomes for *us* a kind of absolute metaphysical alternative to all that in one's experience one wishes to, or must for expediency's sake, redeem from an immediate identification with sensual pleasure. And even these redeemed territories, the gray tundras of duty, pain, or deprivation, are of necessity "watered" by libidinal energies, as if thought itself were sexualized by its own mental endocrine system. The pervasiveness is so elusive, so "metaphysical," that sexuality defeats any one-to-one identification with any single erotic phenomenon, and in an outrageous and eunuchoid statement to which the orgasm is merely the first best retort. But the psyche will have the last word, and there sexuality seems to be not so much a describable state as the mockingbird of states. Sexuality here becomes a state of psychic weightlessness, and perhaps the interpretation of flight as a sexual symbol is saying something like this: I am led to believe that sexuality as a total event is a metaphor, literally a vehicle, for all the unbound elements in our personalities. It is the mode in which we recoup our losses in all our other more restricted or frustrated aims, in which we regain our lost childhoods, lost parents, lost companions, and lost joys.

If, as I have suggested, the artist is nascent among the illegible forms of infancy, it may perhaps follow that his art is the product of the latency period when sexuality must really levitate for want of any organ-complicity and become a circle whose center is nowhere and whose circumference is everywhere. Then the child begins to manipulate the object-world for its pleasures, then starts what is for the artist, as Phyllis Greenacre describes it, his love affair with the world.[5]

The idea of art as therapy is at least as old as Aristotle's *Poetics*, but it is not—particularly as Freud conceives of it in terms of neurotic conflicts, deprivations, and traumas—particularly popular with many artists and critics. Therapeutic art leaves out too much that is positive and sublime and otherwise unaccountable in poetry, the lion's roar of such men as Sophocles, Shakespeare, and Goethe. It conceives of the poet in the unfortunate analogy of the daydreamer, the man with the impediment, the sensitive plant. Art/therapy derives, certainly, from the inevitable perspective Freud gained from the Romantic poet—crushed by the heavy weight of "the weary and unintelligible world," by industrialism, social alienation, the rise of the urban masses. The idea is sustained by Nietzsche's continuation of Schiller's dichotomies of naive and sentimental poetry, a dreaming that combines Greek unities of mind and body with the spiritual well-being of the Gothic. Byron's crippled leg (not the

Devil's clubbed foot after all, but an atrophied calf muscle which mortified him), Shelley's death-instinct, and Heine's consumption are the images before Freud which led him to what has been called "the disease theory of art." Nor is Freud the first to promulgate such a theory. Dostoevsky, for example, considered his epilepsy to be truly the *morbus sacer* which offered him the privileged glimpse of the human spirit as the exalted sufferer, infinitely preferable to "cheap happiness." Certain writers *do* have the authority of their own diseases, and Freudian criticism of necessity postulates a scale of pathologies and morbidities and their social normalizations when a critic inspects an artist's work. Of those who follow Freud, perhaps Thomas Mann, on whom the influence of the psychoanalytic movement is incalculable, first put the disease theory of the creative impulse into a major work of fiction, equating illness, whether of mind or body or even of the State itself, with the emergence of the artist. From *Buddenbrooks* to *Doctor Faustus* the thesis remains a constant one. By the time he composed *Death in Venice*, Mann could describe the pathological etiology of the work of art in crystalline form, when he observes in an authorial aside on the morbid source of Aschenbach's inspiration: "Verily it is well for the world that it sees only the beauty of the completed work and not its origins, nor the conditions whence it sprang; since knowledge of the artist's inspiration might often but confuse and alarm and so prevent the full power of its excellence."[6]

Let me give the disease theory of art its full credit before I qualify it: We have always a tendency to respect sickness; it is the familiar antechamber to the mysteries of death, and with the idea of death we cope with fugitive glimpses of the mental processes of ancient and primitive cultures as they assured themselves of immortality, immunity to further suffering, and reunions with those maternal images whose names are legion. Suffering *does* confer a *vicious* grace upon us. From it comes our capacity for taking identities upon ourselves like crosses.

Whether one's mind is at full stretch, like Shakespeare's, or closed in some pathological contraction, like Strindberg's, makes no difference if the artist can but find a language out of the fruitfulness of a divided talent.

One may safely say without any *immediate* fear of contradiction that death is thrown away upon the dying, but the artist who is confronted with it and is up to its rigorous instruction is apt to become a better artist overnight. The rest of us become at the very least amateur eschatologists.[7]

But one must look beyond the negative aspect of disease for the power of the artist, and this supplement to mere daydreaming is contained in the conception of the work of the artist as a positive act of aggression, a kind of crime committed by the artist against society, which then either acquits him by awarding him its admiring attention, or condemns him by rejecting his work. When we conceive of art as a pseudocriminal activity, we can then more freely conceive of it as something more than an entertainment (a tendency I sometimes discover in Freud), rather as the highest form of moral protest against the inertia of the great world. The poet becomes a minority of one who puts his finger on the precise center of the ulcer; he disinfects the will, he staves off the moral claustrophobia we feel when a single world view seems to be having things all its own way. Again the perspective is Romantic and the mood Promethean, with the artist cast (permanently, it seems) in the role of exile and nay-sayer. The most eloquent spokesman for this view is of course Nietzsche, who celebrates the artist-criminal everywhere, but nowhere so clearly as in *The Birth of Tragedy* when he speaks of the relationship of Aeschylus' Prometheus to Dionysian revolt, and exclaims in *Beyond Good and Evil*: "Dionysus is the God of the artist-criminal! Dionysus, the genius of the heart—the Great Hidden One—The Tempter God and born rat-catcher of the conscience."[8] Otto Rank's violently anti-Freudian and clandestinely anti-semitic *Beyond Psychology* frankly echoes Nietzsche in its distinction between the life-

constricting Jewish guilt-ridden need for and fear of punishment and the "creative presumption" that motivates the "genuine creators of culture," i.e., artists.[9]

But in describing the artist as the moral protester I do not
mean the artist as social critic in any positive sense. The psychoanalytic conception of the union of crime and disease does
not warrant any such straightforward program of reform or
amelioration, and for this reason the limited official imagination conceives of art as immoral, or obscene, or subversive,
when it may, in fact, be at its moral best.

Freudian criticism is constantly measuring its social norms
against, in Mann's phrase, "the creatures of the abyss." The recent revival of interest in the life and the writing of de Sade
commands our interest here. He was, we might say, one of the
creatures of the abyss, and he proposed a hard question to the
champions of individual freedom, who in their blueprints for
personal liberties, rarely take into consideration the sexual deviations of a de Sade. The Freudian critic has perhaps an easier task
of reconciling social norms with personal deviations through
his view of art as a method of articulating crime and disease and
other social disorders. He views these negative and antisocial
elements as distortions of what is in fact a normative and developmental process, whose appearance in life is a nuisance but
whose appearance in art is freedom itself, one might say, a
millennial, speculative freedom, which is perhaps why great
creative works are several hundred years in reaching their most
understanding audience. There is no such thing as an unbound,
entirely free mind. What one admires as a free mind, one that
explores the alternatives of existence in life and art, represents
simply the struggles of a bound mind to free itself from the tyrannies of culture. Cultural tyrannies are not necessarily bad;
they are merely limiting, and limitations to the whole mind of
man, whose chief characteristic, we are told, is freedom, are
categorically unendurable, like the existence of heaven without
hell, or love without hate.

I define a *hero* as a man who asks more from life than it can possibly give him: in the realm of action, a place and power; in the realm of character, freedom of the will; in the realm of thought, an epistemological security and moral justification. Now, in literature, the Freudian critic will argue, the greatest artist will produce such a hero without discounting the abyss. He will combine the "maximum of intensity"—of exposure— that phrase that Hemingway uses with intentional ambiguity to describe bullfighting and writing, controlled by a form. The three circles I have described earlier are useful here. The theater of the exposure becomes the outer circle; the source of the exposure the inner one. Freud's theory of repression, and art as the benign transgression of the forbidden, becomes the mediating agent in the form of the symbol.

The Freudian symbol and the process of symbolization differ radically in at least two respects from the accepted idea of the literary symbol. As it is generally conceived, the literary symbol is a concrete and untranslatable presentation of an idea, or an experience that cannot find its way into consciousness except through the mediation of the symbol. Its main attributes are, then, its concreteness as opposed to the abstraction it represents, and its unique appropriateness to that abstraction. The symbol is under no obligation as to a restriction of the scope and nature of the materials it uses.

In Freud we return to the concept of repression, the existence of unacceptable ideas and their distortion in consciousness, in order to describe another kind of symbolism. Once again there is a forerunner of Freud: this time Schopenhauer, who perceives a contrast between the "dark, impetuous impulse of willing, whose focal point is genital," and the "eternal, freed, serene object of pure knowing, whose focal point is the brain— at their most perfect when they are in balance . . . and like the sun provide heat for the animal spirit and light for the human intellect."[10]

Madmen and geniuses, says Schopenhauer, "leave out of sight knowledge of the connection of things in order (so far as genius is concerned) to try to grasp their *real inner nature* in regard to which one thing represents its whole species and one case is valid for a thousand." So far this sounds like the classical description of the symbol. But then he goes on to describe the creative mind divided against itself ("the antagonism in the heart of the world" is Nietzsche's phrase), the unconscious resistance to the writer's commitment to sacrifice himself to the truth. The psychology of the creative act turns from the traditional idea of the artist struggling against some intractable medium—like the sculptor's struggle with stone—to the artist attempting (like Franz Kafka's K) to justify himself against a body of demonic accusers. For Schopenhauer the supreme symbol of the creative act is contained in the *Oedipus* of Sophocles; Jocasta represents the passive, feminine spirit of conservatism—repression, begging Oedipus for God's sake not to seek the truth.

In Freudian symbolism the symbol evolves from the resistance to the truth of the unconscious. Rather than a unique appropriateness the symbol expresses what one may call a unique *oppositeness* to the unconscious idea. The symbol's common denominator is the meaningful concealment of the truth as the truth promises to emerge as some frightening or forbidden idea. This concept is based on the laws of *tabu*, in which the sacred and the reverential are subordinated to the accursed and the polluted. Metaphor and symbol arising in connection with these concepts tend regularly to falsify: the Furies were designated the Gracious Goddesses, or "good years" to represent plague years. Sexual and excretory acts have likewise gathered together for themselves a vast and picturesque language.

Therefore a symbol, in a psychoanalytic sense of the term, shifts the notion of the symbol as a concrete referent *for* an idea to a notion of the symbol as deriving *from* a concrete referent that has been disallowed.[11] "Originally, we knew only sexual things," the axiom holds here. All the objects that commanded our infantile attention were objects either of desire or loathing, whatever their intrinsic nature as objects. Everything, in short, became a confused reflection of our organs or our desires. The sexual period of early childhood is followed by that uniquely human period, the latency period, in which these early memories of fixation are repressed as dangerous or socially undesirable, or guilt-producing, to all intents and purposes forgotten. When subsequently the child abandons these identifications, the names of such objects, or their images, retain the energies of the original sexual identification.[12] Poetry and art renew these prehistoric identifications through symbols.

Implicit in the legal and moral condemnation of pornographic or obscene art is an unconscious resistance to being pulled back again into this world of original sexuality—to be overcome, as it were, publicly, with a private urge. The Freudian symbol, then, is conceived of as an equation whose more important member is repressed as the result of cultural education, while the other, the less important member, attains to an over-affective significance and becomes a symbol for the repressed one. The world's great symbols, as they emerge in religious icons—symbols of rebirth, rejuvenation, resurrection—are seen as memorials to the anxieties that attend our biological rhythms. The anxiety is mastered by being displaced to a universal religious, scientific, philosophical, or, in pursuit of our interests, a meaningful aesthetic experience. This anxiety is mastered by dint of repetitions, by the substitution of controlled rituals, and by condensation into a unified and benign experience—the tragic drama, for example—that excludes the accidental and the unpredictable.

Thus the Bible transforms the fear, even the hatred, of God into "hymn books which resound with a melodious cursing of God and enduring him forever," as Thoreau mischievously puts it. Tolstoy in *The Death of Ivan Ilych* converts his fear of the "dragon of death" into the love of death; Swift disguises his obsession with dirt and sexuality by dedicating the obsession to public, socially acceptable ends, until it becomes altogether fitting that in denying the totally debased anal eroticism of the

Yahoos, who are forced to eat their own feces, he should dedicate his Augustan stable of horse-sense to the one animal, the horse, whose dung is least offensive to the human nostril.

By extension, the Freudian symbol infers what must be called the Freudian character. By this I mean that Freudian criticism has learned to distrust and look below the manifest intentions of character in action. At times the artist himself invites us to look below these intentions, and to that end under the stimulus of depth psychology, modern writers and readers have developed a morbid accuracy of understanding. At other times, perhaps the best of times, the artist appears to be entirely oblivious to the symbolic drift of his own intentions. Into the definition of the Freudian character we can carry the same qualities we associated with the symbol: the tendency of such characters to pursue courses of action that are opposite to the secret causes of that action, and the tendency of such characters to convert their repressed motivations to some rational, socially acceptable (and social condemnation can be seen as a negative form of acceptance: e.g., murder as surrogate for homosexual love) and seemingly justifiable forms of behavior. In other words, the character tends to proceed from a buried concrete referent to a visible and symbolic one.

Freud's closely drawn analogy between art and neurosis postulates always as the highest form of art the conflict between the artist and his subject, between the primordial demands of the artist's instincts crying out of his unconscious and the repressive demands of his social conscience, bidding him submit. The artist tends, following the model of neurosis, to project his quarrels with himself upon society, his stars, and his relatives. He transfers his infantile loves and hates to gods, kings, presidents, and fathers. In order to persuade himself that his strivings are justifiable, he conceives of bad things—temptations—as happening outside himself. ("And the woman said the serpent beguiled me and I did eat," is the way it began.)

But at the same time Freud's inexorable dialectic will insist that, as Mann has put it: "We are actually bringing about what is happening to us." The illusions that we are victims of life, society, bad luck, are a part of the "externality fallacy." We make the terms of our own victimizings. For Nietzsche this quarrel with oneself is productive of the highest achievements of which civilization is capable: ". . . among the Greeks the conditions were unusually favorable for the development of the individual; not by any means owing to the goodness of the people, but because of the struggles of their evil instincts."[13] For Freud the origins of the quarrel are humble; it originates in the phantasmagoric relations that the infant establishes with its own drives and its immediate environment—its parents. In maturity these fantasied relations, these drives, undergo repression, abandonment, and at their best emerge as purified reflections of themselves in religion, art, and ethics. At their worst they emerge in crime, disease, and discontents. Oedipus Rex—or oedipal wreckage—seem to be the alternatives to the preconditions of infancy offered us.

Great creative activity is always a paradoxical exercise of freedom and response to the tides of existence. Born into an age whose emotional horizons are vast and expansive, in an instant that occurs in every age when the awakening mind sees the grand form of its being and remembers the start as an impression which will survive the careful explanations and ascriptions which will finally contain it, a great artist, Shakespeare, for example, will produce out of his own experience remembrances of things past so profound that they suggest dichotomies of permanence and change, universals and particulars, rather than the dichotomy between a singularly great psychic reality and a singularly receptive external reality.

III

I should like to describe in general terms how Freudian criticism approaches tragic drama, or, more generally stated, a tragic action. The criticism must first clear the immediate foreground of its apparent claim to a realistic motivation, and re-establish the drama's relations with the underlying fantasy. Thus Freudian criticism has an exasperating way of destroying the entire superstructure of a work of art before the critic can get down to analysis. This involves moving the secret cause of the action to a point, not before the play begins, as Aristotle proposes, or when the book begins, but before the original infantile fantasies have been abandoned.

Ella Freeman Sharpe has proposed, in the most ecumenical statement on record, that the life of Christ in its broad outlines provides us with the prototype for all tragic heroes.[14] A child is born to a mother undefiled by any man, and he the son of an unknown and exalted father. The son shows great promise in early childhood. He enters his ministry and is criminally defiant of the debased fathers of the church; he raises up the fallen namesake of his virgin mother; he has private communications with his heavenly father. He enters Jerusalem triumphantly in the hybris of his bold crime; he is arrested and offers himself up as a willing victim to Fate. He is executed, dies, and is resurrected in glory, after which he is reconciled with his father and raises up his mother to sit at his right hand. The life of Christ exhibits at its most complete a number of basic Oedipal fantasies—described in Freud's *Collected Papers*: notably in his "Contributions to a Theory of Sexuality," "A Child is Being Beaten," and "The Passing of the Oedipus Complex" and in Otto Rank's *The Myth of the Birth of the Hero*; Lord Raglan's nonpsychological work *The Hero* is a mechanical listing of the heroic traits and provides on the most disinterested basis a checklist for attributes that mesh organically in the psychoanalytic studies. What is significantly absent, except as renunciation, is the sexual component of the Oedipus legend. The Son redeems his mother, but he does not claim her. It will remain for medieval iconography and the convent's vows to identify the Church itself and its consecrated virgins with the Mother as Christ's consort.

When we move these elements into the realm of secular literature we find that they domesticate themselves readily to a broad variety of cultural and historical situations. Freud found the confirmation to his theory of the Oedipus complex in three widely separated works: the *Oedipus Rex* of Sophocles, Shakespeare's *Hamlet*, and Dostoevsky's *The Brothers Karamazov*.[15] In each there is a parricide, or a parricidal intent; in each there is a maternal figure who is the object of a guilty and incestuous love; in each there is a process by which the crime of aggression is succeeded by an act of submission or self-sacrifice, the reward for which is a posthumous or moral justification. In each the artist has worked through the plenary capacity of mankind for self-exploration to the brink of discovery but no further.

I say to the brink and no further, because, of the three libidinal types that Freud distinguishes, it is in the nature of the tragic protagonist to be above all else obsessive. And obsession tends, for reasons I will develop, to be most obtuse to its own unconscious aims. In the various transactions between the components of the mind, the superego dominates in obsessive behavior. Sexual wishes are subjected to rigid repression, unconscious assertions become conscious as stern prohibitions and unmanageable feelings of guilt prevail. Obsessive thinking and behavior achieves that interesting compromise that our divided minds are capable of: the mind abandons its sexual designs on the object while continuing to retain the object itself. Now, obsessive tendencies in an ordinary person may generate a whole range of good or objectionable qualities—from scientific objectivity to a puritanical hatred of sex, or moral laxity. But in a tragic hero, granted the conditions of dramatic crisis, an obsession can become high tragedy dealing with honor and revenge and moral responsibility. Hamlet's overmastering preoccupation with sexual impurity and his uncle's conjugal habits blinds Hamlet to his own involvement, which the intensity and the pungency of his language betray.

Sophocles' Oedipus pursues his rigidly objective search for his origins and the murderer of Laius as a screen for his own growing sense of complicity and guilt. His violent attack on the aged Tiresias is a reactivation of the original act of parricide. In neither Hamlet nor Oedipus is there a full recognition of the irony of their positions.

Concerning sublime obsessions and forbidden wishes, I wish to quote from two widely separated modern sources. Writing on *Hamlet*, Ella Freeman Sharpe says:

> A satisfying drama is one in which the psyche has accomplished the reconciliation of incompatibles. . . . The magic fulfilment of a deep-lying forbidden wish without the arousing of anxiety . . . contrived by the wish being hidden, securing a balance between hidden forces . . . by the mechanics of symbol formation, personification, projection and reversal. The ego achieves in sublimation a way of accomplishing the fulfilment of id wishes and triumphs by abandoning literal disobedience. In other words Shakespeare has moralized what is at bottom a murderous and incestuous and suicidal fantasy into an obsession with honor and revenges.[16]

My second source is that remarkable work by that not remarkable writer, Norman Mailer, *Miami and the Siege of Chicago*, a report on the nominating conventions of the 1968 presidential elections. Mailer is trying to explain his intuitive distaste for the supporters of Eugene McCarthy, and Mailer falls easily and gracefully into the Freudian explanation of the dynamics of civilized behavior and its hazards. He writes of the McCarthy supporters:

> The moral powers of the vegetarian, the pacifist, and the nationalist have been so refined away from the source of much power—infantile violence—that their moral powers exhibit a leanness, a keenness, and total ferocity which can only hint at worlds given up: precisely those sensuous worlds of corruption, promiscuity, fingers in the take, political alliances forged by the fires of booze, and that sense of property which is the fundament of all political relations.[17]

Both these writers have touched on ambivalences over which Shakespeare appears to have had miraculous control. I am al-

ways aware in Shakespeare of an overriding bourgeois conscience, with its antitragic detestation of force, and obsession,
its sympathy for the fallen and the tincture of guilt that makes
his murderers live with their victims for a long time. In an age
inured to bloody stages I would still suggest that for Shakespeare murder was a symbolic intensification of a relationship,
that it was the psychopathic core of infantile violence, the leg-
acy of primordial solutions, which he invoked to preserve his
tragedies from dissolving into neurotic blurs, which might
have occurred, had he chosen less violent and definitive modes
of action. In Hamlet the tension between regressive aims and
the mature consciousness is stretched to the breaking point, so
that it is with a sense of something more miasmic than pity and
fear that we watch this civilized and restrained young man enter
into the deadly game of the "bloat king." Perhaps this vision as
much as her father's death drove Ophelia to madness and
suicide.

IV

When the Freudian critic turns to the modern writer, the critic
discovers not without surprise that the modern writer returns
his gaze. Where Freud once admired Shakespeare's or Sophocles' or Dostoevsky's *luck* at having grasped the essence of an
unconscious theme, we admire the *cunning* with which Joyce,
or Mann, or Saul Bellow manipulate neurotic characters. We
cannot evade the fact that the translation of Freud into the vernacular has been as material to the emergence of what Philip
Rieff in his study of Freud has called the Psychological Man as
the translation of the Bible was to the Protestant Reformation.
The mind of the artist has had to absorb within its working
confines not only a rational consciousness and a capacity for
judgment but a conception of a working unconscious, perceptions operating usefully at levels that cannot easily be given an
articulate form. When we crawl under a modern work of liter-

ature we emerge with all sorts of Freudian nuts and bolts and the stain of machine oil. Among the soft organic growths, the metaphors of tropical imaginations, there is the hard rattle of the contrived and mechanical, at least to the trained ear.

An oneiric literature, a literature of dream states, of which Joyce's *Finnegans Wake* is the Mount Everest of novels, has emerged quite in keeping with the expansion of the unconscious into our experience. Franz Kafka's symbolisms have the concrete literalness of the dream itself; he represents perhaps more than any other modern artist, the ultimate commitment to a psychological literature, for not only did he plunge himself in the deep well of the unconscious, he most tragically drowned there. It is possible to discover, in studying his work, as if they were the descending rings of a whirlpool, the various levels of the psyche turning around a central core of suffering. There is no symbol of aggression which does not have its antithetical symbol of submission, no advance which does not have its masochistic recoil, no mature and reasoned vantage point of safety that is not undermined by a profoundly regressive fantasy. Beneath Gregor Samsa's horror at his metamorphosis into a monstrous kind of vermin there lurks a sinister satisfaction that no existentialist interpretation can relieve.

A new spirit, born of the Renaissance, with the recession of Christian faith, and fanned to a fever with the alienation of the Romantic poet from the horrors of the Industrial Revolution, seems to be perfecting itself in modern writing. Hegel's conception of the progressive internalizing and spirtualizing of human experience in art and ethics—the higher reaches of Christian conscience—the conviction of sin and the techniques of salvation beyond the clarities of Greek sculpture and Aristotle's Analytics, is today being ironically realized in our literature. With Freud as his guide and Narcissus as his myth, the modern writer explores and exposes himself beyond Rousseau's wildest dreams of confession. "The human soul is an amphibian," cries Herzog in Saul Bellow's novel, "and I have touched its sides." Herzog's ordeal by self-examination has given him a freedom beyond the legislation of freedom, at an historical moment when freedom seems to be joining the rest of the world's illusions.

His remarkable capacity for self-examination has made the modern writer the physician to his age, but it has also created a curious and symptomatic problem: the rejection of the beauty of perfected form as a criterion for excellence and the imposition in its place of an appeal to primitive and kinetic, perverse, and above all personal response on the part of the audience. This is especially true in the visual and dramatic arts. The problem has its crass level today as a forensic issue, involving censorship and morality. To explain the first is perhaps to resolve the second.

A few years ago, the psychoanalyst Franz Alexander told a group of Los Angeles artists that "the naked unconscious is not a suitable way of communication. It must go through the prism of the organizing portion of the personality." The statement is irreproachable in the light of that traditional gentleman's agreement the imagination makes with reality for mutual support, but when its main term, the personality, is violated, the concept falters. The question becomes for the artist, whether, in the world as it is, he can still afford a personality and keep his integrity as an artist. His training and his intuition tell him that most of the world's ideologies are moral or biological fictions in the service of a psychological imperative. His business then must be with those levels below personality—among the psychological imperatives—i.e., the primitive, the kinetic, the perverse. His business is exposure. Delacroix could write in the nineteenth century: "There is no great artist without the friendship of a hero or of a great spirit of some other kind." But we know about Beethoven's romance with Napoleon, and Nietzsche's with Wagner, and the artist is not again to be deceived. He does not look for his oceanic reunion in the great world, because it is a place of social guilt, uneasiness, and fear in which our aggressive and self-destructive impulses have been handed on to authorities who are as venal as they are cruel. In a world which has lost any claim to be a spiritual organism, we are torn merely, as the social historian R. H. Tawney has observed, between the economic advantages of collectivist and individualist societies.

Modern art is the renewal of the perennial resistance to surface realism and plausible rationalism, the delicate postures of men whose balances are being violently disturbed. Art rejects these as they appear in the terrorist structures of authoritarianism in all its manifestations. Rejecting them, the artist imitates his rejection in art by reducing his subject, and even his techniques, below the level of conscious disposition. He turns his violated personality inside out and shows us its lining.[18]

Beauty floats upon the surface of the mind. The unconscious, when it enters art, disturbs or altogether destroys the aesthetic surface, reveals the unbeautiful, and forms free images of the unconscious. Disgust, the sense of the obscene, is merely the alarm bell ringing in our structured egos to tell us that an un-transformed, unconscious idea is getting too near the surface—not a symbol, but the thing itself.[19] The history of the artist's quarrel with censorship would suggest that art serves as a sort of moral sanitation plant, whose present facilities are inadequate. At the end of the last century, when Ibsen's *Ghosts* first appeared on the English stage, the critical response treated the play as if it were raw sewage, revealing with ironic accuracy the anal-sadistic obsessive quality of the epoch along with the shock value of the work.

The modern writer in his experiments with the primal shapes of things keeps reminding me of another period in the history of art when the unconscious seems to have broken through the artist's defenses. Medieval Gothicism was a period when the artist tried to realize through an intense naturalism the reality of human corruptibility, death, and the desperate and illusory hope of life beyond the grave. It was social Darwinism without the optimistic promise of evolution. Grünewald's dead Christ is its most extraordinary achievement. I remember once seeing an exhibition of Gothic sculpture. The figures were wood, polychromed, and every kind of spiritual and physical torment was plastically represented with great sophistication by the artists, so that I finally felt in this sublime doll hospital both the unconscious guilt and sadism, and the unconscious recoil from it, that made up the spirit of the age.

It is the infirmity of our culture that we do not in general feel these atavisms in ourselves with anything like the graphic definition of the Gothic. Our wars tell us that we can no longer afford these confrontations with ourselves. We are prohibited the personal; our feelings are muffled in carbon paper, timetables, and contracts. But the artist-psychologist has developed in this Gothically grotesque time the secret of the Gothic method of self-absolution, derived not from a permanently obtuse system of faith—which is the way of tragedy, faith violated, despair, and death—but from an absolute clarity of introspection, which is the way of comedy. The modern artist is freed from the burden of conscience in the absence of any institution, spiritual or secular, fit to command his loyalty. His is the morally sedentary occupation of a mind contemplating itself rather than outward bound on a positive mission against anyone or anything. He is capable of considering comic alternatives, the possibility of *recovery* rather than moral purgation in the struggle between his instincts and his alleged higher nature. For this reason much of modern introspective art and literature moves toward its conclusions with the solemn gravity of a long and circumstantial joke. The artist has violated the terms of his Oedipal franchise, and the new freedom has made him expansive. He is Ham, laughing at his naked drunken father, rather than Oedipus the parricide. Instead of the classic compulsion to resolve our fates we are content to study our tragic history in a comical distorting mirror.[20]

I would not advise anyone to become a Freudian critic who tended to take himself too seriously. Freudian criticism is an empirical discipline, at one remove from its base in psychology and at one remove from its base in aesthetics—by virtue of the absolute necessity I feel it imposes for preferring oneself to the theoretical or the doctrinaire in either camp. Part of the agony and the excitement of the discipline comes from the fact that one can never be sure one knows what he is talking about, and that one continually runs the risk of becoming what can only be called an *autobiographical* critic.

I know that great art consists of the intuitive grasp of the nature of things, and that inferior art is the studied grasp of these relations. I know that *Hamlet* survives as poetry more readily than it will survive as an Oedipal problem play. I prefer fingerprints to blueprints, and perhaps for this God will forgive me.   [1975]

2.
The Black Art of Psychoanalytic Criticism

Since the psychoanalytic criticism of literature is still considered something of a black art within the academic profession, and if not a black art, certainly a novelty outside the profession, it might be well to introduce this discussion of psychoanalytic criticism the way evangelists these days introduce new religious sects, or the way the Knights of Columbus try to invigorate the Faith: on a kind of "Let's get acquainted" basis, sheering away from hard points of doctrine, domesticating concepts by means of homely precedents and analogies, suppressing as far as it is possible anything that shocks the virgin sensibilities of the neophyte, and above all, offering definitions and applying them to the immediate subject of the literary work of art.

The matters which I will be taking up will include the questions: What is psychoanalytic practice in its broad outlines? What is its relevance to literature? What assertions does it make about reality? the artist? the creative process? What are its limitations? What changes has it effected in literary composition and in the criticism of literature?

First of all, the two disciplines, psychology and literature, are not meeting for the first time; the history of psychology and literature is a continuous chronicle of their meetings, and the division is in fact a forced one. No age has ever existed without having some psychological system to account for the mental states that underlie human actions, and no poetry has ever

33

eluded the implications of such a system. Homer's quaint, pan-
theistic conception of ideas, imaginings, and dreams, true and
false, being implanted by one god or another in the individual
mind, is a primitive psychological system, clearly anticipating
subliminal advertising and nocturnal education. Plato's psychological structure of reason, passions and appetites, embodied in
a commonwealth of philosophers, soldier-citizens and trades-
men, eliminates the poet because he cuts athwart those static
divisions. It is Aristotle who justifies poetic mimesis in psychiatric terms of its cathartic function, its ability to purge the spectator of strong emotions—a concept of psychic relief, which
is as timely now as it was when it was first propounded, and
which contains, latent within it, the ideas of identification, and
projection, and symbolic transformation—all associated with
contemporary depth psychologies.

The history of psychological systems and literature is the history of the conscious, rational mind struggling to retain its su-
premacy against the slow and subtle encroachments of that diminishing dark continent of mental activity, the unconscious.
We may safely say that the differentia between epochs is the
question of what men can entertain in their minds and still
sanction as sane, responsible thought. Aristotle could say that
tragedy relieved men's minds, but he could not say why. Lon-
ginus could discuss the sublime in poetry, as "the soul's proud
flight as if it had itself produced what it had heard," without
being able to trace the connection, and certainly without issu-
ing a round-trip ticket back to the world of sense.

For the Renaissance critic the concept of imagination was the
golden wastebasket for the irrational, and we find typical such
statements as this to describe the relationship between the
creative act and poetry:

> For the body of our imagination being as an unformed
> chaos without fashion, without day, if by the divine power
> of the spirit it be wrought into an orb of order and form, is
> it not more pleasing to Nature, that desires a certainty and
> comports not with that which is infinite, to have these

closes [homophonous line-endings], rather than not to know where to end, or how far to go, especially seeing our passions often without measure?[1]

For the rational eighteenth century, the imagination and its product, poetry, begin by being the golden garbage pail of the irrational. Poetry becomes "decayed memory," which has, for obscure reasons, undergone strange sea changes. But along with this continuing distrust of the imagination comes a sense of internal process, the glimmering intuition that imagination is itself a complex, pseudological system. The metaphors of chaos being ordered by reason give way to metaphors of heat and fusion, the work of art emerging from the crucible: Byron, tracing home to its cloud the lightning of the mind. There was, too, a growing sense of the mutual complexities of creative act and response, each one, as Coleridge puts it, affecting not just the rational, conscious mind, but the whole organism.

In the last half of the nineteenth century, a period of unmitigated scientific materialism, a psychology based on the needs and impulses of the organism became an organic psychology with a vengeance, a psychology of glands, neural responses; and the heroes of the naturalistic novel became a race of sad Pavlovian dogs, salivating, growling, or rutting at the intersection of heredity and environment, stimulus and response. The mind, having sustained itself in an immaterial void for many centuries, finally made a forced landing; it too became a physiological process, like reproduction.

While Sigmund Freud has top billing in this overview, the more I read of his work, the more I am tempted to include the philosopher-psychologist William James as one of those who have been instrumental in the establishment of something like an ultimate psychology of human behavior. Along with Freud, with whom he is roughly contemporary, James fought against the glandular hypothesis which was the hallmark of post-Darwinian psychology, in the name of consciousness and the human ability to alter its conditions, just as Freud was to detach the mind from the biological determinism of natural science. I bring William James in as an ally here for two reasons: first of all as a strategic move against those who feel that Freud has sold us out to the most abysmal bondage to our sexual instinct, and secondly for James's influencing (as I think) the art of his brother Henry, who certainly transmuted the psychological theories into the realms of art.

Both Freud and William James have rescued us from the barbarisms of physiological behaviorism. James's contribution is exclusively on the side of the mind's active, conscious role in electing its destiny. "The moment you bring consciousness into the midst, survival ceases to be a mere hypothesis. No longer is it 'if survival is to occur, then so and so must brain and other organs work.' It has now become an imperative decree: 'survival shall occur and therefore organs must so work!'" Real ends appear for the first time upon the world's stage: "The Spencerians [Darwinians] had attributed social changes to geography, environment, social circumstances—in brief to everything but human control. They had assumed a web of causation in which the finite human intellect becomes hopelessly, hopelessly entangling."[2] And Freud devolved the step that is the complement to the one William James made: to exhibit accurately and with infinite pains the interaction between a web of causation and the human consciousness which more often than not triumphed over causation.

On close examination, we realize that Freud's boldest move, the move that alienated him (and continues to alienate him) from the other physical sciences, is paradoxically a backward step: for he poised the mental process back in the void again. This is not to say he denied the ultimate relationship between the organic and the functional, but he made what seems to be the characteristic leap of all great discoverers over such contiguities in favor of his own vision. As William James was trying to emancipate the consciousness from biological determinism, Freud was also attempting, in what appeared the very citadel of biology, to isolate the unconscious realm of instinctual drives.

Here Freud began to pay the artist that ambiguous compliment which finds its most complete expression in "The Poet and Daydreaming." It is here, I suppose, that psychoanalytic criticism has its origins. One of Freud's associates describes the conflict between medicine and psychoanalysis and the role of literature in its resolution:

> No amount of brain anatomy could dissuade novelists, who view life naively but with sharp eyes, from the idea that mental excitement of itself was capable of occasioning a mental illness. . . . While we doctors were thrashing the empty straw of physiological catchwords Ibsen in his *Lady from the Sea* had made an almost faultless psychoanalysis by which he exposed the origin of an obsessional idea in a psychic conflict. . . . Lady Macbeth's washing obsession has become much more plausible since we have convinced ourselves that our neurotics would also fain wipe away the moral stains from their consciences by the same obsessional actions. Formerly the man of science often made merry over the naiveté of the novelist-poet who, when puzzled for an ending, simply made his hero mad, and now to our shame we have to acknowledge that it was not the scholars but the naive poets who were right. Psychoanalysis showed us that an individual who finds no way out of his mental conflicts takes refuge in a neurosis or psychosis.[3]

Keeping in mind that Freud, in common with all natural philosophers, did not so much discover as he did call to the world's attention certain aspects of human experience that had been observed and either fallaciously explained or left anomalous, let us examine in broad outline his contribution to psychology.

Freud was the first to describe intelligibly the continuities of mental activity between the infant and the man, between the aberration and the accepted norms of social behavior, between the inner psychological experience of reality and the presumably objective scientific experience of reality, between those acts and thoughts which are beyond the "option of consciousness" and those which we can consciously control.

He proposed first of all that the rational consciousness had evolved as an adaptation to natural reality, from primitive unconscious, prerational origins. The child, in some rather raunchy ways that folk wisdom could not foresee, was the father to the man. We begin our mental lives, he observed, in the service of bodily needs, the biological imperatives of hunger and creature warmth. The mind, or, as Freud designated it at this level, the id, is a "mass of seething excitment," unconscious, bent only on the immediate gratification of its wants, which center around the major openings of the body—the mouth in particular, and subsequently the anal and genital regions. The ego develops outward from this mass of undifferentiated energy, producing, and itself a product of, the technics of mastering the strange environment of the world, to become finally the mediator between the world of subjective experience and external phenomena. It is the ego which tests the external world for its reality, its adaptability to its needs; it also tests the inner world of id impulses to determine which of these impulses are feasible, which are a threat, what to postpone, what to suppress altogether.

"We walk," says one of Joseph Conrad's characters, "between the policeman and the butcher," meaning, I suppose, that the food supply and protection are guarantees of civilization. The ego walks, Freud might say, between the robber and the cop, between the id and the superego. The ego's earliest experiences with reality are coterminous with parental restraints and encouragements. When its own boundaries are plastic and permeable it identifies these restraints and encouragements with its own inner experience, and the product becomes the permanently internalized image of the parent—a conscience, a sense of sin, or guilt, whatever we choose to call the inner regulators of our moral lives. The superego censors our dreams, determines the standards by which we live, and at times peremptorily destroys us. We might generalize and say that there are good cops and bad cops, but robbers are all thugs.

Consciousness in Freud's system is in quantitative terms almost an afterthought. It is the final refinement of the ego, and as such, a precious extract of our total experience of life, our ultimate weapon against the urgencies of our impulses and the flagellations of the consciences. But the very continuity of consciousness during the waking day betrays us by running away like water before our eyes. (Like the flight deck of an aircraft carrier, the mind can only accommodate so much consciousness. The rest sinks away into the 'tween decks of habits and reflexes—the so-called pre-conscious, where thoughts not wanted on the voyage are stored.)

One of Freud's most grievous (and to me endearing) offenses against established belief (in itself psychologically suspect) lies in his attributing to infancy a violent, phantasmagoric, erotic existence, in which the infant's experience with reality consists exclusively of sensory gratifications, or their frustrations, around which curious fantasies construct themselves. Here, in this dim prehistoric underworld, occur the infant sexual attachments to the parent, the Oedipus relationship, which Freud calls the "nuclear concept of the neuroses." And, depending on the success or failure which attends the child's passing through this period, are the historical determinants of his future relations with the world.

The amnesia that obscures our infancies from us is a purposeful one. Our early strivings were governed entirely by a pleasure principle, a flight from pain, serviceable enough when nourishment and sleep were our chief requirements. But from childhood on we are taught to renounce our natural impulses until as adults we must accept a whole range of renunciations, involving even the ultimate sacrifice of life itself. All education works toward the suppression of forbidden desires and the substitution of permitted aims. Culture, as one writer rather gloomily remarks, is "the total sum of the frustrations which society imposes on the individual. It recognizes only that part of man which serves it."

To this end, the mechanism of repression works. All unfulfillable wishes, ideas, memories, and fantasies are submerged in the unconscious. Essentially dangerous instincts are turned into useful social channels. Early sexual strivings toward the mother are transferred to acceptably unrelated love-objects. Hatred of the father is tempered by fear, love, and idealization until finally the old fellow becomes a template for one's own identity: ideally, a cosy outlook, but an unlikely one. Instincts are retrograde to the increasingly complex demands of culture, and the old infantile strivings, while repressed, are not fully repressed even in the most untroubled personalities. They survive as memory traces, and the waking and sleeping life of the average man is a reminder of his past: absentminded gestures, little accidents, imaginary pains, blind rages, and ridiculous dreams are all little windows looking into forbidden rooms.

When the ego is seriously impaired, the barrier of repression is weakened, and the consciousness becomes the battleground for an unresolved conflict between partially successful instincts and partially successful repressions. The personality is infiltrated with instincts in disguise, the symbolic transformations of hysteria, compulsive activities, the peculiar imperatives that condition our relationships, our careers, our affinities and fears. Our anxieties become the electrically charged guideposts for our lives, leading us not into temptation but, on the other hand, delivering us only from the greater of two evils. The complete triumph of repressed material over the ego's resistance to it results finally in psychosis, madness, the utter loss of the individual to himself.

At the conclusion of a beautifully integrated analysis of an Ibsen play, Freud writes that the only thing wrong with his interpretation is that it is "too good to be true." It is in this spirit that he advances beyond his elaborately responsible analyses of individuals to speculate on the nature of human society. Culture, as he accounts for its multifarious development, is a magnification of the history of each of its members. Its module is the family; its dramatic struggle is a conflict between the titanic forces of instinctual drives and the renunciation that must be made in the name of order; its character is determined by the degree to which it has eluded the more vicious toils of its Oedipus complex.

If we consider the standard components of a typical theogony, the myths and legends, the customs and literature of any culture, in close apposition to the psychic development of the individual, the analogy becomes clear. Somewhere in the dim past there appears an angry father-God who begets children on the Earth, then either swallows them, expels them from Paradise, or in some way menaces them. Humanity is created out of clay and spittle, or clay and semen, promptly disgraces itself, and is spanked. Whereupon there begins in apostolic succession a long and varied account of heroes, prophets, and patriarchs, all born through the intervention of a god or divine messenger, who slay fabulous beasts, defy tyrannical kings, and inherit the family estate by means of the mother's chicanery. History repeats the process, with sons competing with their fathers or their brothers for kingdoms or concubines, culminating finally in the ultimate Oedipal joke—a cartoon in *The New Yorker* which shows a young man saying to a graybeard behind a desk: "But you can't fire me, sir. You're my father image." What is constant throughout is first of all a theory of creation that inevitably suggests mudpies; second, a family situation in which the mother is conceived of as endlessly protective and loving, and the father as jealous and menacing but, finally, through sacrifice and humility, approachable; third, the theme with variations of the romantic foundling, whose real father was a king or god, or whose mother was still a virgin and who, after a number of incredible exploits, was made king, messiah, or the president of the university.

To explain a cultural phenomenon in Freudian terms is to place it in its proper position of a gradient between psychological reality and external reality, that is, between pure subjectivity and pure objectivity. Neither one of these states can exist ideally; neither one of these states is desirable; the scientific dream of selfless objectivity represents the persistence of an infantile form of thought as egregiously as its opposite.

All theories of reality, Freud leads us to infer, are fictions—anthropomorphic distortions of what Otto Fenichel calls the "microbe of reality." But if we cannot perfect a theory of reality, at least we can improve our relations with reality by learning that the mind has an inalienable share in its existence.

External objects become representations in our minds when we invest the objects with a certain measure of our own psychic energy, when we develop some attitude, ranging between desire and indifference, toward them. Again, pursuing the parallel between the history of the individual and the history of society, we observe that early theories of reality were animistic. That is, the psychic investment obscured the intrinsic nature of the object. "Thou sayest to a stone, be thou my father, and to a stock, by thou my mother," says one of the Hebrew prophets, denouncing the idolators. "Stop projecting your fears and hopes into sticks and stones," the same prophet would say if he had read Freud. In mastering his destructive instincts, animistic man projected them upon nature. He invented Gorgons and Furies to put his night terrors and his conscience at a distance from himself. Thunder reproached him and oracles misled him. When he feared the external world, he reversed the process; he incorporated it to himself. Nature became an extension of his body, which by magical utterances and gestures he could control. He ate God sacramentally.

In an anthropomorphic world science is impossible because nature has a conscious, and unpredictable, will. As one writer puts it, the Egyptians had a splendid grasp of astronomy, but they could not study the sun because he was a god and thus tabu. The great accomplishment of the scientific consciousness is that it could withdraw the anthropomorphic gods from natural things, and with this withdrawal, remove the tabu which prevented their close examination.

I have referred earlier to psychological scientists like William James and Sigmund Freud as men who rescued the mind from the natural scientists, and subsequently to the rescue of nature from the primitive, magical thinking of the prescientific mentality, by natural scientists. The paradox is easily explained. Freud's criticism of animistic thinking applies as readily to the physical sciences as they flowered in their full pride of being in the nineteenth century. They were a bright light in a dark corner; they were a hygienic vacuum cleaner deanimating the physical universe. They systematically removed the tabus from all of nature. But in their fear of what the superstitious mind had done with nature in the past, they created a scientific attitude in which mind itself was the last great tabu. The scientific attitude implied the withdrawal of all emotional involvement from the study of the material world. The effect was similar to the effect observed in schizophrenic subjects, for whom the world, from which emotions have been withdrawn, is a world without color, dreams, feelings, or value. It is the attitude Dostoevsky mocks in *Crime and Punishment* and *Notes from the Underground*. It is a view that Leopold Bloom in Joyce's *Ulysses* succumbs to at a low moment in the day when he thinks: "What is love? A cork in a bottle."

When medical science turned itself to psychology, such science created, as I have said, a glandular theory of behavior, then ignored the interplay of unconscious and conscious, instinctive and egoistic strata of the mind. Freud proposed a psychology that accounted for reality in terms of internal and external qualities, of things and attributes. He removed, if he did not absolutely abolish, the last tabu from nature. It is in these terms that we can account for the immense resistance to Freudian psychology from those paternal institutions which have a vested interest in the mental acquiescence of their subjects.

Out of this synthesis of reality has arisen a new concept of mind in which the artist plays a special and important role. By postulating the mind's perpetual flight from itself, Freud transferred the essential conflict between man and his environment from the traditionally public battlefields of action into the mind itself. The shift is from the prefix "inter" (between) to the prefix "intra" (within). The essential conflicts are within the psyche: their external manifestations are the physical gestures that accompany the conflict.

In Freud's psychology we return to that preference for poetic truth over philosophical truth that Aristotle has expressed, a preference I have touched upon earlier in the choice between Ibsen's play and the diagnoses of medical psychiatry. In the artist Freud has found the comedian of reality. The artist perpetuates the old animisms that enriched the ancient world, but they are fluid and free from the rigidities that accompany religious and ethical creeds and dogmas. Unlike Aristotle who, still in the grip of the magical-medical idea of purgation, defended tragedy for hygienic reasons, Freud saw in the drama the confirmation of a neurotic wish-fulfillment in which the audience participated. He saw, in fact, all literature as a running glossary of forbidden wishes.

He observed that the unconscious mind expressed its desires to the conscious mind in a language of signs: through dreams, waking fantasies, gestures, and physical disorders. More importantly for our purposes, he found in literature the endless translation into language of these same unconscious impulses. His discovery centered itself on that tragedy with which Greek culture seems to have arrived at some ultimate achievement— the conscious creative act in touch with an ultimate human experience—Sophocles' tragedy, *Oedipus Rex*. Freud saw in the play, beyond the public tableau in which a man suffers a series of malevolently determined accidents, a psychological pageant unfold itself in which a man becomes the victim of his own instinct-ridden will. He saw in the play a distorted version of the reality behind the legend, and proposed that the unconscious does tell the conscious mind the truth, but it tells it, especially in poetry, in the form of a beautiful lie.

Freud saw, in the tragedy of Oedipus, the comedy of everyman turned upside down, the body of Oedipus' repressed desires speaking like a ventriloquist from the Delphic Oracle, the sins of the child visited upon the parents. He saw in the tragedy the fulfillment of a series of unconscious wishes, which in all men occur and are more or less successfully repressed and sublimated in the first five years of life: the wish, namely, to preserve the loving attention of the mother to the exclusion of all other rivals, of whom the father is the archetype. In the fantasies that arise about such wishes the father is removed in some violent, unintentional way, after having made the first hostile move. The son then enjoys unobstructed access to the mother. In these terms the playpen becomes the original theater in the round, and *Oedipus Rex* is played out seven nights a week in the suburbs of Vienna. The original version (with the original cast) by Sophocles, tells the story of a son, whose father tried to destroy *him*, who grew up with foster parents and killed his father quite by accident in one of the first traffic fatalities on record. He thereupon married his mother because he has rescued her city from the Sphinx who had killed all the other eligible young men. And it was the inscrutable will of the gods that all this should take place.

The Oedipus legend read as an intrapsychic drama becomes a distortion of the original wish-fantasy in which the child is the sole actor. The terrible fate of Oedipus is the payment in terms of conscious suffering for the enjoyment of forbidden pleasures. In the lexicon of dreams, nightmares are the shipwrecks of unsanctioned desires.

The Freudian symbol ceases to become a straightforward expression in any sense of a universal truth. It comes, so to speak, in a sealed envelope, written backwards. It seems to turn poetic communication on its head—hatred underlies love, love underlies hate, virginity debauches itself—in short, the artist's fiction becomes the truth reversed.

What then gives such a perverse ordering of the symbol its undeniable effectiveness in literature and its validity a universal truth?

The answer may lie in our tracing the evolution of the symbol, as psychoanalysis describes it, in a process that all men share, artist and reader alike. "Originally," I have quoted Freud as saying, "we knew only sexual things." That is to say, all the objects that commanded our infantile attentions were objects either to be feared or desired, whatever their intrinsic nature as objects. Everything, in short, was sexualized, confused equivalents of our organs or our wishes. When, with maturity, the child abandons such identifications, represses them, to be more accurate, the names of such objects, or their images, retain the energies of the original sexual identification. "Poetry and art," writes Sandor Ferenczi, "renew these prehistoric identifications in connection with symbols."

> Only such things (or ideas) are symbols in the sense of psychoanalysis as are invested in consciousness with a logically inexplicable and unfounded affect, and of which it may be analytically established that they owe this affective overemphasis to *unconscious* identification with another thing (or idea) to which the surplus of affect really belongs. Not all similes, therefore, are symbols, but only those in which one member of the equation is repressed into the unconscious. Only from the moment when, as a result of the cultural education, the one member of the equation (the more important one) is repressed, does the other previously less important member attain over affective significance and become a symbol of the repressed one.[4]

Let me generalize, then, from this basis, including in my statement the anonymous authors of myths, legends, and folktales, as well as individual artists. Great literature, rich in powerful symbols, thrives among the inhibitions of the culture that produces the literature. The closer the subject matter of the artist is to the impulses which his culture or his own ego forbids, the more strenuously inverted or disguised is the symbolic expression of that impulse, and more heavily charged with the baffled energy of the original repression. Tragedy may owe its tragic quality, and comedy its comic quality, to the fact that the fatal and the ridiculous represent the debt of conscience one symbolically pays for the entertainment of a wish.

The much-argued question of the morality of art may perhaps find some solution here. A good work of art is like a good nightmare; it leaves both the reader and the artist aghast at the horrors that are alien to human existence. The artist never abandons that austere standard of normality which he unconsciously raises agains his own desires, yet at the same time retains the courage to confront and render his own mind in all its unredeemed complexity. Franz Kafka, for example, in his profoundest nightmares, strives toward an almost banal ideal of sanity. Thomas Mann's artist-heroes, poised always between the devil and the bourgeoisie, declare for the lesser of the two evils.

If literature falls to the unrestrained libido, it lapses into morbidity, into the works of Edgar Allan Poe. If it closes the libido out altogether, literature consigns itself to mere insipidity, the low altitude flights of Mrs. Lindbergh. What makes, in any case, the statement of a philosophical truth a passionate utterance in the work of the artist lies in his unconscious inversion of that truth. As spectators we follow him intuitively through the whole process, being ourselves committed to the identical fantasy.

By extension, the Freudian symbol suggests, if I may coin a term, the Freudian character, to whose care the manipulation of the symbol falls. It is truistic to hold that one of the highest achievements of a writer's craft is to create a living character. But there are not so many that one can take them as a matter of course, or that one can easily account for them. The question is an open one, and complicated.

Dostoevsky's characters, for example, have such life almost forced upon them. The epileptic exaggerations of their roles force us to recognize, as if we were witnessing some hyperbolic laboratory demonstration, the synthetic process by which fiction accomplishes the sense of felt life, by the unfiltered flow of the artist's energies into his characters. It is because we have come to accept within our own mental lives the function of the "complex, that cluster of emotionally charged ideas which reflect neurotic conflict," ideas which are, as Jung describes the creative act itself, independent of the "option of consciousness," that we have come to insist on this function as a sign of life in the characters of fiction. This complex mediates between the world and the individual, and both determine the quality of the inner experience and the use to which one puts the raw materials life puts before one. It is the complex that manifests itself in a fictitious character when he avoids the mere tropisms of behavior. It is the impression these characters give that even in their most trivial and unrecorded actions their minds are fixed upon matters which take priority over these fortuities. The complex emerges in Hamlet's sudden exclamations; his "how all occasions do inform against me!"; his baffling anomalies of response. Such a complex emerges in the demonstrable consistencies, without the sacrifice of complexity, of Holden Caulfield and Portia. Such characters convey an almost physical sense of motion, as if one were holding a spinning gyroscopic top concealed within a handkerchief.

By thinking to expose the unconscious forces that he thinks thereby to conquer, the artist reveals not his victory but the strength of the forces with which he wrestles, and the degree to which he shares our complicity.

Complicity between the artist and his audience leads us to speculate on what special distinction separates the two. Let me sketch briefly a composite description of the artist as a psychological entity. I will begin by urging you to dissociate in your minds the fact that artists are psychologically interesting, from the fact that to be psychologically interesting in this day and age is to be considered neurotic. Freud rather cheerfully suggests that we are all neurotic anyway, so perhaps the dissociation is unnecessary. His intensity of disposition makes the artist what he is, and the fact that he may be neurotic, or even psychotic, in certain quadrants of his life, has no bearing on that intensity as it manifests itself in his art.

The language of literature—associated as it is with symbol, poetic diction, the connotative aspects of words—is identified in psychology with the prelogical thinking of children, primitives, and psychotics. Similarities become identities, the part substitutes for the whole, the objectively perceived incident undergoes distortion. The artist thus intentionally shares in the fantasy life of the nonartist, so far as his metaphorical grasp of experience is concerned; the more essential affinity lies in the relationship of the finished work to the unconscious wish-fulfillment behind it.

Like the nonartist, the creator's wish-fantasy life is built ultimately around his original involvement in the family constellation, and the residue of guilt that inheres in the Oedipus complex. But here the resemblance to the neurotic stops. Where the neurotic finds himself deadlocked in a conflict between repressed instincts, his egoistic urge toward self-preservation, and the gratuitous remorse of conscience, the artist sublimates his drives, releases his bound energies in the performance of a substitutive function in which, because others participate in it and recognize it, he frees himself of what might have eventuated in neurosis. The work of art is an act of restitution, a token of love, a substitute for the futile masochistic acts of contrition one associates with neurotic behavior. Freud observed that Dostoevsky mourned his father's death by having epileptic seizures, losing all his money at cards, and writing such novels as *The Brothers Karamazov*.

In short, a successful work of art spares the artist the formation of neurotic symptoms. Perhaps one can estimate the greatness of an artist by the degree to which he can work freely and within the bounds of his discipline without confinement in the shallows of mere pleasure-seeking, the fiction of adventure and sexual titillation, or without remaining in the depths of pathological morbidity. His ability, as I expressed it to begin with, to entertain ideas that lie on the limits of thought, without destroying the mind in the process, provides a measure for assessment.

But the artist must pay a price for being a superior organism. He is hyperimpressionable, allergic to the shocks of existence to an alarming degree. He has, one might say, absolute psychological pitch. And this sensitivity becomes at once the artist's

greatest instrument and a heavy burden, which, like a Frankenstein monster, can destroy the artist. Thomas Mann's *Death in
Venice* is perhaps one of the happiest statements of the artist's
two-edged nature.

He possesses a greater accessibility to his unconscious processes; he is closer to the strata of his psyche where the primitive impulses rule. He can contemplate enormities (murders
and perversions) and absurdities (the ridiculous, the dreamlike)
with more freedom than the nonartist. He is more at home
with his instinctual drives, and such proximity makes him peculiarly susceptible to internal trauma. These experiences, especially infantile memories and associations, trouble him and
threaten to raise anxieties he cannot deal with except as an artist. Freud's designation of the threefold nature of anxiety bears
an interesting affinity to the subject matter of literature. Our
fears relate, he says, to the fear of the loss of love, and thus the
vicissitudes of its pursuit; to the fear of castration, which may
be rendered as the loss of power, and thus the whole range of
ambition and defeat; to the loss of social esteem, and thus the
complex problem of honor and disgrace. Human anxieties are
the loom of literature.

The artist is susceptible to certain trauma, which he repro-
duces continually in some benign, controllable form. In this
way he accomplishes what the neurotic accomplishes when he
exposes himself to the same experience in order to prove to
himself that the experience did not destroy him. Hemingway's
repetition-compulsion in his writing (as well as in his life)
shown by his concern with violent death, is a dramatic demonstration of this bargain the artist strikes with his work. Thomas
Mann (and Goethe before him) likens it to a pact with the
Devil. When the artist has completed his great work, he is con-
signed like lesser men to the destruction that awaits him.

Now, such a rich inner life is what allows the artist his insights into natures alien to his own. He is constitutionally narcissistic, intent upon himself. But he preserves within himself
the record, long extirpated from most of us, of the alternatives

the Oedipus complex offers us as imperfect resolutions: the flights toward bisexuality, the ambivalences we entertained toward our parents. Such memory traces carry their proportionate burden of guilt; in writers like Dostoevsky and Kafka their fiction creates again for them, in its masochistic, ambivalent components, the crises in their psychic lives.

For all artists the eye or the ear is the favored sense. They are the tools of the trade, the distance senses, the ones connected with the aesthetic experience. We say of a work of art that it makes us "feel" the sensations that are being rendered, essentially into sounds, or words *seen* on the page. Again the artist's faculty for retaining the remnants of infantile processes separates him from the rest. We know from bittersweet experience that the eyes and ears are *almost* tactile senses under certain circumstances. The Bible, when it forbids us to look upon our parents' nakedness, or Oedipus, when he removes his offending eye, identify sight with touch; and we can infer that at one point in our lives the two were confused. One of the legacies of the unresolved fixations of childhood is a morbid curiosity about the lives of other people, particularly their sexual lives. This does not imply that all artists are voyeurs but merely that their extraordinary capacity for seeing returns that sense to its original affinities with touch, and with sexual pleasure, yet liberates it from its practical involvements in the performance and excitement of the act. The gist of the psychoanalytic explanation for the power, fluency, and adaptability of language is its ability to displace what were originally physical, sexual activities to the mind. Metaphor enjoys its rich, textual freedom of allusion precisely because it has separated itself from solid things. The book-burner has not yet made the separation.

There is, finally, in the artist a strong drive to possess, by means of experience, the "real" external world. He accomplishes this possession by an act of incorporation, of identification. He becomes the world, as Shakespeare and Balzac are said to have created worlds within themselves. It is this sense of possession, identification, and with it the sense of omnipotence, that is called "the oceanic reunion." Again, it is in touch with very primitive formations. It ranges from the omnipotence of the infant, who cannot define the boundaries between oneself and one's environment and who therefore conceives of omnipotence in terms of getting milk when wanted, to the tendency of individuals to identify themselves with some substitute parent figure—patriotic nationalism, or the Church—and so share in some institutional omnipotence. The quality of the artist's capacity for conveying this ultimate experience of reunion and its devastating opposite, alienation, is again superior in its methods and effects. It is, I feel, one of the most pervasive themes of art—*Oedipus Rex*, which casts out the blinded king, is brought to its oceanic reunion in *Oedipus at Colonnus*. *The Divine Comedy* and *Crime and Punishment* are tragicomedies of separation and return. The lonely catcher in the rye, giving Janey a buzz, is looking for his lost connections with the great world.

What, then, is the psychoanalytic critic? At first glance, psychoanalytic criticism would seem to be a perverse art of benevolent contradiction. It would seem to deny the artist his high notes, by calling attention to his anal eroticism, or to deny him his low notes by pointing to his castration anxieties. It examines the moving drama of *Oedipus Rex* and shifts its action from the stage to the interior of the mind. The skeleton in the closet has become the bat in the belfry. This criticism has removed the lid from the id in defiance of the artist's will. Such reading invokes more primitive levels of mind and experience than do other modes of criticism in connection with works that are not in themselves primitive or archaic to the uses of civilization. It is an art restorer's nightmare in which the underpainting of everything from the Sacrifice of Isaac to the Rape of Europa turns out to look something like Whistler's Mother.

Psychoanalytic criticism's greatest fault is perhaps its commitment to the pastness, the historical origins of action, its tendency to make all art into an archaic tragedy of secret curses. The existentialist, for example, grows physically ill at the thought of Thomas Mann's bondslaves of fixation, and Jean

Paul Sartre's criticism of Faulkner's morbid fascination with the "super-reality" of the psychological past may well stand as an indictment of the tendency psychoanalytic criticism encourages. It irritates Sartre, as an existentialist, to see his problematic, debatable present, and his impeccable future, sinking into the quicksand past. What if one does not want to operate along the lines of pastness?

Finally, there are the easy analytics of the artist and critic making free with the catchwords of neurosis: the "psychic sex scar" of one of Dreiser's characters, or Faulkner's painful description of why the parents of a twelve-year-old boy cannot explain a sexual relationship to him, the over-attentiveness to the more sensational forms of fiction, the unrelieved degradation of the creative act into an infantilism. "A novel needs a hero and all the traits for an anti-hero are expressly gathered here," writes Dostoevsky at the end of his *Notes from the Underground*. This statement of perverse intention signals the need for a critical discipline that will not balk at such perversity. The subject matter and the forms of modern literature, in fact the modern temperament at large, are recalcitrant to the older canons of behavior. Psychological realism as we now approach it is like academic figure painting, presenting with a correct regard for substructure the anatomy of action.

The relations that subsist between literature and criticism are constantly in transition. The traditional role of criticism, especially in connection with such forms as poetry and drama, has been admonitory. The critic has become the watchdog of decorum. The flexibility of narrative fiction, its essential formlessness, with regard to any tight linguistic structure, or decorum, has resulted in a new relationship between criticism and fiction, which psychoanalytic criticism is prepared to explore. It sets itself to examine the anomalous, the tentative, the experimental in modern fiction, and in so doing, gives the artist the courage to explore new paths. It has serviced also the resurrective function of discovering, beneath the archaic surfaces of older literary works, the vivid and familiar tones of life.

"The prophetic spirit of art," the psychologist Jung writes, "has turned from the old object relationship toward the dark chaos of subjectivism." It has done so at the bidding of the psychologists and philosophers who, within recent times, have reaffirmed the subjective nature of experience. Under their impulse, art has ceased to imitate literal, observed reality. Instead, it has begun to externalize the innermost feelings through some palpable medium. The world becomes the projected psyche of the artist; the whole psychic experience of the artist enters into the work. We must, in order to interpret works of art whose stage is the mind itself, become experts in the natural history of the mind. If this be a black art, then we critics must make the most of it. [1970]

II

ON AMERICAN
LITERATURE

3.

The Red Badge of Courage

I

In *The Torrents of Spring*, Ernest Hemingway's ribald parody of Sherwood Anderson, the hero Yogi Johnson remembers the war:

> In a good soldier in the war it went like this: First, you were brave because you didn't think anything special could hit you, because you yourself were something special, and you knew that you could never die. Then you found out different. You were really scared then; but if you were a good soldier you functioned the same as before. Then after you were wounded and not killed, with new men coming on, and going through your old processes, you hardened and became a good hard-boiled soldier. Then came the second crack, which is much worse than the first, and then you began doing good deeds and being the boy Sir Philip Sidney, and storing up treasures in heaven. At the same time, of course, functioning always the same as before. As if it were a football game.[1]

The passage is surprising for a number of reasons. It is anomalous to *The Torrents of Spring*, which is entirely farcical, in the seriousness of its tone. It is a concise description of a process that preoccupied Hemingway through all of his literary career. And it follows, with certain minor differences, the developmental scheme Stephen Crane appears to have set up for himself in connection with his hero Henry Fleming in *The Red Badge of Courage,*[2] even to his finally racing over the battlefield, ducking "his head low like a football player" (p. 90).

The parallel extends finally off the printed page to the lives of the two authors. Both men were subject to that "thirst for abstract danger," as Malcolm Cowley calls it, to an excessive degree. They followed violence with that uneasy trust in a courage that must continually be tested, making even the experience of war as instrumental as an athletic event to their self-evaluation. Both were at one time or another war correspondents. "Neither ever quite got over the death of his father," writes Philip Young, "and both rebelled in various ways against their families. Each childhood was marred by the painful experience of violence; and it was eventually in warfare, sought out and embraced, that each man found a fascinating formulation of violence, and his essential metaphor for life. . . . Chiefly they were compelled to learn what it had to teach them about themselves, and to test themselves against it. . . . They worried at great length the problems of the relation of fear to bravery."[3]

Charles Fenton describes Hemingway's callow eagerness to be torpedoed by a German U-boat on the way to Europe, and his joy at his first heavy bombardment, like a small boy in a spring thunderstorm.[4] "It is almost certain," writes John Berryman of Stephen Crane, "that Crane tried to be killed, and it is probable that he consciously tried to."[5] At one point Crane was described by an eyewitness in the Cuban War: "Suddenly Crane, who was incapable of bravado, let himself quietly over the redoubt, lighted a cigarette, stood for a few moments with his arms at his sides, while the bullets hissed past him into the mud, then as quietly climbed back over the redoubt and strolled away."[6]

Out of these experiences each man produced at least one masterpiece in that exotic genre, the war novel. The essential difference between the two men lies in the fact that Hemingway's responsibility for the inner responses of his embattled protagonists derived from his own experience of war, and that

Stephen Crane (who holds a place with Henry James and Mark Twain in Hemingway's pantheon) derived his experience of war from research and intuition, and felt battle was something to be corroborated, like a scientific hypothesis, after *The Red Badge of Courage* had been written.

While Crane's novel has been universally praised, it has also been the subject of a number of controversial readings, in each of which (with the possible exception of Robert W. Stallman's solipsistic dream of a work inspired by a novel of the same name)[7] the question of the process by which Henry Fleming achieves his manhood has been crucial.

Assuming that Hemingway's formulation of the steps by which one becomes a veteran (or at any rate masters fear) is empirically correct and that it follows with reasonable accuracy Crane's own formulation, then we can reasonably assume that both writers have in their own way struck on a psychological process whose accuracy may be objectively determined. The addition of a verifiable psychological process to the criticism gathered about Crane's novel will perhaps serve to give the body of that criticism an axis from which other less naturalistic considerations may then radiate with some confidence.

II

Psychoanalysis tends in its method to dull the bright immediacy of poetic statement. It surveys the ground over which the poet has flown; it polarizes with reason the clear white flare of revelation. But in the long run psychoanalytic criticism succeeds in giving the work of art its fullest measure of importance, its relevance to universal human experience, by exhibiting analytically the demonstrable truths on which it is based. *The Red Badge of Courage* appears to be describing a predictable process, Crane's explicit intention in the work, namely, to depict "a psychological portrait of fear."[8]

Crane's method, as we know, was largely intuitive, a synthesis of hearsay and introspection, born of that callow and orgiastic pleasure the young take in the tales and mementos of wars they are too young to remember. The literature of psychoanalysis in connection with the experience of war and the soldier lends itself to the examination of such a synthesis in that it makes only a quantitative difference between the peacetime experience of fear and crisis, and the more vivid experience of battle. Psychoanalysis recognizes too that the modern army mobilized for war is not composed of character types predisposed to seek honor in the cannon's mouth, but that war consists of all men, and thus constitutes, if only for an agonizing and brief historical moment, a universal experience, worthy of the artist's service.

John Berryman's vivid biography fails, I think, in its attempt to account psychoanalytically for the habitual motifs in Crane's fiction. Berryman's critical insights are indeed brilliant, but the psychological connections he makes are doors away from them. "Why," he asks, "did the child born belatedly into a peaceful Newark parsonage on November 1, 1871, spend his life imagining, chasing, reporting, remembering War?" He begins by tracing Crane's "Negro-War" obsession to several sources in Crane's childhood.

There are, first of all, two childhood memories: a dream and an incident. The dream is of "black riders on black horses charging at him from the surf," frightening and recurrent, later to appear, almost as remembered, as the title poem in his volume, *The Black Riders*. The second memory of childhood is of being placed upon a white horse, recollected with great fear, and being enjoined by his mother to be brave.[9] A later recollection relates to seeing a Negro stab his white mistress with a knife, a vision which is followed by Crane's panic flight from the scene and the repression of the incident.[10] Last, there is the inferential construction in Crane's infancy of an Oedipal relationship out of which Crane emerged permanently involved, so far as his adult relations with men and women were concerned, with the unconscious sanctions of the incest tabu and the threat of paternal punishment.[11]

Crane was the sickly last child of a large family. His father was a mild naif, a pious minister, his mother strongminded, militantly Christian, and unconventional. Oedipal strivings must, unless one has finely detailed information, be hypothesized from observed behavior in later life. Berryman hypothesizes for Crane the Oedipal fixations which, Freud says in his essay "A Special Type of Choice of Object Made by Man," determine the social relationships of certain types of men. It is in effect an unconscious attempt to recapitulate in one's adult life the Oedipus triangle of infancy, with the addition of a disturbing element, the superego's strenuous prohibition of such a return.

Thus, the maternal image both attracts and repels, and the relationship with women is a disguised and repetitious flight both from and toward such images. Such men have ambivalent fixations on older women who have well-established prior attachments to husbands or lovers. Strongly defensive of female virtue, these men nevertheless associate themselves with women of questionable repute, degraded love objects, whom they then "rescue," as Freud puts it, from their general disesteem, and even from their own fallen penchant for sin. *Camille* is the banal archetype of such fantasies.

For these men, the other man in the case, "the injured third party," as Freud calls him, closely resembles the stock type of Roman comedy—the outwitted *senex* or *mercator*, who loses his concubine to his wily son or younger, poorer rival. They are the necessary rivals from whom the woman is "rescued" or stolen, and if they do not exist substantially they must be invented.

Crane's own life and the preoccupations of his fiction can then be seen to derive in part from such a psychic prehistory. His own sympathies with the poor and degraded, which, when women were concerned, resulted in the shabby gossip that developed around his name in New York, resulted too in his irregular but eminently successful affair with a woman whose mere life-history shouted *demi-mondaine* to the world.

In Crane's fiction, Berryman writes, the theme of degradation and rescue is transferred to a multiplicity of situations. *Maggie: A Girl of the Streets* contains a degradation and, truncated, a rescue by the artist himself from the squalors that actually destroy her. "The movement in youth from innocence to experience, seen as a degradation," moved Crane to begin a novel, *Flowers of Asphalt*, a Huysmans-like study, but uncompleted, lost, which was going to deal with a young boy whose prototype was an adolescent, mascara-eyed male prostitute (who had accosted Crane in New York), coming to the city and there succumbing to the general vice.[12] *The Red Badge of Courage* describes Henry Fleming moving through the degradation that his cowardice subjects him to in his progress toward manhood.

Berryman isolates in the black riders, the terrible white horse, and the Negro's crime, the horrified fascination with violence, the necessity for facing it, and the identification with the degraded innocent, the outcast, ultimately the exiled artist. The horse itself is the symbol of abstract danger, and also the aggressive, murderous son, trampling the father. To ride the white horse is to be brave and gratify the mother. To be the black rider is to be the sinner, the outcast. To be the horse is to destroy the father. In "The Blue Hotel," which Berryman considers correctly to be one of the most brilliant of American short stories, these visions culminate. Every son, or "foster" son—the Swede, Johnnie, the Cowboy, the Easterner—is a "Crane-mask." The father, old Scully, is an avatar of all the fathers, beginning with Crane's own ineffectual father and including the highly-principled but ineffectual Dr. Prescott of "The Monster." In "The Blue Hotel" Crane thrashes himself when the Swede thrashes Johnnie, then goes to the saloon where Crane kills himself when the professional (and therefore social pariah) gambler kills the Swede. In "The Open Boat," again, the Correspondent, who is this time Crane himself, rides the "white horses" of the cruel sea with a sense of the tonic effect of such an experience on his mastery of fear. The belated, bungled rescue fails to save the oiler, who joins in death the other sacrificial victims of a cruel father-fate: Jim Conklin, Maggie, Henry Johnson (of "The Monster") and the Swede of "The Blue Hotel."

Somehow it all fits, but fits badly, like a child's outgrown clothing. In Crane's life we can see more constantly, for example, the line of magdalens raised above their dusty reputations, but the rescues and degradations, the rescuers and degraded, of Crane's fiction are removed from what is mainly such a sexual realm of activity. The images of terror and mindless force make more sense within the context of war and violence, but again they are wrenched to serve as parricidal impulses, especially as they are directed at the rather benign shade of the Reverend Jonathan Townley Crane, whose pious life might evoke guilt in his strayed son, but hardly an unconscious wish to destroy the father that expresses itself with such violence. It would be more readily possible to postulate (as I do) hostility directed against an older sibling, for the mother's love, than against the father. In the criminal calendar of neurosis, fratricide deserves some billing.

The answer to this poor fit is perhaps paradoxical to the received uses of psychoanalysis. The imprint of biography on fiction is like *trompe l'oeil* painting. Now you see it in its substantial outline; now you see it as a welter of the objects you would reasonably expect to see within such a scene. To be biocentric, as Berryman necessarily is, is to sacrifice diversity of the product for the sake of its unitary origins. The artist too, I believe, when he grasps the Proteus of his imagination, must of necessity lose sight of the fact among its transformations that he is really holding on to the Old Man of the Sea.

Consequently, I prefer in the analysis of literature to take half a leaf of the page of the new critic, to begin at least with the psychological dynamic of the work, as if its authorship were unknown, then later to return to the corroborative data of the life of the artist. The ability to write well indicates that a certain liberation has taken place, that earlier fixations have found a certain measure of freedom. It pays in literary criticism to neglect the artist in considering his work, for in his creation of a character not himself, he "sends forth his soul into unknown arts."[13] His imaginative life dwells at those levels just below personality, where the man becomes an essence. In earlier times he was a mythical essence. Now he has become an ethical essence, or a psychological essence. In the modern novel genus *Homo* at times becomes genus *Homo neuroticus*.

It is on this basis that I propose to deal with the psychological structure of Crane's fiction.

III

The psychoanalyst W. H. Frink writes about the emotions: "An emotion, one might say, is an undischarged action, a deed yet retained within the organism. Thus anger is unfought combat; fear unfled flight. Perhaps it would be more accurate to say that an emotion is a state of preparedness for action, which, however, in many ways is almost action itself."[14]

What is perenially impressive about *The Red Badge of Courage* is its innerness of experience, comparable in its handling of developmental changes to the subjective ordeals of Richard Feverel and Stephen Dedalus. It is an epic imitation of an emotion rather than of an action, and so becomes, as Frink suggests, another form and, I suggest, perhaps a more intense form, of action. Crane's veracity is less a matter of reconstructing a historical event which may have accompanied it. As we shall see, Crane's grasp of the sense of fear did not change when he found his war, and *his* profoundest study of terror, "The Blue Hotel," has nothing military about it. Crane's success lies in his having achieved the crystalline essence of the emotion he set out to describe.

We may begin by generalizing on the situation in which Henry Fleming finds himself. He is a part of a social group that is confronted as a group with some palpable threat of physical danger. To men who are for the first time in such a situation, the normal anxieties are predictably twofold: the first is the anxious anticipation of physical danger and possible destruction—a personal, intrapsychic anxiety; the second is outwardly directed, a matter of relationship, a social concern, involving one's self-esteem and loyalty to the small group in which one serves. Such a situation proposes an immediate challenge to how well the individual has formulated his sense of himself, and the modifications that attend his response to such pressures are an index to the quality and strength of this formulation.

Fleming's tender youth, as we might expect, precludes his achieving the serenity of his friend Jim Conklin. He is, we might say, the delicate neophyte, carefully chosen for precisely those qualities he is most deficient in, and for the one quality, "that craven scruple of thinking too precisely on th' event," that will make his initiation an affair of some moment rather than a casual transition. Literature is, of course, full of Henry Flemings. One thinks immediately of Conrad's captain in "The Secret Sharer," wondering as he stands his quixotic anchor watch, "how far I should turn out faithful to that ideal conception of one's own personality every man sets up for himself secretly." As for the others (and the captain's thought gives the lie to "every man"), "they had simply to be equal to their tasks." So Henry Fleming, at the first intimations of battle, feels himself an "unknown quantity" (p. 111), and begins immediately to look for himself, "continually trying to measure himself by his comrades, looking for kindred emotions" (p. 14), yet at the same time with the baffling sense of alienation, the sense of being "separated from the others" (p. 17).

Berryman comments brilliantly and definitively on the introspective candor of Crane's characters, their Hamlet-like awareness of the polarities of seeming and being. "There is regularly," he writes, "an element of pathos, therefore, in his ironic (oppositional) inspection, and an element of irony regularly in his pathos. A Crane creation or character normally is *pretentious* and *scared*—the human condition; fitted by the second for pathos, by the first for irony. If the second feeling can save the first, as in Henry Fleming, the first can doom the second, as in the Swede (in 'The Blue Hotel')." [15]

Henry Fleming's search for some standard by which to measure himself, his "ideal conception," settles itself on the "tall soldier," who is, even after he dies, oracular to Henry's expectations, anxieties, and hopes. Yet we must anticipate that Jim Conklin's reassurances are finally false reassurances, the identification which is only the penultimate step toward identity. Claims of pretension and fear, to use Berryman's counters, must give way to some more viable position.

Heroes in literature are, as I have suggested, heavily endowed with a faculty for self-concern, to which we may add those handmaidens to intelligence, the faculties of interest and curiosity. Henry Fleming is so endowed; it is his major differentia. Interest and curiosity are ill-suited to the life of action in almost the same degree that they are well-suited to the learning process. They are onlookers' faculties, passive, receptive, requiring always a safe distance between subject and object. To the interested and the curious the wholesome state of preparedness for danger is lacking, and any untoward activity on the part of the observed object leads to terror, flight, and with it a radical loss of interest. Henry Fleming's interest and curiosity are the elements which attracted him to the war, for he sees it as an anachronistic survival, and in his fantasies he goes into battle as if he were going into a museum of antiquities. War is a matter of the past, a "Greek-like struggle," a Homeric fantasy. "Men were better or more timid. Secular and religious education had effaced the throat-grappling instinct" (p. 10). He has, in other words, set up an aesthetic and historical distance, a strategy of denial, between himself and the actuality. He has not yet left the classroom.

Crane, we may observe here, elects at all times, for his soldiers, this role of spectator in the presence of hostile *objects*. In his battles the agents of death—weapons, a tangible enemy, the errors and coups of strategists—become a negligible aspect in the individual's struggles to master his anxieties. Henry Fleming's first successful stand against the enemy is not a stand against anything. His interest and curiosity, when they are challenged by the resistance of the "phantom" enemy, result not in anxiety, which is a state of preparedness, but in panic, which is an intolerable excess of unanticipated emotion.

This, then, is the hero that Crane sends into battle. The hero's response to danger, like that of his comrades in arms, will have been conditioned from childhood into patterns of defense and aggression, whose strengths and weaknesses will be found out under stress. He will, like his comrades, face a limited number of more or less determinate alternatives of response; a psychological naturalism will assert itself, less subject to the options of consciousness, because levels of mind and experience archaic to the uses of mature and peaceable culture are being invoked exclusively. The restrictions of Henry Fleming's point of view, his personal response, would do Henry James credit.

We must, let me assert parenthetically, rule out one alternative response, the one most associated with war and calamity, the fully developed traumatic neurosis. In such cases, better suited to clinical than to literary description, all adaptations to the world and all the higher motor and mental functions are swept under in the psychological debacle of trauma. We are dealing in Crane's novel with adaptations that are familiar to us, by which men under pressure maintain their equilibrium both within themselves and in relation to the world of friends and foes, of dangers and refuges from danger. The simplified, monothematic conditions under which Henry Fleming operates give these adaptations a greater clarity than they would possess under other conditions.

IV

The overall motif in *The Red Badge of Courage* is Henry Fleming's obsessive need to purge himself of fear. The novel is in psychological terms a study of anxiety-defense mechanisms working under pressure to establish some tolerable adaptation to a dangerous reality. Whether Crane knew or did not know at first hand about the consecrated nightmare of war is secondary to the fact that he had experienced some event in which massive fears in the presence of imminent danger were produced. The athletic contest comes immediately to mind, since Crane himself draws the comparison: "The psychology is the same. The opposite team is the enemy tribe."[16] His imagery of conflict seems mainly to be drawn from sports. At least one psychologist has commented on sports as an activity in which defense mechanisms are as observable as they are in anxiety-ridden neurotics; but anyone who has ever known the fine agony that precedes an athletic event needs no professional backing to corroborate Crane's perceptions.

Anxiety is classically described as "undischarged excitation," an emotional state attendant on the expectation of some failure, loss, or threat to the body or mind, in which the impulse toward flight is, at least for the moment, checked, or futile. Its referents are varied, environmental or psychic, but the feelings of mental and physical discomfort that anxiety arouses are known and constant. Freud discerns three basic danger situations conducive to anxiety: the fear of the loss of love, the fear of castration, and the loss of social or superego esteem—these anxiety situations being capable of infinite translations in adult life into situations which may plausibly warrant anxiety. Loss of love may range in apostolic succession from mother to nanny to mistress, the fear of castration from father's hardhanded discipline to the oppressor's wrong, and the loss of social or superego esteem from the agons of the chamber pot to "disgrace with fortune and men's eyes."

If anxiety attaches itself to three realms of activity, anxiety has also varied forms of relief, of which several will command our attention. Anxiety has been described as an anticipatory emotion, a mental preparation for danger. Given some motor discharge for the tensions of such a state, anxiety dissipates itself in purposeful activity. Deprived of motor activity, the body, as the psychoanalytic metaphor has it, is "flooded" by unmastered excitation, and the response is panic—mindless flight or paralysis. In the program Ernest Hemingway has set up for the good soldier, it is between the first and second phases of his experience of war that panic may supervene. In *The Red Badge of Courage*, likewise, it is after Henry Fleming, his anxieties at their spurious ease, has been lulled by a sense of his invulnerability and apparent victory and bodily fatigue, that he is taken by surprise and flees from the battle. He has surrendered to panic.

Cowardice and courage are imprecise public entities; fear (and I use the word as a more dynamic synonym for anxiety) is a strictly personal emotion and may lie, like libido, at the roots of love or hate, behind either cowardice or courage. The central problem becomes, ultimately, the mastering of fear, for which cowardice and courage come to represent mere extremes of adjustment. Panic, for example, is an adjustment to fear—and a very bad one since it represents the total abdication of the ego from the problem of preserving itself. But there are other, less drastic adjustments which manage to a more or less successful degree to preserve the integrity of the individual, and among these is to be found Henry Fleming's relief from "the red sickness of battle."

The mastering of fear anterior to the mastering of a danger situation involves inevitably the denial, not only of the fear, but of the situation which has produced the fear. The technics of denial, described as counterphobic defenses, are in some respects literally charms against danger, in that one adopts an attitude toward a situation which then will presumably control it. Such an attitude is plainly a regressive one, involving the denial of the world in its most palpable reality when the ego cannot master it. The psychic adaptation to external danger and internal anxiety is a recourse to those mental processes which either ignore reality or finally substitute a system of delusions linked to reality only as magic formulae are linked to the phenomena they control.

A study of Henry Fleming's ordeal reveals, as I have suggested, a medically valid depiction of the psychology of fear. Such a study follows, too, allowing for certain interstitial variations within the categories the author sets up, Ernest Hemingway's description of a process by which the civilian becomes the good soldier. But *The Red Badge of Courage*, and let us add Hemingway's *A Farewell to Arms*, describe not merely a generic response to danger, but an idiosyncratic and ultimately moral reaction to violence.

Generally speaking, a man becomes a veteran at the expense of a certain emotional and moral finesse. The alternatives of sheer self-preservative panic flight, reckless self-sacrifice, and a sensitivity to the sufferings of others are all denied him. The veteran soldier is prudently aggressive, merciless toward his enemies, and loyal to his comrades; he is a primitive, a Fortinbras rather than a Hamlet. Neither Crane nor Hemingway appears to have made any such sacrifice of emotional and moral finesse. It is interesting that Hemingway should choose "the boy Sir Philip Sidney" as the ultimate product of the military process. Sidney, it will be remembered, died not in a charge but in an act of compassion: "Poor fellow, thy necessity is greater than mine." Hemingway himself began his career in the army as an ambulance corpsman rather than as a combatant. The novel which most directly incorporates his own war experience shows us a lieutenant, Frederick Henry, a noncombatant ambulance officer, whose revulsion at the meaninglessness of the slaughter he witnesses leads him finally, as another one of Hemingway's characters puts it, to "make a separate peace."

Without doing much more than muse on the identity of surname and Christian name and the reversal of the initials of Henry Fleming and Frederick Henry, I should like to consider Henry Fleming in the light of both an extended study of the

psychology of fear and the suggestive headings that Hemingway offers us from *The Torrents of Spring*.

One is aware, in *The Red Badge of Courage*, that an individual,
unique characterization threads its way through the studiously
generalized experience suggested by the contrivedly anonymous and unbounded framework of the novel. The "youthful
private," in spite of the suggestion, finally, that the field is
checkered with such types, is perceptibly styled out of the class
to which belong the "tall soldier" and the "loud soldier," the
"tattered man" and the "cheery man." It is true that the ordeal
he undergoes and, to a certain extent his responses, are true to
type, but at a significant juncture he exhibits a unique deviation
from the standard that armies propose as their norms. We return, in short, as we do with Hemingway, to the literary hero
rather than the military hero.

"First, you were brave," Hemingway writes, "because you
didn't think anything could hit you because you yourself were
something special, and you knew that you could never die."

In every group of men confronted by a common danger (and
this may include athletes as well as soldiers) morale is a massive
denial of danger, an assurance of invulnerability, a coral atoll of
security built up out of many individual solutions to the problem of personal fear and one's ability to face danger with grace
born of a sense of being "something special." Crane's novel begins with a survey of men, a varied lot, constructing mental
earthworks of security for themselves. At the beginning of the
novel we find Henry Fleming constructing his private fantasy
of invulnerability out of his schoolboy experience of life, in
which he has learned that war is a matter of the past, a "Greek-
like struggle," a "blue demonstration," the academic strategies
noted earlier in connection with the spectatorial role. Nothing
can happen, Henry Fleming tells himself, because the war is a
Homeric archaism, removed from the present (p. 7). The very
fact of war itself is ingeniously projected into the past and into
literature. Such a stratagem bears comparison, does it not, with

Tolstoy's use of such a projection in *The Death of Ivan Ilych*, when Ivan Ilych tries to project, unsuccessfully, the fact of his death to the syllogism of Caius' mortality in "Kiezewetter's *Logic*"? As Freud observes, noting the easy expendability of lives in literature and the pleasure we take in these painless fatalities, war challenges "this conventional treatment of death." [17]

A second personal adjustment on Fleming's part involves another projection, this time the projection of his own fears onto his friend Wilson, the "loud soldier." One way of collecting reassurances is to impute fear and cowardice to others. He is frightened; I am not. Wilson and Fleming exhibit both sides of the same counterfeit coin. Fleming impugns Wilson's show of bravery and assurance by attributing his own fears, quite accurately, to Wilson and so intimidating him. Wilson, on the other hand, is denying his fears by acting out, magically, the victory he wants desperately to be reassured of. The one proceeds by disparagement, the other by self-encouragement to the same temporary sense of security. "Gee rod! how we will thump 'em!" (p. 18).

A few hours later, Wilson, confessing himself "a gone coon" (p. 26) less inhibited about expressing his fear, speaks Fleming's anxieties *for* him just as the brigade goes into action.

But these are minor adaptations, which exhaust themselves in discharges of irritability on Fleming's part, in accesses of morbid despair on Wilson's. The momentous process in Fleming's ordeal is removed from these incidentals, although his relationship with Wilson in particular deserves and will receive further mention. Rather, a continuous and unified structure of indentifications and relationships carries Fleming through his ordeal and to the threshold of his personal deliverance.

What makes Crane's grasp of the psychology of soldiering something less than miraculous, yet a marvel of intuition, involves his recognition of the subtle affinities between adolescent strivings in the toils of the Oedipal family involvement, and the regressive atmosphere of the military situation. Crane, we must suppose, flung his youth into the retort out of which

The Red Badge of Courage emerged, making use of, indeed advertising, the relationship between adolescent fantasies of deadly struggle and real violence to create a novel about the experiences of war. In Fleming we see represented a young man attempting to throw off the benevolent swaddlings of his strong-minded, protective mother and the atmosphere of school. He seeks, like Sohrab, to demonstrate his manhood in that ultimate proving ground of manhood, the battle, before a nebulous image of the father whom he barely remembers and who for that reason is everywhere and everyone who breathes authority or assurance. The real drama of the novel lies not so much in the achievement by Henry Fleming of courage (that, as we shall see, is supposititious) as in the extent to which his particular and separate peace with the "red sickness of battle" is rigidly determined by his character.

Army life (and I add, for the last time, any similar group activity) encourages an extension of regressive aims. It provides a moratorium on maturity. The stereotype of the escape from responsibility into the Foreign Legion is well known, and it is more than a schoolboy's dream. Otto Fenichel, for example, describes the "infantilization" that takes place in the mental lives of individual soldiers. The army becomes the institutionalized version of both the protective and the punishing parents. In exchange for giving up his independence the soldier entrusts his life and well-being to his superiors, fashioning the relationship out of its analogy with his earlier dependence. It is a trust, Fenichel observes, "which may give place to a sudden and severe disappointment." [18]

Henry Fleming's sense of invulnerability gives place to such a disappointment at the moment the enemy troops re-form and advance against him. It can be explained in terms of the extension of the Oedipal situation. The unconscious irony of *The Red Badge of Courage* lies in the fact that Henry Fleming never does throw off his swaddling bands. He extends their coverage. To consider only the events between the opening of the novel to his running away from the battle, we may observe that he has found his mother again in the collective activity of the army, and has found his father in those men Crane isolates, now here, now there, who represent aggression, assurance, and convey a sense of their omnipotence.

Just as a mother, by holding her fearful child's hand, shares her presumed omnipotence with the child, so Henry Fleming, when the battle forms, is engulfed in the collective security of the regiment. The metaphors of domesticity and enclosure describe his safety. The regiment is a "composite monster;" he was "in a moving box." Images of the schoolroom, the farm-yard, the world of women, pile up: the officers are like "scold-ing" birds and "schoolmistresses," the soldiers are like women trying on "bonnets"—all these represent desperate attempts to master the alien, wholly fearsome situation with the verbal magic of metaphor (pp. 29, 30).

It is more, though, than a matter of metaphor, which leaves the subject still a little vantage point of individuality. Crane draws still another insight from intuition and recognizes that the maternal embrace does not stop at symbols of enclosure; it demands some ultimate complicity on the part of the man. Maternal omnipotence is a passive virtue, an invitation to lie down. The suggestion of sleep and self-forgetfulness, as we shall see later, invites the unwary to confuse death itself with some final form of invulnerability. This invitation becomes fi-nally the crucial experience in *The Red Badge of Courage*, and its resolution for Henry Fleming becomes his inevitable response to it.

V

The rhythm of the novel may be described as an alternation of sleeps and wakings on the part of Henry Fleming. It may, in these terms, be described as an illustration of the Schopenhau-erian conflict between the principle of individuation and the slumbering Will, or between the primordial Female in her passivity and the striving Male principle. Henry Fleming's first "battle sleep" relieves him of the agonizing burden of self-consciousness he had borne in the preceding days. He loses concern with himself "in the common crisis." He is part of the "battle brotherhood," he is a "little finger on a hand" (pp. 31, 32).

Psychoanalysis, not always happy in the terminology it uses to describe phenomena, has hit upon a term that does poetic justice to the sensations of collective, ecstatic omnipotence that Crane decribes, which are characteristic of the religious, patriotic, and other concerted activities of human beings. It is the "oceanic reunion" (see above, p. 52), a feeling technically referred to as secondary narcissism. It represents an attempt to recapitulate the sense, now outgrown, of omnipotence felt by the infant whose libido has no object but itself (primary narcissism). In secondary narcissism it is the parent or his symbol who renews this sense of power, this sense of an "oceanic" (biology would suggest amniotic) reunion. One holds the Great Mother Herself by the hand. One regresses, psychically, to the community between the mother and the child at her breast, when the infant takes, along with her milk, the omnipotent mother herself into its body. It is the fantasy latent in the dying speech of Shakespeare's Cleopatra, when the serpent at her breast becomes at once the child nursing, who "sucks the nurse asleep," and the nurse who lulls the child. As it synthesizes itself out of the heat and unanimity of battle, Henry Fleming achieves briefly his oceanic reunion.

"Then you found out different," writes Hemingway. "You were really scared then, but if you were a good soldier you functioned the same as before. Then after you were wounded and not killed, with new men coming on and going through your old processes, you hardened and became a good, hard-boiled soldier."

Henry Fleming's panic occurs when he experiences his first surprised disappointment, that in his "battle sleep" his invulnerability is not unassailable. It is material to our understanding of his unconscious denial of fear to note that on all occasions when he fights, he fights like a child in a fantasy of war, firing without aiming, at a "phantom enemy." The prospects of actual conflict with real men like himself, capable of retaliation, jar him awake from his dream of perfect immunity. In his narcissistic world, he is alone, "something special," enclosed in the mother. External objects owe their existence to his will, tractable or else intolerably insurrectionary. The enemy must fall dead on command.

In his waking interim, however, it is no such matter, and in the hours following his flight certain unconscious recognitions and revisions take place in him conditioned by external events, the most important of which is the death of Jim Conklin. It is possible now to consider elements which lie within this "moving box" of maternal omnipotence. These will include certain relations and identifications, as well as a certain sinister latency connected with what I have described as the maternal invitation to "lie down."

In Oedipal terms we may epitomize the situation in this way: maternal omnipotence promises safety without effort on the part of the son. The powerful, authoritarian father, himself omnipotent, apotheosized by Crane in his brilliant expressionistic description of "the gigantic figure of the colonel on a gigantic horse," framed "black and patternlike" (difficult, I suggest, to reconcile with the "black rider" as Berryman sees him) against the sun, introduces a sterner note of duty (p. 21). The mood is active, strenuous, and dominated by the drives of conscience, and the conscience in this case is the colonel internalized.

What happens to Henry Fleming on the first day of battle amounts to a debacle of family relations. The mother has failed him; the Rebels fought back. He has failed his father, the gigantic colonel. Henry is plunged into a limbo of nullified relationships and ponders desperate remedies, rationalizations which offer slight comfort and do not touch the profound psychic adaptations which must take place. On the one hand, the mother has cast him out into the autonomous world of self-determination; on the other hand, the father, as remote on his horse as one of those patriarchal absolutes Franz Kafka is good at depicting, points an accusing finger at Henry, as coward.

We have so far discussed Henry Fleming in his role as son to the neglect of his relationships with his brothers-in-law, and even his foes, who constitute the siblings in this extension of the family. I have mentioned Wilson and Jim Conklin only briefly, indicating the extent to which Wilson represents the minor variation on Henry Fleming's fears, and Conklin some standard by which he can measure himself. Both men, in fact, the whole regiment below the rank of officer, as well as the enemy, may be designated the siblings of Henry Fleming, and, as siblings, subject to the same vicissitudes as he.

Jim Conklin is, and we need not labor the point, the good soldier, and as such becomes for Henry Fleming his sibling ideal, the son he would like to be, the dutiful son in whom the colonel is well pleased. To discriminate between Jim Conklin and all the rest of Fleming's comrades, we might suggest that Fleming exhibits the tendency of the younger brother to transfer to the eldest some of the love and idealization which would otherwise fall to the father. The travesty of assurance his friend Wilson displays arouses only rivalry and contempt in Henry Fleming; Jim Conklin he loves and admires to the extent that Conklin shows some of the assurance which characterizes the omnipotent parent, yet he remains the sibling in that he too must move on command and is subject to an uncertain fate. He is Fleming's Aristotelian hero.

Let us assume that Henry Fleming both consciously and unconsciouly elects Jim Conklin as his ego ideal. The conscious election is apparent enough in the respect Henry shows Conklin as an oracle of the coming battle. The unconscious electives are more dispersed, and their influence more pervasive. To Henry Fleming's conscious perceptions, Jim Conklin presents the model for a sensible, realistic, and above all active role in meeting the ominous threat of the battle. The only trouble is that Henry Fleming is unconsciously predisposed against such a role. He must, as I have suggested before, work his salvation out his own way.

What interests Henry Fleming more than *how* he will do (here Conklin provides a certain template for Henry) is *what* will happen to him. Here Jim Conklin can only direct Henry to an attitude which he can take only on speculation; by living or dying himself he will confirm or deny the fears that beset him. Of the two major anxieties, the loss of life and the loss of esteem, Henry Fleming has repressed the more pressing of the two. It haunts him from the cellarage. I have mentioned, as a sinister latency in the idea of maternal omnipotence, the confusion of death with invulnerability. Fleming's tentative identification with Jim Conklin is complicated by the unconscious appeal this confusion makes to him. Before the battle he thinks: "Regarding death thus out of the corner of his eye, he conceived it to be nothing but rest and he was filled with the momentary astonishment that he should have made an extraordinary commotion about the mere matter of getting killed" (pp. 25, 26). The idea, not only of rest, but of invulnerability, manifests itself to him when he sees the dead soldier: "The invulnerable dead man forced a way for himself" (p. 22). The troops must march around his inviolable body.

Now, although there seems to be some continuity between Fleming's bland attitude toward death before the battle and his reckless wish to die after his return, certain recognitions have intervened, bound up with the fate of Jim Conklin and his own shameful flight. "He jests at scars who never felt a wound" is the spirit which governs Fleming's first *conscious* reaction to the thought of his own death. He is too thoroughly entrenched in his own sense of invulnerability to be able to accept the idea of personal destruction as anything beyond a verbal concept. There is nothing to prevent his standing up, like Jim Conklin, to the enemy.

It is when the enemy rises up against him that the idea of death, and with it the consequences of being Jim Conklin, occur to him. The true, rather than the mythical, implications of the descent into the grave appear, unrelieved by the compassionate veil that regression throws over the experience of death. Here, suddenly, there is no "moving box," no collective security; there is only one's own cold-blooded mutilation. We confront here the permanent paradox of men at war who are most manly when they have become demonic children fighting under the aegis of some protective deity. In Homer's *Iliad*, Achilles defeats Hector when the former becomes the infantile berserker. Deprived of the concerns of adult life, he is more capable of the ultimate effort of war. Hector fights like a man against him, incapable of the ecstatic sense of immunity Achilles derives from the identification grief induces with Patroclus and its discharge as rage. Hector's recognition of the regressive adaptations of battle makes him refuse to return to his wife the night before he is killed. Such, too, was the impulse of Uriah the Hittite, when he fought against the Ammonites. Admittedly, Henry Fleming is no Hector, but, as I have suggested earlier, his youth and his predisposed temperament render him unfit for the aggressions war demands. The seasoned soldier, we are told, converts his fear of death into hatred and aggression. He will suffer death in order to inflict it. Toward the dead there exists not a sense of compassion, but a sense of scorn (repressed naturally) that they have succumbed, and a wish for revenge, whose magic objective, like Achilles' sacrifice of twelve Trojans to the shade of Patroclus, is to restore one's fallen comrades to some nebulous sort of life.

The Henry Fleming who shrieks and runs from the corpse in the "religious half light" (p. 42) of the woods is not the Henry Fleming who earlier has made his way around the "invulnerable dead man." Nor is he the young man who a moment before has found nature to be a "woman with a deep aversion to tragedy" (p. 41). His fear of death has been completely activated by his flight and is for the moment denied the palliation it requires.

VI

The death of Jim Conklin, including the peculiar ceremony that accompanies it, is the turning point, but only the turning point, in Fleming's slow coming-about to his final mastery of fear. He turns again after Conklin's death to the old task of mastering his fear, but this time his technics are limited by his experience and by the unconscious latencies in his identification with Jim Conklin. We may summarize (without, however, shirking an explanation) Fleming's reactions to Jim Conklin's death by saying that Henry overcomes his fear of death by the strength of his identification with Conklin. Once again death has been domesticated; Jim Conklin becomes retroactively all dead men. The living in this ocean of the dead and dying are anomalous to the normal order of things, and the old invitation to sleep takes on more somber tones. In his death, seeking with antique formality (*Oedipus at Colonnus* comes immediately to mind) his fated piece of earth, Jim Conklin directs Fleming to an intuition that was inchoate when he saw the "invulnerable corpse" and conceived of death as "nothing but rest."

Fleming's actions immediately following Conklin's death are symptomatic of unconscious adjustment. His first thoughts involving his disgrace, are along the lines of what has come to be called the "world destruction fantasy." It accompanies, paradoxically enough, that cozy sense of collective security that men experience in the face of a common crisis. The fantasy amounts to a projection outward of the fear of personal destruction, the establishment of an inverted norm, like the felicities of the early dynastic Egyptian underworld where the deceased exclaims, "I am the boy in the fields, the young man of the city is my name." Fleming briefly considers such a world destruction: "In a defeat there would be a roundabout vindication of himself. A defeat of the army had suggested itself to him as a means of escape from the consequences of his fall" (pp. 57, 58).

He again seeks for the reunion with omnipotence he had

briefly enjoyed, but now it is complicated by his recognition that it cannot be his without a struggle. We may describe it again in terms of childhood experience, terms sanctioned by Fleming's own predisposition to revert to certain patterns of childhood dependence. Maternal omnipotence is passive. It lulls the sense of individuation. Like Jocasta it mocks the reproaches of oracles and denies the existence of duties and dangers. It thrives in a fatherless world. But the way to this reunion with the mother is blocked (and the organization and function of an army at war are a magnification of this process) by a stern and equally omnipotent father, with whom reunion is possible only through a process of imitation and identification and, if this process proves impossible, through an act of self-immolation. In Oedipal terms, this is a reunion through a masochistic identification with the mother.

We recall that Henry Fleming's mother has invoked his dead father's memory along with her own prayers that he will behave honorably. He has, because of his youth, and his tendency to accept the role of the dependent son, fled from the battle. His dead father cries from his conscience; the gigantic colonel glares from his horse; Jim Conklin reproaches him from his burial place; his mother mutely waits with folded hands for him to act, since it is to her, in any case, he must return. The question his dilemma raises is *How?* His cowardice has driven him from the charmed circle his comrades inhabit and from any substantial identification with the colonel.

The hazard of an identification with some omnipotent being, or some ego idea, lies in, as we have seen, the fact that such figures tend to become confused with fate itself, a fate in which one has trusted. The loss of such a being (e.g., the initial scattering of the regiment) is in itself traumatic. Such powerful figures, when they are sufficiently individualized, (the maternal army is too vast, too oceanic, the colonel too awesome, too remote, to become more than titanic abstractions—"the Indefinite Cause, whatever it was responsible for him") are describable as "magic helpers" who take over the executive functions of the individual soldier who needs then only blindly to obey in order to be preserved.

The ordering of events between the time of Conklin's death and Fleming's rejoining the regiment impinges directly on the loss of Conklin as "magic helper." Fleming's irritable rejection of the pitifully wounded "tattered man" is as symptomatic as it is reprehensible. Henry's grief at the loss of Jim Conklin is exacerbated by the fact that Fleming has lost his most accessible source of omnipotence. He cannot help; he must be helped. The second event that takes place is understandable in the regressive logic of neurosis. Without ceasing to wish for and finally to obtain a new magic helper, Fleming identifies himself with Jim Conklin. But it is a qualified identification. He tries for a moment to see himself "throw off himself and become a better . . . a blue, desperate figure leading lurid charges with one knee forward and a broken blade high—a blue, determined figure standing before a crimson and steel assault, getting calmly killed on a high place before the eyes of all. He thought of the magnificent pathos of his own body" (p. 55). The vision fails him: "He had no rifle; he could not fight with his hands, said he resentfully to his plan" (p. 56). Again the fine ironic play between the "pretentious and the scared."

What is wrong with this fantasied identification with Jim Conklin is the element of aggression involved. I have indicated certain consistencies in Henry Fleming's character. They begin now to take positive shape. The one major consistency is his constant deflection away from aggression toward the masochistic submission to fate and authority. It is out of this most unpromising nettle that Henry Fleming must pluck the flower safely. His identification with Jim Conklin turns not on Jim Conklin's presumably heroic fight but upon his being dead. What obsesses Fleming for a while is the idea of his death in the presence of some Awful Superior. Crane very subtly indicates the ambivalence and temporary quality of this obsession by a telling use of the limited point of view. "He now *thought that he wished* he was dead. He believed that he envied those men whose bodies lay strewn over the grass of the fields" (p. 54, my italics).

In his identification with Jim Conklin, Fleming has discovered momentarily a way out of his disgrace and separation, a method of placating his conscience. One has only to die before the father, the colonel on the horse.

> It was clear to him that his final and absolute revenge was to be achieved by his dead body lying, torn and glittering, upon the field. This was to be a poignant retaliation upon the officer who had said "mule drivers" and later "mud diggers," for in all the wild graspings of his mind for a unit responsible for his sufferings and commotions he always seized upon the man who had dubbed him wrongly. And it was his idea, vaguely formulated, that his corpse would be for those eyes a great and salt reproach [p. 102].

This consummate act of moral masochism, this offering of oneself, as Freud puts it, as a "willing victim to fate," is under certain circumstances the neurotic solution to Oedipal strivings. If the process by which one comes finally to identify one's interests with the father and so effect some atonement with him is interrupted, aggressions developed on the way to such an atonement direct themselves against their possessor. The alternative becomes a flight in the direction of a passive, feminine submission to the "good" father image, to a point where the filial is equivalent to the maternal position, as regards the father.

We may regard this new anxiety (over the loss of paternal esteem) and the defense against it as representing a higher stage of development from Henry Fleming's initial fear of having lost maternal protection, a mere concern for safety. Now conscience, the superego, has come onto the scene, and Fleming is posed between the imperatives of his impulse to fly and his sense of guilt, which demands expiation in the form of his death.

The connection between Fleming's original sense of immunity to danger and his present dangerous resolution to die forthwith rests in his need to be reunited with the potent supe-

rior beings, both maternal and paternal, who have either abandoned him or cast him out. Personal safety has gone by the
board; with Jim Conklin as the precursor, Fleming may now
pursue honor in the cannon's mouth. Thus his present urge to
destroy himself is the reverse side of the immunity obtained
through identification with a superior. The lost omnipotence is
renewed in the very act of being destroyed or in destroying
oneself. This is particularly true in situations where one's self-
esteem has suffered a severe blow by virtue of some act of cowardice which has separated one from the group.

"The attempt to get rid of the pressure from the super-ego,"
writes Otto Fenichel, "is the aim of all self-destruction. . . .
The ascetic pride of self-destruction and self-sacrifice is for the
purpose of regaining participation in the omnipotence of the
powerful authority figure, or its representative in the superego. It is a passive-receptive merging with the omnipotent
person." [19]

The wish to be destroyed for the sake of forgiveness and
reconciliation is augmented by a consideration which over-
determines the desire for death—the identification with Jim
Conklin that can meaningfully be interpreted as an act of
mourning, the expression of a wish to be reunited with the
dead. To this intense wish to participate in the life and death of
Jim Conklin belongs the only wound Henry Fleming is to suffer. It would be ridiculous to explain the minor head wound he
receives as absolutely of his own devising, but the use he makes
of it allows no ambiguity as to its function. After he has been
struck, "he went tall soldier fashion." He imagined secluded
spots where he could fall and be "unmolested" (p. 61). He is, in
fact, Jim Conklin.

Part of the grim comedy of Henry Fleming's patent defenses
against fear and disgrace lies in the fact that they pass off in repetitious fantasies which must be practically unsuccessful in
warding off these anxieties. He survives his own daydream of a
heroic death. His wound, to which he has been masochistically

receptive, is after all a safe, mitigated version of Jim Conklin's mortal wounding, a spanking rather than a death.

What Henry Fleming returns to finally is Henry Fleming, in need of the magic helper he has lost. He regresses always, in terms of erogenous zones, to the toothless stage of oral receptivity. It is a stage which finds its characterological foundation in the early sucking stage of infancy. Here, aggressiveness is replaced by an infinite willingness to receive. Self-assertion and independence are replaced by self-abasement and dependence, or by an intuition of luck and immunity from the dangers that others must face alone. Such helplessness is a component of mourning, institutionally recognized in the apparent incongruity of the funeral feast prepared for the mourners. Henry Fleming's thoughts return, after Conklin's death, after Henry has been struck, to the magic helper he left behind him—his mother, and particularly to "certain meals his mother had cooked at home, in which those dishes of which he was particularly fond had occupied prominent positions" (p. 62). He remembers, too, swimming with his school friends in the river. More than hunger and thirst induce these memories; they are the yearnings of loss and separation from breast and womb. Just as the mother returns to nostalgic reflection, the "cheery man" comes along in actuality to return Fleming to his regiment. He is recognizedly the answer to an unconscious need. He "seemed to possess a wand of a magic kind" (p. 63). One is led to suspect, by the ease with which this stranger finds his way back to Fleming's regiment, that the extent to which Fleming is lost is relative to his own regressive loss of orientation. He has become in this bleak interim the little boy entire.

"Then came the second crack," writes Hemingway, "which is much worse than the first, and then you began doing good deeds and being the boy Sir Philip Sidney and storing up treasures in heaven. At the same time of course functioning always the same as before. As if it were a football game."

VII

Looking back over the events that have taken place thus far, we are aware that a certain dramatic unity has asserted itself, governed by the intricate consistencies of Henry Fleming's character and driving inferentially toward some inevitable conclusion. With mythical simplicity the fact of death and the need to face it present themselves to our frightened neophyte until, all denials and rationalizations failing him, he turns and flees toward it, whereupon it loses its terror for him and he returns to life.

With Henry Fleming we are in the epic tradition of the *Gilgamesh* and the *Odyssey*, whose heroes descend into Hell to rescue Enkidu or learn their fates, and learn among other things that death is neither blissful nor noble, and return more resolutely to life. Within other contexts, but I think in ways that psychologically have striking affinities, D. H. Lawrence has described the "drift toward death" and the recoil from it in *Sons and Lovers* and *Women in Love*, and Thomas Mann has dealt at great length with such an experience in Hans Castorp's long dalliance beside the "ocean of time" and his final emergence.

The strictly psychoanalytic view of these events has revealed an equally impressive unity, even more rigidly determined by the character of the hero than by the timeless and intrinsically mythical quality of armed conflict. Henry Fleming transfers his Oedipal strivings to his need to remain within the charmed circle of maternal protection, his inability to meet the stern demands of the paternal superego, his self-destructive bid for reconciliation and forgiveness, and his need for magic helpers, to the field of battle.

It may be thought that now in this developmental schedule Henry Fleming should emerge the happy warrior. But about the hero of *The Red Badge of Courage* as about the hero of *Oedipus Rex* it is enough to say that he emerges without claiming the superhumanity of perfect adjustment. We can say about both heroes that they discover the conduct proper to their na-

tive qualities as men. There are, in fact, certain affinities between Henry Fleming and Oedipus that I shall touch upon.

I have described the rhythm of *The Red Badge of Courage* as a
rhythm of sleeping and waking, "battle sleep" preceded and
followed by a period of self-conscious anxiety. It is equally describable as a rhythm of reunions and alienations in connection with some omnipotent superior power. It may finally and
most comprehensively be described as a rhythm of alternating
"flights."

Hamlet, too thoughtful to be a baroque hero, considers

> Whether 'tis nobler in the mind to suffer
> The slings and arrows of outrageous fortune
> Or to take arms against a sea of troubles
> And by opposing end them.

If we recognize the *Hamlet* of Freud's and Ernest Jones's studies
as well as Shakespeare's play, and grant that his anxieties are in
excess of the realistic motives of revenge for murder and usur-
pation, then we realize that what Hamlet is considering here is
not a plan of attack against a real adversary, but a defense
against his own nebulous anxieties; not how to change his fate,
but how to face his fears. He exhibits throughout the play his
neurotic ability to face real problems realistically, and his behavior consists of alternate "flights" to activity and passivity which
are productive of nothing but useless murders and unhappiness
and a morbid paralysis of will.

Anxiety has been described as a state of preparedness for a
danger situation; panic and terror as disorganized responses to
unexpected dangers, the "flooding" of the system with undischarged anxiety. Both states are liable to exaggeration into
attitudes of hair-trigger readiness and the most abject helplessness, the one to prevent the other. Hamlet's electric gibes
and plans and his inability to premeditate a definitive coup are
symptomatic of his state. Helplessness under certain circumstances, the loss of volitional powers, or the illusion of such a

loss, becomes the most painful of feelings. It is, we intuitively surmise, because the survival of the ego depends upon our feeling at all times that we take an active part in the ordering of our destinies. Those ecstatic moments of collective self-determination, which come in our oceanic reunion with others, are of necessity temporary states.

In a mind overcharged with anxiety, denied the pathological release of mania or unconsciousness, one is driven to deny either the anxiety or the situation which gave rise to the anxiety. The flight to activity denies fear and danger by the paradoxical strategy of exposing one to the very thing one fears. To prevent and forestall the terror of surprise and the annihilative sense of being a hapless victim, one seeks actively the feared situation, preferring even destruction to the dread of destruction. Thus Ovid is being psychologically accurate in his description of fear-crazed men in a plague-ridden city who

> *Hung themselves*
> *Driving the fear of death away by death,*
> *By going out to meet it.*

Such exposures and responses to danger are not always so drastic.

If one survives the initial onslaught of outrageous fortune, one then returns to meet it again compulsively, to prove to oneself that the thing one feared might happen did not in actuality happen, while all the while the original and unresolved anxiety forbids final proof. In effect one strives to ritualize, to enclose within a rigid framework of intention, what had originally been a unique and unforeseen accident. Thus one may be induced to rush blindly into a battle because of a profound fear of battle, or to incur in some mitigated form what might first have been a serious injury.

VIII

I have discussed, in connection with the "magic helper," the regression of Henry Fleming at that point to the stage of oral receptivity, a passive suckling stage. The flight to activity similarly elects an oral regressive stage in which mastery is achieved not by suckling helplessness, but by a destructive biting. Such destructive biting, as it applies here, finds a felicitous apposition in the Icelandic sagas that often depict the "berserker," the bloodlusting fighter (who is very often defeated by his more prudent antagonist), literally champing on the edge of his own shield in his murderous frenzy.

Here the flight to activity involves the primitive logic of becoming the thing or the person one fears and then proceeding to intimidate others. Reassurance is bound up with the obsessive display of fierceness; seeming *is* being, pretensions are genuine. The encouragement of one's friends is merely a benevolent variation on identification with the aggressor. One offers one's friends the encouragement one stands desperately in need of for one's self. Such cheers and threats are as readily observable on the playing fields of Eton as they are on the battlefield of Waterloo. In all these instances of the flight to activity the stress is laid upon the active as synonymous with the intentionality of the act performed. Perhaps the best instance of volition *in extremis* is afforded by the ancient world's recognition that suicide was the most dignified form of execution in capital crimes.

In connection with the flight to activity an oblique reference to the collection of trophies (the cups, banners, scalps of sports and battles) will bear interesting fruit when we apply it to Henry Fleming's final appearance under the hard-won banners he has collected. Otto Fenichel remarks that the trophy is a palpable attestation to the fact that one has in reality "run a risk without incurring the consequences." [20]

Having outlined the flight to passivity in terms of Henry

Fleming's readiness to accept protection, to yield rather than to advance, we may now chart in their alternating order the flights he undertakes and describe his final synthesis. "Regarding death thus out of the corner of his eye," by what valid means does Henry Fleming master his fears? Whatever toy slings and rubber-tipped arrows of a not-so-outrageous fortune he has suffered in the past, he has developed a characteristic response to them, which persists in his experience of war, and which finally perfects itself to become the ark of his salvation.

The true direction of Henry Fleming's flight is, we may safely say, toward passivity. The exigencies of his situation drive him into activity, but it is inevitably a spurious flight, a pantomime of activity from which he turns back with a sense of relief, back to his old dependencies. To say, however, that there is no final and elevated stasis awarded him in the role is to ignore both the course of the novel and the psychological directive that underlies it. The *mathema*, the education of King Oedipus, is an education not only in submission to the gods, but in his own identity. The "self-made," active man of Scene I takes refuge in his "unthinkable fate" at the last because at the last he knows who he is, and therefore what his fate is. Fleming, at the end of his ordeal, accepts his role as the passive spectator of the conflict because it is entirely in accordance with his sense of himself.

To stretch the mantle of King Oedipus a little further over *The Red Badge of Courage*, I would suggest still another analogy. Oedipus' arrogance early in the play derives from the protection and encouragement he receives from his wife-mother. Jocasta offers him a false security. His prophetic anxieties, his father's blood crying from the oracles, and his own conscience lead him to self-discovery, expiation, and a final abdication of any active control of his fate. His accounts are rendered in full.

Henry Fleming's activity first proceeds from his being in the maternal security of the regiment. He is the spoiled only child of an indulgent and protective mother. His trial flights to activity are tentative and mean-spirited. He intimidates poor

Wilson for his own aggrandizement, just as Wilson drowns his fears under his own loud self-encouragement. Jim Conklin holds out an image of some integrity, but the battle destroys it as a possibility, for Fleming's conduct on the first day of battle is the aimless destructiveness of oral sadism. The mere appearance on the horizon of his consciousness of hostile siblings renders him again impotent, passive. He is suddenly wearing "invisible mittens" (p. 36) (the image will be used in other stories); death is "about to thrust him between the shoulder blades"; "destruction threatened him from all points" (pp. 36, 37); and he takes to ignominious flight.

If he is not Henry Fleming the gallant soldier, who is he? His fear of destruction has alienated him from the false security of the mother; his cowardice awakens the sense of the paternal reproach. The father dominates any attempts, first of all, to excuse his cowardice to himself—"he had fled early because of his superior powers of perception" (p. 57)—to give his flight a virile framework of intention, and second, to expiate his guilt by taking belatedly Jim Conklin's road to dusty death. Both these alternate flights to activity are abandoned, as in a moment of physical and moral exhaustion Fleming yields himself up passively to the magic helper, the "cheery man," who leads him back to his regiment, the helpless, dependent, lost boy.

The subsequent stages of Fleming's development introduce two new elements, one of them undreamed of in *Oedipus Rex*. This final act of *The Red Badge of Courage* may be said now to become a *fraternal* competition for the love, protection, and esteem of *both* parents, in which Fleming's role is qualified by its being exclusively filial and submissive. His flight to passivity acquires an ethical dimension. This does not at first seem apparent until we measure his new-found valor against his new-found protectress, the flag, in terms of his inner satisfactions.

Fleming's second stand in battle is suspiciously like the first; the differentia is the degree of anger he feels, and this can be accounted for in terms of revenge. Again there is the mindless destructivity, the uncontrollable shooting at "tormentors" who are more like vermin than men. He continues to fire long after the enemy has retreated. Again there is, at the end, the sense of impotence—"in a dream it occurred to the youth that his rifle was an impotent stick" (p. 80)—a sense that previously had sent him into flight.

IX

Gregory Zilboorg, writing about troop morale in World War II, describes the sanction of anger in the process:

> It is a well observed fact that "green" troops become "seasoned" as soon as they become angry—that is, as soon as they begin to convert their fear of death into hatred and aggression. This usually happens after the baptism of fire, not so much because the soldiers become accustomed to the fire of the enemy, but primarily because their anger begins to be aroused after they have lost some of their brothers in combat. It is the mechanism of revenge, of overcoming death by means of murder, that proves to be the most potent psychological force.[21]

It is here, precisely at what would seem to be the moment of his apotheosis as the soldier-hero, that Henry Fleming makes his final adaptation, not to his fears but to his nature, for reasons I assume must ultimately rest with Stephen Crane. Far from being the hardened veteran, Fleming has turned entirely toward the higher moral and softer emotional sensibilities of the noncombatant.

I have described him as being endowed with the "faculties of interest and curiosity" to an extraordinary degree, and with the susceptibilities of youth and sensitivity given to submission to and identification with figures of authority. These qualities are alien to, or rather can only contribute to, "the delirium that encounters despair and death and is heedless and blind to the odds" (p. 87), and may possibly terminate in the same sense of impotence and terror as before.

Those who elect passivity as their release from anxiety are characterized as more dependent upon the power and good will of others. Their aggressions demand their weight in feelings of guilt, and one pays for one's supply of love and security by accepting along with the gratification a certain amount of punishment. As a fighter Fleming knows only delirium. It is only when he sees the flag which he endows obviously with the intermingled trappings of maternity and divinity—"a creation of beauty and invulnerability . . . a goddess . . . a woman, red and white . . . because no harm could come to it he endowed it with power" (p. 90)—that he falls finally and easily into his role. His real pleasure and mastery come when he seizes the flag and is "deeply absorbed as a spectator" (p. 101) of what has now become for him as it was in the beginning, a remote "blue demonstration," with other regiments fighting "as if at a matched game" (p. 99). To the lieutenant rallying the troops, Henry becomes the passive helpmate and builds not an identification but a filial, almost daughterly relationship with the man of action. "Between him and the lieutenant, scolding and near to losing his mind with rage, there was felt a subtle fellowship and equality. They supported each other in all manner of hoarse, howling protests" (p. 92).

As a fighter Fleming's behavior is autistic, infantile. His fraternal competition for the flag is an entirely different matter. It bespeaks relationships, the rivalry of brothers for the love of the parents. The fact that he wrests two flags from the hands of dying color guards and struggles with his friend Wilson for one, subsequently exposing himself to enemy fire, would lead me to postulate a fantasy psychologically equivalent to the facts (the incident is itself the elaboration of a true one): a fantasy in which the younger brother supersedes the elder because of the elder's death or wished-for death, and who then expiates the guilty aggression by taking up the same dangerous position, yet in a passive role. Such a fantasy would then extend the identification I proposed in connection with Jim Conklin, whom Fleming replaces with the clear intention of dying as a "salt reproach" to the colonel. The rival flag is Fleming's trophy to show that he has come through, that he has achieved a new invulnerability, a renewed reunion with the parents.

Read with the concepts stated here in mind, the end of *The Red Badge of Courage* makes somewhat more sense in its repudiation of all that Fleming has struggled to achieve. The close turns away as Fleming turns away from the "red sickness of battle. He had been an animal blistered and sweating in the heat and pain of war" (p. 110). The ending turns away in short from more than cowardice; it turns from "delirium," the "battle sleep," and presumably the bloodshed, to "images of tranquil skies, fresh meadows, cool brooks—an existence of soft and eternal peace" (p. 110). The novel ends not with the formulation of military courage following cowardice, but more with the formulation suggested by Freud in his "Thoughts on War and Death"—that death realized becomes "life-conditioning."

Fleming has succeeded in effecting a sublimation of impulses that had hitherto been blocked or exercised with disastrous effects. He has sacrificed activity without the loss of self-esteem or social alienation. He has fulfilled some socially acceptable ideal conception of himself. What had been an apron has become an aegis; what had been a flight has become an individual choice of mode.

I have not, except for one quoted passage, alluded to more than literary analogies with regard to *The Red Badge of Courage* as a military experience. But certain interesting parallels, which invite our consideration of Crane's later fiction in the light of his military experience and Ernest Hemingway's treatment of the war, emerge from psychoanalytic studies of combat neurosis. A study of the action of *The Red Badge of Courage* first shows us Henry Fleming standing in mortal fear of destruction, with the expressionistic (animistic) uses of color and appearances as ominous. He is next shown witnessing violence, or the effects of violence, with feelings of anxiety. In his last position as color bearer and spectator the similitude of the game, the "football" player, the "matched game," predominate.

Abram Kardiner, describing the recovery of a victim of a battle-incurred traumatic neurosis, offers as symptomatic of the patient's recovery a progression of dreams which follows a scheme similar to the one I have outlined. The first dreams were the most terrifying dreams of personal annihilation, accompanied by great anxiety. These dreams were followed by those in which the patient from a vantage point of safety watched violence, again disquieting, but less so. Finally the patient dreamed of witnessing merely sports and refined combat accompanied by minimal anxiety. In both the novel and the case history the transition is from actor to spectator, identification to projection, violence to controlled activity.[22]

Another parallel from the literature of war and neurosis seems at first in the light of Crane's novel, and what I have said about Henry Fleming's sublimation, to contradict my supposing him capable of making a successful adaptation. Gregory Zilboorg takes a dimmer view of the essentially passive character in wartime.

The neurotic is incapable of fighting, Zilboorg says, because his identification with the dead is too great, "because of a severe sense of guilt which antedates his military service." He feels "unconscious compassion without corresponding scorn. He succumbs to a passivity from which he is unable to escape *except by way of fantasy* . . . into that magic megalomanic type of passivity by means of which they avoid both death and murder but are unable to escape the fear of either. . . . The paradoxical ethicosociological implications of these reactions are clear: those who are the most conspicuous misfits on the battlefront appear in actuality to be ethically the most sensitive people" (my italics).[23]

Admittedly it is clear that the orally receptive individual does not make a good soldier in any active, combatant sense of the word. At best he will serve effectively behind the lines or in a humanitarian role. It is precisely this consideration that makes Henry Fleming's final role interesting and provides us with some extension with which to consider both Crane and

Hemingway as men and artists. In assigning Henry Fleming to the role of standard-bearer Crane is, with great and perhaps unconscious ingenuity, accurately representing the extent to which *The Red Badge of Courage* is compounded of hearsay and unobstructed fantasy. Real carnage in the novel is curiously impressionistic, and Henry Fleming, otherwise wakeful and alert, becomes on the firing line a somnambulist shooting at nothing in particular.

X

When Crane finally got to see *his* war, it was not as a combatant but as a war correspondent, a *spectator. His* behavior under fire was, as his biographer points out, "somnambulistic," passive, made up of useless gestures. As we shall see, the essential nature of his description of war changed very little. Thus the equation evolves: Henry Fleming, color sergeant, equals Stephen Crane, war correspondent. Having beaten his pen into a sword in *The Red Badge of Courage*, he subsequently beats it back into a pen.

Philip Young is at some pains to prove that the Ernest Hemingway hero—Nick Adams, or Frederick Henry, or Jake Barnes—is a "sensitive, humorless, honest, rather passive male,"[24] and that, by and large, both the characters' and Hemingway's own personalities derive from the traumatic experience of the Great War in which Hemingway, an ambulance officer, was severely wounded.

Hemingway suffered, Young says, from the traumatic neurosis commonly associated with wars and other catastrophic events, a nervous disorder following a shock or an injury. The effect of the original shock is such that any subsequent excitation, no matter how far removed from the traumatic experience, arouses the most intense anxieties, the waking nightmares of insomnia and troubled dreams. The mind, fighting always to master these excitations, retreats to simple, primitive functions—games, mechanical occupations, fishing, the performance or enjoyment of ritual or ceremonial activities.

A second effect of traumatic neurosis is the compulsion of the sufferer to return to some mitigated version of the original injury. If he is a writer, he may write about it obsessively. Or he may in his own life find analogues to the original violence—sports or hunting—and project these experiences, too, in his fiction. And finally he may create a hero who can stand up to these fatalities with a courage that lies on the far side of thought.

Young accounts in these terms for certain biographical salients of Hemingway's own life. Not presuming to contain either the man or his work within this necessarily narrow framework, nevertheless he explains Hemingway's inexhaustible zest for the bullfight which provided him with a spectacle which allowed the controlled and perpetual exhibition of courage within a ritual framework, as opposed to the formless accidentality of war. Young explains, too, in view of Hemingway's physical restlessness, his obsessive devotion to this art.

I feel, however, in the light of the analogies between Crane's and Hemingway's lives and fiction, that Hemingway's poetics of violence did not require the sledgehammer blows of traumatic neurosis to shape it. The young ambulance corpsman Fenton described languishing on shipboard because the German U-boats were neglecting to torpedo him seems to have been already far on his way to becoming Nick Adams. In much the same way Stephen Crane could synthesize in Henry Fleming the foolhardy correspondent who stood on the redoubt at San Juan and lighted his cigarette.

XI

There is, finally, in connection with *The Red Badge of Courage*, the corroboration afforded by those other works of fiction in which Crane treats of war and violence, particularly those which follow his adventures in Greece and Cuba where, presumably, he activated his prophetic fears. It is safe to say that the psychological texture of these later works remains the same. War continues to speak to the uneasy sense of invulnerability that Henry Fleming felt. The same bronze father images stand guard, and the same maternal regiments enclose whole pods of frightened siblings. The same passive neophyte (behind whom now stands the war correspondent) remains the ironist of his ordeal.

"The Price of the Harness," written out of the Spanish-American War, contains these elements: "The whole scene would have spoken to the private soldiers of ambushes, sudden flank attacks, terrible disasters, if it were not for those cool gentlemen with shoulder straps and swords, who, the private soldiers knew, were of another world and omnipotent for the business." [25] The hero of the story, Nolan, combines in his character and the effect of his death on his comrades, qualities inherent in both Jim Conklin and Henry Fleming. Nolan is at once the passive spectator and the good soldier. Crane describes Nolan as if, having overlaid the original fantasy with fact, he could not for the sake of his integrity obscure either. Nolan, actively engaged in the charge which costs him his life, thinks: "He had loved the regiment, the army, because the regiment, the army was his life—he had no other outlook; and now these men, his comrades, *were performing his dream-scenes for him; they were doing as he had ordained in his visions.* It is curious that in this charge he considered himself as rather unworthy. . . . His part, to his mind was merely that of a man who was going along with the crowd" (p. 296, my italics).

"The Five White Mice" illustrates with more intimate directness the relationship between fraternal competition and paternal omnipotence than do their institutionalized versions in *The Red Badge of Courage*. The New York Kid, whose companion, the drunken Frisco Kid, has jostled a proud Mexican, is challenged to fight. He has just bluffed his way out of losing a bet on a throw of the dice, and now his bluff is being challenged in an invitation to mortal combat. Again, as in *The*

Red Badge of Courage, the same massive inhibitions against self-assertion and aggression turn the Kid's gun into an "impotent stick." The gun he draws feels "unwieldly as a sewing machine. Some of the eels of despair lay wet and cold against his back" (p. 210). At the same moment he thinks of his father:

> He witnessed the uprising of his mother and sister, and the invincible calm of his hard-mouthed old father, who would probably shut himself up in his library and smoke alone. Then his father would come, and they would bring him here and say, "This is the place." He pitied his old, financing father, unyielding and millioned, a man who commonly spoke twenty-two words a year to his beloved son. The Kid understood it at this time. If his fate was not impregnable he might have turned out to be a man and have been liked by his father [p. 209].

Behind the passage is Henry Fleming, who has decided to die, a "salt reproach" to the colonel, exchanging a plausibly heroic death for a speculative manhood. With this flashback in his mind the New York Kid draws his pistol, convinced that he will be killed. The Mexican and his friends step back in fear, and the Kid realizes that the "tall," "stout" Mexican, "a fine and terrible figure," is vulnerable:

> He had never dreamed that he did not have a complete monopoly of all possible trepidations. . . . Thus the Kid was able to understand swiftly that they were all human beings. . . . He was bursting with rage because these men had not previously confided to him that they were vulnerable. . . . He had been seduced into respectful alarm by the concave attitude of the grandee. And after all, there had been an equality of emotion. . . . An equality! [pp. 208, 211].

"Had he not resembled my father as he slept," says Lady Macbeth (her dagger as "unwieldy as a sewing machine"), "I had done't." We can, with Crane's heroes, as we can with Hemingway's, postulate a closed season on fathers. The Kid's flight to activity (out of character with the gambling man

Crane has described) is inhibited by his recognizing in the "Spanish grandee" the authoritarian figure of his "unyielding and millioned" father. The inhibition is released when he recognizes that he has only to deal with a vulnerable sibling like himself. Here, rage is the equivalent of laughter, a violent release from tension.

Even beyond *The Red Badge of Courage* and the other studies of violence, "The Blue Hotel" is, as an intensive study of fear, the finest thing Crane created. It has been compared to Hemingway's "The Killers," which is interesting, since psychologically they are diametrical opposites meeting only at the antipodes—fear itself, for Ole Andreson in "The Killers" exemplifies in almost pathological terms the flight to passivity in his fatalistic resignation to death, and the Swede is the other side of the coin, a pathological flight to activity.

The one weakness of "The Blue Hotel" is perhaps its rational framework. The widespread assumption on the part of Easterners and Europeans in the 1890s that the Western United States were inhabited solely by cowpokes, Indians, and bandits is used by Crane as a foundation for the Swede's immediate suspicion of everyone. But the Swede is, like Bartleby the Scrivener, an "Isolato," the very mask of fear, and not to be measured by normal standards.

The Swede arrives, with some other travelers, at the Palace Hotel, Nebraska, convinced from the start that he will be robbed and murdered by the proprietor, Pat Scully, his son, Johnnie, or one of the cowboy transients about the place. At first he is timidly apprehensive, then hysterically frightened. Scully calms him down and invites him to play a friendly game of cards with the group. The Swede now undergoes a complete change of personality. He plays cards with manic verve, "board-whacking" as he takes his tricks. The card game is upset when he accuses the proprietor's son Johnnie of cheating, and then beats him in a fist fight. Flushed with this triumph, he extends his circle to the local saloon where, trying to browbeat the local gambler into drinking with him, he meets the death he has long feared.

The Easterner speaks the epilogue. Johnnie, he says, *was* cheating: "And you—you were simply puffing around the place and wanting to fight. And then old Scully himself! We are all in it! . . . Every sin is the result of collaboration. We, five of us, have collaborated in the murder of this Swede" (p. 197).

In considering "The Blue Hotel" in its psychological apposition to *The Red Badge of Courage*, we face first of all an archaeological problem. Excavating for the characterological sources of Henry Fleming's actions, we have run across a structure that is obliquely but intrinsically a part of the counterphobic techniques examined previously in the novel. Digging for the battlefield of Homeric Troy, we have found a city below the ancient site.

The Red Badge of Courage presented a reasonably normal youth making a tolerable adjustment to an unreasonably tough situation. His anxieties were finally and convincingly assuaged when certain psychic imperatives found satisfaction under the shelter of the flag. Certain shadowy relationships, parental and sibling, resolved themselves in the process, with nothing more untoward in their nature than would be compatible with the ambivalences of adolescence—identifications and projections and flights, all in the service of an urgent adjustment to danger.

In "The Blue Hotel" the firm ligature of counterphobic defense technics unites the story with the others that have been considered, but now they are in the service, not of a real danger situation, but of a paranoid delusional system, and all that such a system implies. *The Red Badge of Courage* can be called a strategic fantasy of fear overcome. "The Blue Hotel" is a nightmare.

XII

In discussing *The Red Badge of Courage*, I touched upon Henry Fleming's attempts, first and last, to still his excitement by seeing the war first as the above-mentioned "blue demonstration" and finally as a "matched game." As a defense against a danger situation, either one's own rebellious impulses or an environmental threat, the game satisfies the compulsion to repeat in a mitigated, controlled form an experience which was originally terrifying. Children's games often play out deaths, murders, and mutilations, with the child playing the active role in a drama which originally cast him as its passive, frightened victim. Such games, as we all know, are played with a frantic joy that comes close to being pain. It is, in fact, a joy that celebrates a release from painful anxieties.

There is, in the stories we have considered, a sort of "game syndrome" that operates in this way. We have seen it in the imagery of the novel. It shows itself briefly in "The Price of the Harness," in Nolan's relegating the charge he is involved in to a level of "dream-scenes." In "The Five White Mice" the game is more ambitiously employed; it is an analogous foreshadowing of the main action. The New York Kid in a friendly dice game in the Mexican bar puts fifty dollars, sight unseen, on a die. There are no takers; the die is a low number; he would have lost. The incident passes off in good-natured teasing.

The same bluff and backing down take place in the street, in what the Kid thinks of as the "unreal real" (p. 209). This time the Kid himself is the losing die, and the Spanish grandee is the timid bettor who will not call the Kid's bluff. The full psychological function of the game as a release from anxiety is subordinated to its value as a symbolic statement of self-evaluation. The Kid says, in effect, "I am not what I seem to be, but only my father will call my bluff."

In "The Blue Hotel" the play's the thing, and Crane apparently knew it, the same way he knew something about the inner workings of the Swede somewhere between conscious and intuitive grasp. As a man the Swede is past redemption; the game of cards is not his undoing. It merely serves as the last scrap of reality on which the Swede can found his delusions of persecution.

When the Swede enters the hotel, Scully's son Johnnie and an old farmer are playing cards for fun. Serious money-gambling is too close to reality for mock hostility to function as it does in child's play. Playing for fun, Johnnie and the old man are engaged in serious quarrels over their game. Following each such quarrel the Swede laughs nervously and makes some remark about the dangers of Western life, incomprehensible to the others. When he is first invited into the game, he plays nervously and quietly, while the cowboy is the "board-whacker." "A game with a board-whacker in it is sure to become intense," and for the Swede the intensity, because all occasions inform against him, becomes unendurable, and he voices his fears: "I suppose I am going to be killed before I can leave this house" (pp. 171, 172).

Old Scully, with a fine sense of the problem, exhibits the domesticity of his life to the Swede, shows pictures of his wife and dead daughter, gives an account of his sons and the life of the town. He draws the Swede into the circle of fraternal fellowship to which his son, the cowboy, and the transients of the Palace Hotel belong. The Swede, finally induced to take a drink (which he first rejects, as Scully says, because he "thought I was tryin' to poison 'im'") (p. 179), discharges all the energy that was part of his anxiety in an outburst of false relief. He becomes a part of the family with a vengeance, presiding over the supper table with a joyless, feverish joy: "The Swede domineered the whole feast and he gave it the appearance of a cruel bacchanal. He seemed to have grown suddenly taller; he gazed, brutally disdainful, into every face. His voice rang through the room" (p. 181).

When he plays cards again with the group, he becomes the "board-whacker," while the cowboy is reduced to a sad silence. It is the discovery of Johnnie's cheating that precipitates the tragic sequel. The Swede is mad; he "fizzed like a firewheel" (p. 180); but the game of cards is a benign way for him to work off his aggressions harmlessly, his hostilities intelligently displaced to the card table. Ironically, however, the game is denied its therapeutic value. The scrap of reality that will nourish the Swede's original delusion, which he has not relinquished, merely mastered, is provided by the fact that Johnnie is *really* cheating. *Real* cheating in a game for fun violates the make-believe, like acid in a water pistol. For the Swede the cheating restores the game to the world of outlaws, professional gamblers, and gunmen. It then follows, with maniacal logic and poetic justice both, that the next and last victim of the Swede's attentions should be the town's professional gambler, whom the Swede unwittingly but unerringly singles out. He is the institutionalized reality of which Johnnie was merely the precursor.

I have reviewed here those elements which relate most apparently to Henry Fleming's actions in *The Red Badge of Courage*. The Swede exhibits, albeit madly, alternate flights to passivity and activity. Wary apprehension succeeds to panic and a passive acceptance of annihilation, to be succeeded by a triumph of mastery, an identification with the aggressor, the pursuer, and no longer the pursued. And above all there is the framework of the game, danger passing off in play, only to return again as danger.

There are other resemblances, however, obscured, not by their existing in "The Blue Hotel" as traces, but because in "The Blue Hotel" these elements are more intense. They have the vividness of mania.

The inference in connection with paranoid delusions of persecution is that the subject is defending himself against his own homosexuality. In his relations with other men he denies his love by substituting an equally dynamic attraction—that of hate. He then denies the hate itself, since it lacks any foundation in reality, and puts upon him moreover the guilty burden of aggression, and projects his hatred upon the object of his original desire. The ego in such cases regresses from its ability to test reality to the archaic delusional systems, the animistic world of childhood, in which all nature is equally sensate. Thus the wish to be the passive victim of some homosexual violation may express itself in the fear of such violation—which displaces itself to other body openings. The fears arise in connection with being poisoned, invaded by dangerous rays, brainwashed. The paranoid may also identify *with* his persecutor in order actively to do to him what he might otherwise have suffered himself. The transformation of the repressed erotic attraction in favor of an overt sadistic aversion finds its literary expression in such relationships as Prince Hal's and Harry Hotspur's, "I will embrace him with a soldier's arm," or Claggart's persecution of Billy Budd in Melville's story.

The Swede's emotional swing from apprehensive depression to manic elation reflects, internalized, the same battlefield as that on which Henry Fleming fought his fears. The problems of self-esteem, alienation, and reunion with the omnipotent superior present themselves, along with the technics of mastery involved. We can only add, tentatively, in view of the Swede's paranoid delusions, that the Swede's anxieties involve the mastery of his own homosexual aggressions rather than a threat from the external world.

Anyone arriving in a strange town will experience that sense of narcissistic starvation that comes with the feeling that one is a social cipher in the life of the community. The Swede, psychotic to begin with, arrives already prejudiced, in a small Western town, bringing with him a massive and insatiable need for reassurance against his own unfathomed wishes.

"We'll git swallowed," says a soldier meekly, just before a charge in *The Red Badge of Courage* (p. 86). It is perfectly descriptive of the oral level of fixation that prevails in a raging battle. Eat or be eaten. The Swede's repressed oral fixations involve "swallowing" the world in order to be reunited with its omnipotence, the way a hungry child cleaves savagely to the breast that comforts it. But the obverse side of the coin is his manifest fear that the world will just as savagely attack him.

In this spirit he refuses the first drink Scully offers him as if Scully's teeth were at his throat. But Scully's kindness and the drink itself, once the Swede has swallowed it and found it harmless—experiences which would, with a rational man, effect a pleasant reunion with society—return the Swede's impulse to its original uninhibited form. Scully behaves like a father to the Swede. What is more, he offers him the oral satisfactions of a drink. "'Drink,' said the old man affectionately. . . . The Swede laughed wildly. He grabbed the bottle, put it to his mouth; and as his lips curled absurdly around the opening and his throat worked, he kept his glance, *burning with hatred*, upon the old man's face" (p. 178, my italics). The image is the image of a fierce baby, its feeding long overdue, glaring over the nipple at the source of its relief.

The combined gestures are the symbolic fulfillment of a deeply repressed fantasy. Scully has, in effect, "adopted" the Swede, whose exaggerated need for assurance and oral sadistic drives will extend themselves to the absorption of everything and everyone in sight. His foster father, Scully, he swallows at one gulp. A few minutes after he has drunk he is contradicting Scully "in a bullying voice," or has "stalked with the air of an owner into the executive parts of the hotel" (p. 179). He must enter into this cannibalistic relationship with everyone at once. In the card game he takes all the tricks. At supper he almost impales the Easterner's hand as they reach for the same biscuit. His fight with Johnnie is a still more intimate encounter, a sibling struggle for the attentions of the same father, the translation into sadistic (and therefore socially plausible) activity of the Swede's repressed homoerotic drives. There is no clear line here between the various components that move the Swede to action. His mind is a graveyard of decaying realities, baseless fears, disguised desires, and futile strategies.

Manic elation is the literal rendering of the ancient "Whom the gods destroy they first make mad." Its shrill laughter and high spirits and a sense of unlimited power are a celebration of the release of the ego from the bonds of a self-derogatory conscience. Now the ego has become the lord of its own misrule and embarks on defiant pursuit of forbidden pleasures, which here involve the aggressive humiliation of other men. The Swede discharges his new, liberated energies in cards, drinking, and fighting. He has achieved his reunion with omnipotence at the expense of his intellect. He had begun in all self-effacing humility by fearing for his life; he ends bloated with his triumph over his imagined persecutors. He *is* the group. His commanding the gambler to drink with him, the sadistic counterpart to Scully's earlier, kinder command, is his moment of *hubris*. He has become the manic travesty of the father. The gambler knifes him, the knife itself a translation (and therefore socially acceptable, more so, at least than its phallic equivalent) of the Swede's repressed wish for sexual violation, and like an enchantment dispelled, the Swede reverts to his former role of the passive, hapless victim of another man.

The Easterner's self-accusatory indictment of all of them as murderers—"every sin is the result of a collaboration"—is too oriental, too transcendental a statement to be confined within a blue hotel or a platitude of social consciousness. It has karmic ramifications, whose psychological equivalents are consistent with that omniscient "Indefinite Cause" which threatens to seal Henry Fleming's doom, that fascinated dread and disbelief with which Crane's characters enter onto the stage as spectators and actors both. In summing up "The Five White Mice" John Berryman writes: "The Kid's faith, in substance—Crane's new faith—is in Circumstance as *not* making impossible the individual's determination of his destiny." It is, we may say, Crane's vision of normality, a mind turned outward upon the world, away from its own crippling presentiments. The Easterner's epilogue, as it gestures inward towards an infinity of secret causes, is Crane's cry of resignation.   [1965]

4.

Shedding His Sickness in Books: Sherwood Anderson's Literary Case History

My own interest in American literature is conditioned by my prior experience with the broader, richer body of European literature, in which the issues of class struggle, the whole fabrics of experience, are subordinated to the concern with reproducing them in literary form; in European literature the abiding concern is aesthetic, style the attempt to define reality in terms of a mimetic art. There is no equivalent in American literature, for example, of a work like Joyce's *A Portrait of the Artist as a Young Man*, the *kunstler roman*, the developmental novel— *Tonio Kröger*, for example—except perhaps *The Education of Henry Adams*, which is less a novel than it is a dramatized autobiography. When an American writer deals with his development, it usually takes the form of his slow conversion to the Socialist party, as it does in Frank Norris and Upton Sinclair, or his acceptance of a world view as a philosophical certainty. My position then is that whatever the social or economic situation is de facto within which the artist works, what really matters is the extent to which he is capable of rendering that situation. I regard it as an absurd law which forbids us to love or admire anything because it is relative or arbitrarily homogeneous to our own limited condition.

The novel's immediate concern, if it is to meet the challenge to render life realistically, is with what Lionel Trilling calls the "social texture" that is intrinsic to the work of fiction. And "social texture" must necessarily include such considerations as class, wealth, intellectual levels, religious sects, political, military, cultural activities, from which a large part of the population, particularly the lower orders, is excluded.

"It would seem," writes Trilling, "that the Americans have a kind of resistance to looking closely at society. They appear to believe that to touch accurately on the matter of class, to take full note of snobbery, is somehow to demean themselves."[1] I consider it, then, central to our consideration of these American writers, to study and evaluate them in terms of the moral and psychological realism they achieve in the presence of whatever happens to be the body of their fiction. "Moral realism" is Trilling's term for a benign ambivalence toward any and all characters and actions; not moral relativism, but a 20/20 point of view. Such an approach will preclude the provincialism that inheres in the popular notion of what reality is and what realism is—the fallacious notion that reality must live in the slums where the noises are louder and the smells more noisome, and that realism is an onomatopoeic rendering of sounds and smells.

Reality is not an *absolute* term. It should not constitute the immediately recognizable, but should come to us, as it does to scientists and poets, as a surprise, a treasure suddenly uncovered, or as it does to Hamlet, as a ghost in the cellarage. Reality is primarily the gift of consciousness, whatever else it is not, and the history of a literary era and the realisms it achieved is a history of a series of consciousnesses whose moral and psychological perceptions help shape our reality.

Within these parameters, the American writer Sherwood Anderson bears particularly close scrutiny. There are two approaches to Anderson: his own and your own. He is like D. H. Lawrence in that respect; he seeks to impose a belief to which his art is an argument. With Lawrence, who has more substance than Anderson, it is possible to accept the author fruitfully on his own terms, to become a disciple, to be washed in the blood of *Lady Chatterley's Lover*. But Anderson never brings off anything like a religious commitment. He is more like a high school graduation: warm June night after a rainfall, girls looking like moths in white organdy. When we try to evaluate Anderson in terms of himself, we find very little to say.

In a passage from his *Memoirs*, he sums himself up as an emotion in search of an idea:

> There was a young woman who came to wait on us, and occasionally when our eyes met something happened between her and me. I had, again, as she came toward us, made a picture of her life but this time the thing had really happened. What I had imagined about her, the picture I had made of her life so swiftly, was true. This I knew and she knew. She knew when our eyes met. It was almost as though the woman and myself had lived together in great intimacy for years. There was nothing about her I did not know.
>
> But how shall I explain all of this? There is, sometimes, this sudden, half mystic bond suddenly set up between people, deep knowledge of each other, something deeply felt, something known. All my life it has been happening to me. It is love. What else can it be called? It is one of the thousands of marriages people make. It is something that is always happening between people, but they dare not or will not know it. When men and women dare let themselves know it there will be a new life on this earth.[2]

And elsewhere Anderson states very simply his objections to the literature of the nineteenth-century writers Howells, Hawthorne, and Mark Twain, objections that Van Wyck Brooks and Vernon Parrington were to labor. The approach is thoroughly unhistorical and one-sided; Anderson writes:

> They are all of them, Howells, Hawthorne, Twain, too much afraid. . . . In all their writing there is too much of life left out.
>
> There was, for example, the matter of sex. My own experience in living had already taught me that sex was a tremendous force in life. It twisted people, beat upon them, often distracted and destroyed their lives.[3]

Now it is only poetic justice that we can turn this comment back upon Anderson: in all his writing there is too much of life left out. There was, for example, the multiplicity of ways in which people might relate to one another or to society—relationships as perceptible and important as the sexual relationship—as well as the life of art, the ramifications of marriage, education, urbanity, social changes, wars, with the sexual relationship pervading all this as some generalized Eros of civilization.

But for Anderson, due I suppose to the heightened consciousness his generation acquired of the importance of the sexual relationship stimulated by the Freudian discipline, the sexual relationship per se became his all in all. Take for example the character of Louise, from "Godliness" in *Winesburg, Ohio*, who "was from childhood a neurotic, one of the race of oversensitive women": "Before such women as Louise can be understood and their lives made livable, much will have to be done. Thoughtful books will have to be written and thoughtful lives lived by people about them."[4] The world has turned bottoms up for Anderson, and the prospect so enchanted him that he can observe nothing else. Thus, there is a curious lack of content in his fiction. People say many, many things, or a piece of paper is filled with many figures, or people are making something, or they think about many things. Only the natural world is valid and is described with considerable brilliance, not as Lawrence or Shakespeare describe it, with the names of flowers which are like the flowers themselves, or accurate renderings of topography as James places the reader in his novels, but certainly with a great nose and ear and sixth sense for the quality of the Ohio countryside.

Lionel Trilling is tougher on Anderson than I am. I tend to be grateful to Anderson for his ability to capture the emotions of the inchoate sexual experience. But for Trilling this is all kid stuff, and he wishes none of it. In this connection Trilling delivers himself, unless I'm reading it wrong, one of the silliest sentences I have ever read.

> But although the visitor from Mars might be instructed by Anderson in the mere fact of bisexuality, he would still be

advised to go to the Italian opera if he seeks fuller information. For from the opera as never from Anderson, he will
acquire some of the knowledge which is normally in the
possession of natives of the planet, such as that sex has certain manifestations which are socially quite complex, that
it is involved with religion, politics, and the fate of nations,
above all that it is frequently marked by the liveliest sort of
energy.[5]

But I gree with the statement in substance; Anderson appears, like one of his characters in "Loneliness," to be "confused and disconcerted by the facts of life."[6] We are more often
than not at the mercy of his vagueness.

> No. I do not think that any of us at the time wanted to
> over-play sex. But we wanted in our stories and novels to
> bring it back into real relation to the life we lived and saw
> others living. We wanted the flesh back in our literature,
> wanted directly in our literature the fact of men and women
> in bed together, babies being born. We wanted the ter-
> rible. . . . Was I not later to be called by one of our Ameri-
> can critics "The Phallic Chekhov"?[7]

Yet it is not this program of sexual rehabilitation that im-
presses us in the long run but those extraordinary moments
when some concrete data of experience are before him and he
presents them to us, or when instead of using the Freudian unconscious, the Freudian unconscious uses him, as perhaps it
does in "The Man Who Became a Woman."

Poor White, generally speaking, is a poor novel. Its main
character is implausible, a shambling allegory of a man whose
discovery of bisexuality is the magnification to absurdity of the
sexual theme of *Winesburg, Ohio*. Hugh McVey appears almost
to be a prototype of that other allegory of the modern man,
Clifford Chatterley, with a powerful upper body and a passion
for the machine, but with paralyzed or clumsy legs.

The novel does, however, have features that redeem even its
allegorical program which—while it constitutes the skeleton of
the novel and so makes it into a plot very close to Bunyan's *Pil-*

grim's Progress, a rhetorical rather than a poetic instrument—is decently clothed with something of Anderson's sensuous feeling for nature and for relationship.

The novel can be divided into three areas of discussion. The first and simplest is Anderson's description of the historical moment, the turn of the century when Populism, the old agrarian economy, was yielding to the new order of things—the rise of industrialism, the worship of bigness, the poison of eastern capitalism. Second is the allegorical level, in which this process takes places within the characters particularly of Hugh McVey and Clara, who loom archetypally in the novel. The third may be called the psychopathology of small town life, and includes all the neurotic and psychopathic symptoms observable in *Winesburg, Ohio*: the halfwits, the obsessions, the frustrations, the rituals, the perversions.

The populist background of the novel is most easily dealt with, as the preface deals with it. Anderson is a rustic Hesiod who describes an age before our own, an arcadian society of country folk: "Between the acres of the rye these pretty country folk would lie," a moonlighted, pastoral setting, inhabited by dreamily psychopathic farm lads and their gingham-aproned sweethearts, ploughing up the deep virgin soils of mid-America in a spirit of optimism and courage, listening to stories by men who had, in the Civil War, "climbed fighting over hills and in the terror of defeat had swum wide rivers." And, "Friendships begun between boys and girls in the fields ripened into love. Couples walked along residence streets under the trees and talked with subdued voices. They became silent and embarrassed. The bolder ones kissed. . . ."[8]

Yet the Anderson myth continues, with the same lucidity that characterizes the myth from Hesiod to William Faulkner. At the height of this silver age of sweet authority, new, disquieting elements were at work. "The minds of men were turned in upon themselves. The soul and its destiny was spoken of openly in the streets. Robert Ingersoll came to Bidwell to speak in Terry's Hall, and after he had gone the question of the divinity of Christ for months occupied the minds of the citizens."[9]

The new force at bottom was industrialism, the machine. There is a certain force to the Marxist insistence on the economic roots of religion and ethics. Faulkner and Anderson are positively medieval in their sense of the rightness of the feudal system whose apex is the farmer gentleman who reads his Virgil and his Keats with calloused hands, and whose fieldworkers differ from him only in degree and according to the lengths their own ambitions drove them.

The machine destroyed all that. The distribution of reward for physical effort was no longer observable to the lay mind; it sank into economic abstraction, became high finance. The process by which one man became master and the other slave took place now in the vault of banks and the Wall Street Canyon.

> The new force stirred and aroused the people. It was meant to seal men together to wipe out national lines, to walk under seas and fly through the air. . . . Already the giant that was to be king in the place of old kings was calling his servants and armies to serve him. . . . Thought and poetry died or passed as a heritage to feeble fawning men who also became servants of the new order. Serious young men in Bidwell and in other American towns whose fathers had walked together on moonlit nights along Turner's Pike to talk of God, went away to technical schools.[10]

The Bidwell tycoon, Steve Hunter, is victimized (like Dos Passos' J. Ward Morehouse in *U.S.A.*) by the conspiracy afoot to create the "myth of greatness" in order to justify the consolidation of great capital and great holdings among the new millionaires.

> At the seat of the American government at Washington hordes of somewhat clever and altogether unhealthy young men were already being employed for the purpose. . . . Having befouled their own minds for hire, they made their living by befouling the minds of others. . . . As the politicians of the industrial age have created a myth about

themselves, so also have the owners of dollars, the big bankers, the railroad manipulators, the promoters of industrial enterprises.[11]

Arcadia, or Bidwell if you wish, is subdivided, industrialized, and the men and women who used to walk in the woods are, as Anderson describes them, ". . . like mice that have come out of the fields to live in houses that do not belong to them. . . . Now and then a bold mouse [Eugene V. Debs?] stands upon his hind legs and addresses the others. He declares he will force his way through the walls and conquer the gods who have built the house."[12]

Village prophets emerge who cry woe unto Jerusalem, like Judge Hanby, who says: "'There's going to be a new war here. . . . At first it's going to be a war between individuals to see to what class a man must belong; then it's going to be a long, silent war between classes, between those who have and those who can't get it. It'll be the worst war of all.'"[13] The tone is tendentious. Anderson is speaking for the early socialist-labor movement in this country, in an era in which any kind of idealism had died with Wilson, and in which Harding normalcy and Coolidge conservatism were inane travesties of both those qualities. One can see the fervor and the rhetoric of Anderson's statement justified by the social conditions under which he wrote. The American writer in Anderson's generation had to take a stand. Only a scoundrel would have been disinterested enough to ignore the situation. James Branch Cabell and Joseph Hergesheimer did, and they earned obscurity for doing so. Henry James, who viewed life from the vantage point of eternity, did not ignore the social forces. He was able, however, to represent them in a little room and to keep the strenuous note of the reformer out of his novels.

There is something of this quality in D. H. Lawrence. At a time when he was on the verge of some quasi-political activity in his relationship with Bertrand Russell, Lawrence in *Sons and Lovers* and even more so in *Women in Love* describes very much the same process taking place in the midlands mining district, with the machine—in this instance the mining machinery, and the mechanical man—with the Gerald Crich of *Women in Love* and the Clifford Chatterley of *Lady Chatterley's Lover*, superseding the old bucolic way of life.

Beneath this populist vision of the decline and fall of the American dream lies Anderson's grasp of the natural and economic philosophy of Herbert Spencer. "I always did believe in the survival of the fittest and I got a daughter to support and put through college," Tom Butterworth says to Steve Hunter, in order to justify his canniness in a financial deal.[14]

Opposed to this predatory philosophy of social anarchy lies Thorstein Veblen's essentially humane, socialistic philosophy in which control must lie with the maker and not with the promoter—an extension of the roles of farmer and farmhand into the industrial future. Veblen's *Theory of the Leisure Class*, with its catchword "conspicuous consumption," its denunciation of the economic middlemen—the advertisers, the promoters, the financiers—of useful industry, is the guidebook to Anderson's conception of his novel.

Veblen's work lies behind Clara Butterworth's grasp of the difference between her husband and the others:

> "He's not like Father or Henderson Wooburn or Alfred Buckley," she told herself. "He doesn't scheme and twist things about trying to get the best of someone else. He works, and because of his efforts things are accomplished." The figure of Jim Priest working in a field of corn came to her mind. "The farm hand works," she thought, "and the corn grows. This man sticks to his task in the shop and makes a town grow."[15]

Joseph Conrad expresses this philosophy of honest work in his writing, in the difference between Kurtz's hollow idealism and the fact that even the second-rate helmsman at least steers the boat, in *Heart of Darkness*. Anderson's personal reverence for honest tasks honestly performed is partially explained by a passage from his *Memoirs*:

I was an advertising man for years and as an advertising
writer was compelled to attend many of the meetings called
"conferences," sitting often in them for hours . . . throw-
ing words onto paper to try to help sell some damn soap or
toothpaste . . . men in such conferences afterward to be remembered, say, as one might remember seeing a dog tear
at the flesh of a long dead horse beside a desert road.[16]

Now out of these observed and doctrinaire components
Anderson has fashioned his benevolent Frankenstein monster,
Hugh McVey, who lacks the dimensions necessary to real humanity. There is some fumbling attempt to give McVey a character, a personality, but it is a rubber mask—Huckleberry Finn
in McVey's childhood, Abraham Lincoln when he grows up.
Psychically McVey has inherited the single plaintive note of
Winesburg, Ohio's sexual frustrations. He has come to Bidwell
"to live and to try to work out his problem!" And his problem
is as far as we can make out a sexual problem, extended to a
wish to get into touch with other people: "It did not seem to
him at the moment that it was worth while for him to go further east or to try to find a place where he would be able to
mingle freely with men and women, or where such a wonder-
ful thing as had happened to the man in the barnyard below
might happen to him."[17] Beyond this, if we accept McVey
without a struggle, as an allegorical figure—a mythical figure,
a folk hero like Paul Bunyan—we get something rather impressive, very close in spirit to the sculpture of Rodin—the
thinker, rude, twisted, clumsy, and incapable of intellectual
refinement.

It remains then to examine McVey's allegorical verisimilitude.
Veblen's hand is apparent in the character's physique and in his
origins; he is a Missourian, from the area where elements from
north and south, east and west, meet on the banks of the great
American river, and industry and agriculture, industriousness
and indolence, can flourish equally well. As the man of vision and invention McVey is a giant whose legs are weak and
whose upper body is strong, and whose mind discovers and in-

vents but cannot hold and administer. He is Veblen's image of the veblen hero, the engineer, the bridge builder.

> The clouds blotted out the sun from the earth and darkness descended on the land, on the troubled towns, on the hills that were torn open, on the forests that were destroyed, on the peace and quiet of all places. In the country stretching away from the river where all had been peace and quiet, all was now agitation and unrest. Houses were destroyed and instantly rebuilt. People gathered in whirling crowds.
>
> The dreaming man felt himself a part of something significant and terrible that was happening to the earth and to the people of the earth.[18]

Thus runs McVey's vision to which he is intrinsic as its cause. And we are subsequently shown how America emerges from McVey's dream, or from his idle calculation of all the pickets in the town's fences, and the ability of the trees to yield an equal number, or from his bodily mimicry of the actions of a cabbage planter. He is at once a figure of terror and a messianic figure, as when Wainsworth is torn between murdering him with a stone and touching "with his finger the hem of Hugh's coat." Within the sheltering form of allegory the halfwit Allie Mulberry becomes plausible, the mindless tool of mechanism, able to do one thing and do it well and only for the sake of doing it, a sort of fragment of the composite figure of Hugh McVey.

The theme is remarkably akin to D. H. Lawrence's apocalyptic vision of a struggle between the old organic structure of life and the new mechanistic synthesis of life. It is represented in this novel, rather splendidly and successfully I think, in two descriptions. First is the long, extended simile of Jim Priest's comparison between the trotting racers Geers and Doble and the generals Grant and Lee. Geers and Grant are men of the earth, Emersonian common men, Lawrence's primitives, who receive "life direct through the senses."

> There he sits hunched up like a sleeping dog. He looks as though he cared about nothing on earth, and he'll sit like

that through three quarters of the hardest race . . . he sits still. . . . He waits. . . . He looks half asleep. If he doesn't have to do it he makes no effort. If the horse has it in him to win without help he sits still . . . and if that Bud Doble has a horse in the race he's leaning forward in the sulky, shouting at his horse and making a holy show of himself.[19]

Jim Priest—Pop Geers, Tom Butterworth, Steve Hunter, and the rest, Bud Doble. Clara the trotting horse. And supernally representative of the sleepy power of Pop Geers over nature: Hugh McVey. To expand the trope as Shakespeare expands his metaphors, Hugh McVey's relationship with Clara finally becomes the mystical union of passive matter with the shaping force of the man; the achievement of their sexual union resolves a mechanical problem for McVey. Lawrence's *Women in Love* contains many similar symbolic actions; the mechanical brilliance of Gerald subdues horses and women, but he dies of his own inhumanity, just as Birkin and Ursula find their atonement in the organic world.

Now there was no defeat, no problem, no victory. In himself he did not exist. Within himself something new had been born or another something that had always lived with him had stirred to life. It was not awkward, it was not afraid. It was a thing as swift and sure as the flight of the male bird through the branches of trees and it was in pursuit of something light and swift in her.[20]

Very Lawrentian.

The second event also relates to the struggle between the mechanistic and the organic: the long automobile ride through the countryside which culminates in the madness of Wainsworth the harness maker. "In her mind the harness maker had come to stand for all the men and women in the world who were in secret revolt against the absorption of the age in machines and the products of machines."[21]

The novel ends in a tableau very much in the order of Ibsen, very much, I suspect, the product of the late nineteenth-century

Weltanschauung. The harness maker's bite has delivered Hugh McVey over to another dream: from being the Promethean demiurge, the worker for the people who has brought the machine, he becomes interested in the purpose, the ultimate serviceability of the machine to mankind. He becomes, we might say, a socialist.

All ideological literature tends to end like Ibsen's *Enemy of the People*. The man who has given his community a great gift regrets the gift because the community has abused it. An outcast, he reverts to the most fundamental of relationships, the family. And the wife, like Mrs. Stockmann or Solveig, is larger than life, an earth mother, whose unruly son has been rejected. "To her then and forever after Hugh was no hero, making the world, but a perplexed boy hurt by life. He never escaped out of boyhood in her consciousness of him. . . . Sensing his troubled state her mother spirit was aroused." [22]

The third aspect of Anderson's accomplishment, which I have called the psychopathology of small town life, is certainly the most difficult to evaluate or even to describe. It is partly a conscious, strenuously post-Freudian investigation of social-sexual maladjustment, whose observations are based on the assumption, cited above, that "sex is a tremendous force in life. It twisted people, beat upon them, often distracted and destroyed their lives." About the robin's-egg renaissance of literature in Chicago, Anderson writes of "the terrible importance of flesh in human relations also revealed again." [23]

At the same time, Anderson positively disclaims any real experience with the Freudians beyond their general philosophy and their subject matter. This is not hard to believe in light of his callow description of his friends "psyching" one another in Chicago, in his *Memoirs*, and from his rather broad handling of the Oedipus complex in *Winesburg, Ohio*, along with the confusions of mothers and sweethearts, the naturalistic regularity with which the inchoate sexual experience begins with unconscious incestuous longings and anti-incestuous revulsions on the parts of the parents and the children alike. The relationship between Tom Butterworth and Clara is an excellent example of this use of Freudian overstatement to make a relationship clear. But this does not explain some things about Anderson's choice of subject matter. It merely contributes.

Like that other great prophet of sexual hygiene, Lawrence, Anderson in his fiction (as Trilling has noted) points to the promised land—over the hill to maturity—but can only represent feelingly the sense of frustration and deprivation peculiar to an adolescent nympholept, who could not possess the object of his love even if it were handed him. There is a permanent arrest of development, and it would seem to implicate not only the work but the artist himself.

At its best, as I think it is in "The Man Who Became a Woman," it has a quality that approaches the Dostoevskian atmosphere of literary madness, in which the unforeseen reaches rare heights. At its most consistent, it informs Anderson's work with a flavor, a set of symptoms as it were, which finally become predictable, and at the same time, uncontrollable. Anderson taps the contents of his own psyche, which when it begins to flow into his fiction allows nothing but frustration and the signs of neurotic conflict to come under his conscious artistic control.

Those elements which I would term *symptomatic* in Anderson's work are roughly classifiable under three headings: the sense of omnipotence (the "oceanic feeling"), scoptophilia (voyeurism), and bisexuality. That these three elements are quite characteristic, in benign form, in all artists lends strength to their appearance in less sublimated form in Anderson's fiction.

Let me recast briefly the standard description of the artist as a psychological entity. I will begin by urging dissociation of the fact that artists are psychologically interesting and the fact that to be psychologically interesting in this day and age is to be considered neurotic. It is his intensity of disposition that makes an artist what he is, and the fact that he may be neurotic or even insane in certain quadrants of his life has no bearing on that intensity as it manifests itself in his art. One fact, however, qualifies that statement: some writers—and Anderson is one of them—make a dead set in the direction of what we have come to recognize as the standard neuroses, the Oedipus complex being the central one, of course. In these instances we are justified in analyzing their fiction in terms of its neurotic content, and if there is available biographical evidence, reconciling it with the artist's life. This is what I will do with Anderson.

The language of literature, associated as it is with symbol, poetic diction, the connotative aspects of words, is identified in psychology with the prelogical thinking of children, primitives, and psychotics. Similarities become identities, the part substitutes for the whole, the objectively perceived incident undergoes distortion. The artist thus shares in the fantasy life of the nonartist. He constructs his work from unconscious fantasies which express wishes.

Like the neurotic, his wish-fantasy life is built ultimately around his original involvement in the family constellation, and he shares in the guilt feelings about his role which are the regular components of the Oedipus situation. But here the resemblance to the neurotic stops. Where the neurotic finds himself deadlocked in a conflict between repressed instincts and his law-abiding ego, the artist sublimates his drives, releases his energies in the performance of a substitutive function, in which, because others participate in it and recognize it, he frees himself of what might have eventuated in neurosis. The work of art is an act of restitution, a token of love, a substitute for the futile masochistic acts of contrition one associates with neurotic behavior.

The last element I wish to take up, the concern with looking at things, especially at forbidden things, is particularly interesting in connection with Sherwood Anderson. For all artists the eye or the ear is the favored sense. The eyes and ears are of the distance senses, the ones connected with the aesthetic experience. But in Anderson the sensitivity becomes pathogenic and postulates some extraordinary traumatic occurrence in his life. In a remarkable way, to understand Anderson's autobio-

graphical view of himself (often an invented view) is to understand his fictional view of Hugh McVey in *Poor White*.

Anderson's critics have remarked on his inability to strike a
note beyond a certain permanent adolescence in his fiction. His
young boys daydream of lovely, anonymous, faceless young
girls, or they have misgivings about their manhoods. His
women and men have strong voyeuristic, or exhibitionistic,
tendencies along with a certain instability that makes them
euphorically in love with the world one moment, and suicidal
the next.

To the extent that they are trustworthy, Anderson's memoirs
furnish us with all sorts of clues as to why there should be this
emotional arrest in his development, an arrest for which his art
has suffered, but in spite of which he has achieved a certain level
of excellence.

Four entries command our attention in the *Memoirs*. They
are related. There is first of all his relationship with his parents.
For his mother, blind adoration and anguish at her having to
slave as a washwoman, his feeling that she was beautiful rather
than any objective conviction that she was beautiful. For his father an ambivalence of shame and admiration. He describes
what Freud calls the Family Romance; young Anderson, the
memoirs recall,

> was filled with bitterness, and sometimes I wished he wasn't
> my father. To protect my mother I'd make up stories of a
> secret marriage that for some strange reason never got
> known. As though some man, say the president of a rail-
> road company or maybe a Congressman, has married my
> mother, thinking his wife was dead and then it turned out
> she wasn't.[24]

This is the material of the fairy tale, the foundling son of the
King of Thebes.

The relationship with the father was climaxed by a strange
ceremonial atonement of father and son. Anderson's father took

him out one dark night in a rainstorm, told him to undress, and together they swam naked in the pond. From that time forward, Anderson writes, "I knew that I was the son of my father . . . I laughed, knowing that I would never again be wanting another father."

A second entry describes his being invited by another boy to watch a girl undress before a stove. Again, as in the first description of the experience with the father, the tone is lyrical, enrapt. Anderson struck the boy beside him in the face and ran from the sight. He associates it in his *Memoirs* with "Death in the Woods."

A third entry describes a peculiar experience, a visual aberration that Anderson experienced as a young boy. It consisted of seeing things disappear as if they were looked at through the wrong end of a telescope. Objects floated away, then returned suddenly, accompanied by a psychological deafness that made him incapable of replying to questions. At the same time, when he was in bed at night the faces of women and girls, beautiful and ugly, crowded to his bedside and troubled his sleep.

When Anderson's mother died, his sister Stella took her place. In a fourth entry, Stella is described as attractive, and imaginative to the point of living in a fantasy world. Anderson describes an evening when she took him out for a walk in the moonlight and cast him in the role of a suitor, kissing him and calling him "James."

How are these connected? How do they bear upon Anderson's work? The reminiscences as they appear in the *Memoirs* have a certain lyrical beauty, but it is the finish that consciousness can give to more sinister, less appetizing but, I think, more exciting latencies. We must examine his *Memoirs* in the same way we examine his fiction, as one step still removed from life. Anderson invites us to do so, professing that he is inaccurate, in order to quiet the objections of his friends who remember incidents as having occurred quite differently from the way he relates them. "I was continually falling in love. I saw a woman walking in the street, followed her at a distance. Had she no-

ticed me, turned and spoken to me, I would have been frightened."[25] We can, I think, on the integrated evidence of Anderson's *Memoirs*, his life, and his fiction, describe the fixations
which motivated him, and the forms they took in his writing.

There is, first of all, an unresolved conflict in connection
with his Oedipal attachment to both his parents. On the one
hand, there is a strong incestuous attachment to the mother, in
which the fantasy of the father's not having any connection
with his mother guarantees him an unobstructed right to her.
On the other hand, there is what is termed the negative
Oedipus, in which the son, relinquishing his right to his mother,
accepts a passive, feminine role and submits instead to the father. In both these roles there is involved a threat to one's manhood: in the striving for the mother the fear that the father will
exact revenge, in the submission to the father an identification
with the emasculate, effeminate mother. The wish to be like
one's father may grow, as Otto Fenichel puts it, "into a kind of
love which may best be described as an apprentice complex, a
temporary feminine submission to the father in order to pre-
pare oneself for a later masculine competition with him."[26]
Both these strivings give rise to what may become a permanent
anxiety about one's manhood. And the symptoms which best
reveal this anxiety are the related ones of exhibitionism, voyeurism, and fetishism.

All three of these disorders are calculated to allay the fear of
emasculation and to reassure the subject that he is, so to speak,
all there. They are very often the rather high price one must pay
for being bisexual.

Both the voyeur and the exhibitionist are equally fixated on
scenes which either arouse anxiety or give reassurance. The exhibitionist is most easily explained. He attempts to deny that he
is emasculated by obtaining a positive reaction of fear or surprise from the onlooker. For the man exhibitionism constitutes
an exposure of his virility, in a gross, criminal way, or in the
more socially acceptable way of being, as Sherwood Anderson
described himself, "a great lover."

The voyeur returns always to a childhood experience which aroused his anxiety and envy—the sight of his father's nakedness or his mother's. His eye becomes the focal point for an erotic experience, a lesser gratification for the one which has been denied him.

These two forms of reassurance and gratification may, in neurotic personalities, result in peculiar physical symptoms. The one I am interested in here is connected with Anderson's description of his eyes failing him during his adolescence, objects rapidly diminishing and vanishing, accompanied by psychic deafness and the fear of death. Such psychogenic blindness and deafness derive from the forcible repression of the wish to see what one has been forbidden to see. Freud describes the process as a punitive one: "Because you wish to see something, you shall not see at all." Anderson's description of his looking into the window, while it may have been a true experience, is certainly a screen, a coverup for an earlier experience of seeing, of which he has no memory.

Fetishism is more of the same. It is attributed to a child's anxiety at realizing that his father and mother are differently endowed sexually, and the inference he draws that his mother has been altered by an act of violence. The child's anxiety centers on his fear of being similarly altered. In his prelogical, archaic mind, he develops the identification between his mother's missing organ and some equivalent object, most notably a shoe (as we see it in the Old Testament book of Ruth), or some other object. The fetishist then cherishes this concrete proof that all's right with the world.

Anderson describes his own fetishism:

> I used to take little things to worship. Now I am talking about a time when I was a young man. It might be just a young tree. I remember once a man gave me a little wooden figure. . . . I kept the little figure in a box. Sometimes at night, when I was depressed, I crept out of bed and knelt by a table. I felt about in the darkness until I had

got out the figure; then I caressed it with my hands. The figure was of no importance. I did not dare look at it in the daytime. At night, when my fingers played over it, my imagination was aroused.ʼ . . . Once, when I was in love and could not find a woman who satisfied me, I bestowed my love on a young tree that grew in Chicago, in Jackson Park. I used to walk there in the darkness, never going too near the tree. One night when I was very sad and lonely I did approach the tree. I touched it with my fingers. A thrill ran through my body.[27]

Freud, in his *Interpretation of Dreams*, identifies the tree regularly with the woman, and pagan antiquity records the regular mating of farmers with their fruit trees as a fertility rite.

Or, after a particularly distressing experience of being bullied and ragged by some men, Anderson says: "But, following some obscure impulse, I went from one to another of the livery horses, touching each with my hand. . . ."[28] Similarly, Hugh McVey responds to corn and to farm animals, as do many figures in Anderson's *Horses and Men* stories.

I have left till last the discussion of the oceanic feeling earlier described. In the schizophrenic, whose grasp on the distinction between his ego and the external world is weak, and who slips back into the objectless world of infancy, the ecstatic reunion with the world is futile and unproductive. The process itself is transparent: it is a massive regression to the omnipotent state of infancy. Anderson described this ecstatic reunion frequently in his memoirs and in his fiction. It relates best to the mystical participation he described in connection with his father. In submerging his own drives and aims with those of his father he achieves the sense of omnipotence, the ecstatic.

We come now to consider how these neurotic aims and symptoms have transferred themselves to Anderson's fiction. They are all patently observable in his work. The Reverend Curtis Hartman is the voyeur of *Winesburg, Ohio*, and Hugh McVey listens to the lovers in *Poor White*. Alice Hindman exhibits herself in *Winesburg, Ohio*. Joe Welling, the Man of Ideas in *Winesburg, Ohio*, is the schizomanic who can solve the problems of the world with his ideas, just as Hugh McVey becomes the corporate image of spirit that moves in America. The young boy who looks in the mirror in "The Man Who Became a Woman" and sees a girl's face, reflects the anxieties I have discussed in connection with the *Memoirs*.

In all cases, these symptoms have been displaced to other, fictitious characters. The reality has been creatively falsified. The frustrations and repressions have been spread around to include men and women alike, while at the heart of *Winesburg, Ohio*, for example, the character of George Willard, closest in terms of identity to Anderson himself, emerges purified of these abnormal strivings. "One sheds one's sickness in books," D. H. Lawrence used to say. Anderson creates in his fiction a fractional distribution of his psychic components, with his purified, rectified self sitting on the sidelines—George Willard, for example, or the prophetic heroic ego-ideal Hugh McVey, suffering all, overcoming all, being at once the precipitate and the release from these psychic maladjustments.

What limits such works as *Winesburg* and *Poor White* in their achievement of a final excellence is that Anderson has not been successful in mastering those elements which remain, even in his work, neurotic symptoms rather than artistic statements. It is basically the reproach Lionel Trilling levels at him, for neglecting the sublimated social manifestations of sexuality in favor of an adolescent phallicism. I should like to examine two stories which, equally committed to studies in pathology, exemplify Anderson's failure and his success.

The first, "The Man's Story," presents in first-person narrative a reporter's experience with a strange murder case. A man named Edgar Wilson, something like Hugh McVey, the typical lonely, primitive poet, comes in from the prairie where he has found a woman, equally lost. In Chicago, the wife gets a job and Wilson writes poetry. His theme is the theme of *Winesburg,*

Ohio, the metaphor of the wall, or wells. Men kept building walls around themselves, or digging themselves into wells: ". . . the wells getting deeper and deeper and the voices growing dimmer and dimmer in the distance. . . ."[29] Wilson's poetry and his actions bespeak the oceanic union we associate with schizophrenia, the sense of omnipotence, the illusion of body magic, the tendency to exist at some distance from the physical body.

> The firm grip of my fingers on the thin paper of this cigarette is a sign that I am very quiet now. Sometimes it is not so. When I am unquiet, I am weak, but when I am quiet, as I am now, I am very strong.
>   . . . Very suddenly and completely the knowledge has come to me that I could grip the sides of tall buildings as freely and as easily as I now grip this cigarette. . . . I could hold the building between my fingers and put it to my lips and blow smoke through it. . . . When the feeling comes over me there is a directness and simplicity in me that makes me love myself. To myself at such times I say strong sweet words. . . . I could take a row of houses standing on a street tip them over empty the people out of them, squeeze and compress all the people into one person and love that person. . . .[30]

Meanwhile a very sensitive hunchbacked girl in the next room peeps through a keyhole at this couple. She lives vicariously with the man. His power has made the two women instrumental to him; in making love to the woman he made love to the whole world.

The couple goes out for a walk one evening and a workman, crazed for love of the woman, shoots her in the heart. The man is oblivious to the fact that she is shot. She walks back to their flat, falls dead at his feet. He is still oblivious, steps over her body and goes out again, walks in the street, stops before a moving picture house where a picture called "The Light of the World" is playing, stops and begins to scream. He is arrested and tried for murder, appears indifferent to his fate, and is saved by the confession of the stagehand.

Anderson sums it up by describing the man as having been raised from the sea of doubt to the surface of life by the woman's hand, and having sunk again into it. Now he continues to sink, in spite of the attempts to bring him up.

I consider the story a failure in that it willfully abandons that austere standard of normality which the artist must hold sacred and which Kafka, even in his profoundest nightmares, strives toward. In this story Anderson sentimentalizes a schizophrenic oversimplification of human experience. The peeping hunchback and the mute relationship between the man and the woman become an unchallenged norm, while the rest of the world is by implication inferior, because it is less intense in its relationships. Anderson, in this story, invokes unchanged, unconscious tendencies in himself. The story is less a story than it is an acidulation of his own memoirs, prior to the final transformation into art.

"The Man Who Became a Woman" I regard as a successful work of fiction, in which neurotic symptoms are transformed into symbolic actions, delineation of character. The story has form, direction; it accomplishes the revelations and reversals that are the concomitants of the literary act. The narrative structure is reminiscent of Mark Twain; the boy moves in a world of homely, familiar things. The hallucinatory change of sex is accomplished through drunkenness, as is the mistake on the part of the blacks. The resolution of the story involves a passing through the ordeal of adolescence, with its incipient falterings into passive homosexuality, and the final entrance into the realistic state of manhood.

Anderson begins with doubling of his narrative persona. Tom Means is the boy who loved horses with a mystical passion. Tom Means went off and became a well-known writer. The present narrator both shares and avoids the identification of the author with the main character.

But the story is still an explicitly therapeutic confession. "It will be kind of like confession is, I suppose, to a good Catholic, or maybe better yet, like cleaning up the room you live in if you are a bachelor . . . and your room smells sweet and you feel sweetened up and better inside yourself too."[31]

The flight from masculinity, in the direction of passive homosexuality, is urged on the boy by a series of symbolic representations. Shy and sexually deprived, he indulges in fantasies involving women. But the actuality frightens him. The black man in American culture has come to represent and symbolize to the white man all his own repressed and rejected sexual strivings. The boy, already sexually insecure, finds himself driven into a passive, feminine role in the company of a black man. His best friend Burt treats him protectively as if he were a delicate girl.

Only with the delicate gelding, Pick-it-boy, can he feel male. But even here the relationship is tenuous, epicene, boy-and-girl love. The symptoms described elsewhere in the *Memoirs* are introduced here: the fading away of sights and sounds, which the psychiatrist calls micropsia, a clinically observed hallucination in neuroses connected with looking.

The vision of his face in the bar is like the experience called déja vu, in which an actual experience is associated with a repressed one, and becomes a substitute for it. The repressed memory is that of the wish to be a girl, or the fear that one *is* a girl, to which the image in the mirror is the fulfillment.

What precipitates the identity is the terrifyingly huge apparition at that moment in the barroom brawl of the father image, in all his raw maleness, who first threatens the boy, then deflects his cruelty to his tormentor. In psychoanalytic terms Anderson has created a pantomimic situation involving a choice of roles. To the boy who has already seen himself as a woman, the alternatives are clear. If you avoid the challenges of manhood and accept the passive role—take care of the baby—you will not be harmed. The man who teased the giant is destroyed, as an object lesson.

The boy flees the harsh reality of the man's world, back to his fetishistic world of the horse, where he can enjoy his pregenital relationship with Pick-it-boy, a matter of caresses.

But the alternative, becoming a woman, proves equally disagreeable, since the practical consequences, being attacked by the two drunken horse-handlers, is worse than standing up to the red-haired man or to a woman.

> So I had invented a kind of princess, with black hair and a slender willowy body to dream about. . . . I suppose I fancied that if I ever found such a woman in the flesh I would be the strong sure one and she the timid shrinking one.
>
> And now I was that woman or something like her, myself.[32]

The boy's panic and actual flight, his falling into the skeleton of the horse, dissipate his fantasy. The reality tests and disproves the subjective conclusions the boy has come to. He is symbolically reborn, a boy, from the skeleton of what had become for him an ego-ideal, a mother image. In its precise and yet symbolic psychoanalytic accuracy, its startling yet homely scenes and images, "The Man Who Became a Woman" shows Anderson—in ways he only gropes toward in "The Man's Story," *Winesburg, Ohio*, or *Poor White*—as an intuitive psychological writer of fiction on a level of achievement equal to Mann and Lawrence.   [1970]

5.

Ernest Hemingway: The Stylist of Stoicism

I

Ernest Hemingway, who died by his own hand, has in his suicide written his signature across his own life, and it is impossible in terms of this final act to avoid a reappraisal of him and his work. This is not to say that one must think better of his art for his having died with such a brave and terrible flourish (there *are* writers whose works are past redeeming), but only that the importance Hemingway attached to violence and death and courage in the face of defeat deserves reconsideration. Two generations of his readers, admirers and detractors alike, have been intrigued by the brilliant comedy of his career—his dedication both in his life and in his work to the importance of being Ernest. Now in a moment of time the obsessive concern he evinces in his fiction, and the perennial ingenuity with which he courted death in his life, find an unexpected validation.

Hemingway appears consciously to have patterned his life on some obsolescent Renaissance dream of the whole man. Like Byron, Hemingway lived his works and wrote his life. This, at least, is the semi-popular notion that neither Hemingway nor most of his critics have done much to discredit. And it is only when we look into that very late, very bad novel—*Across the River and into the Trees*, where all his ideas are in complete decay, reduced to a handful of mannerisms, where the style that sustained him in his frailest moments, is a little deposit smeared on the end of a pen—that we realize that Hemingway's stature as a writer is more attributable to his craft, his concern with style, than it is to the rich material of his experience.

It is possible, almost essential, that one be of two minds about Ernest Hemingway's achievements. Any writer who lives a reasonably long and productive life must run the hazard of surviving his best creative moments, but with Hemingway it is not so much a matter of decline from excellence as it is a matter of his being at all times a melánge of elements, any one of which by itself lacked the quality we associate with a high order of genius. He is one of those writers through whose works one must walk carefully. Like Rudyard Kipling, a man of genius whose devotion to masculinity, militarism, and the British Empire on which the sun also sets, Hemingway betrays us occasionally to his own unworthy or questionable objectives; at times, as in the case of Kipling, a meanness reveals itself, or a simplification, that makes us turn away for shame. He leads us by means of his splendid gift for statement along some exciting paths which end to our distress in some second-rate shrine—on the steps of a gymnasium, at the gates of the bullring, in the oversized cot of the great white hunter.

The alert reader is able, in reading Hemingway, to discriminate among these elements. One observes first of all a great talent born of hard work, employed in the service of a monolithic, primitive, and at this late date, simpleminded philosophy of life. This is the stoic fatalism for which Hemingway is best known. Seen clearly, it lacks the firm sobriety of a philosophical statement: the philosophy of men free from passion, unmoved by joy or grief and resigned without the complicity of a genuine religious belief such as the *bismillah*—in God's name— of Mohammedanism, which has been called a soldier's religion. Nor does his fatalism have the sustaining power of some uncomplicated cultural ethos—the "bend the bow and tell the truth" that summed up the Persian catalogue of manly virtues.

No, it is rather the lyrical and childlike obsession of Greek tragedy, or of the Preacher in *Ecclesiastes*, with the futility of human hope in the face of death. It is the hysterical fatalism of the frightened chorus of Aeschylus' *Agamemnon*:

> The black Furies stalking the man
> fortunate beyond all right
> wrench back again the set of his life
> and drop him to darkness.
> There among the ciphers there is no more comfort in
> power.
>
> [*Agam.* 463]

or the morbid gloating of *Ecclesiastes*: "There is a just man that perisheth in his righteousness, and there is a wicked man that prolongeth his life in his wickedness" (Eccles. 7:15).

It is the ancient theme of the ordeal by sacrifice, the yielding of the good man, the hero, to the inexorable claims of time, or to the infinitely corruptible nature of all human institutions and societies. All of Hemingway's heroes go down in the dark, like Homer's Achilles, Hector, or Agamemnon, victims of their own or others' errors or malevolences.

Such a theme in our time, when presumably we have moved to higher ground *vis à vis* fate, becomes a hollow echo of something like Tolstoy's belief in the salutary nature of degradation. "It is in defeat that we become Christians," says Frederick Henry in *A Farewell to Arms*. ". . . I don't mean technically Christians. I mean like Our Lord. . . . That is why the peasant has wisdom because he is defeated from the start." [1]

What emerges here is a masochistic version of Christian doctrine denied the unction of salvation. Even Christ, who, as the centurion in "Today is Friday" describes him, "ain't lucky, but he looked pretty good in there today," becomes another battered boxer or matador going down in defeat. Life is a form of penance, and Hemingway's characters rush with an unhealthy eagerness toward the lions, the bulls, and the arena we associate with Christian martyrdom.

Hemingway best sums all this up in the end of *A Farewell to Arms*. The short happy lives of Catherine Barkley and Frederick

Henry, redeemed from the external threat of war, end with the death in childbirth of Catherine. Frederick Henry speaks the epilogue:

> If people bring so much courage to this world the world has to kill them to break them, so of course it kills them. The world breaks everyone and afterward many are strong at the broken places. But those that will not break it kills. It kills the very good and the very gentle and the very brave impartially. If you are none of these then you can be sure it will kill you too but there will be no special hurry. . . . Poor, poor, dear Cat. And this was the price you paid for sleeping together. This was the end of the trap. This was what people got for loving each other. . . .
>
> That was what you did. You died. You did not know what it was about. You never had time to learn. They threw you in and told you the rules, and the first time they caught you off base they killed you. Or they killed you gratuitously, like Aymo. . . . But they killed you in the end. You could count on that. Stay around and they would kill you.[2]

In his grand vintage style Hemingway puts it well. But look at it again, when the style has begun to creak with age in *Across the River and into the Trees*. The Colonel, writes Hemingway, "only loved people who had fought or been mutilated. Other people were fun and you liked them and were good friends, but you only felt true tenderness and love for those who had been there and received the castigation that everyone receives who goes there long enough."[3] What were originally stigmata of suffering turn out to be the wound stripes and hash marks of an exotic class distinction.

As a corollary to this intentionally crass evaluation of Hemingway's philosophy of defeat, I should like now to consider the "code" as it has come to be called, by which the conventional Hemingway hero lives. The code and its practitioners are best described, not in his fiction, but in his book on bullfighting, *Death in the Afternoon*.

In Spain and the running of the bulls, Hemingway appears to

have found a culture in which his own beliefs, archaic and inadequate to the complexities of peace and urbanity, found normative acceptance. Just as T. S. Eliot, the local boy who made God, looking up from the waste land of postwar Europe, found in the Catholic mass the poetics of religion, preferring its ritual to the spontaneous and untrustworthy effusions of lesser Christian sects, so Hemingway found in the *corrida* the poetics of violence. It provided him with a spectacle that allowed the controlled and perpetual exhibition of courage within a ritual framework as opposed to the formless, uncontrollable accidents of the war. "The formal bullfight," he wrote, "is a tragedy, not a sport, and the bull is certain to be killed."

No matter on which side of the *muleta* one looks, whether it be bull or matador, one will find the protagonist Hemingway fashioned for his admirers to marvel at. The bull is the generic, the matador the particular, antagonist of fate, and their roles, as the number of eulogistic epitaphs in *Death in the Afternoon* attest, are interchangeable. Bravery is the quality most valued in both, the difference lying only in the extent to which the man must learn to "ignore possible consequences," or "not only to ignore them but to despise them." The word *noble*, Hemingway tells us in his glossary of bullfighting terms, describes a bull "that is frank in its charges, brave, simple and easily deceived."[4] It is this same quality that he looked for in his human characters, having only to translate these abstract virtues into the vernacular of individuality. Of the matador Maera, whom Hemingway admired, and who was killed in the ring, Hemingway writes: "He was generous, humorous, proud, bitter, foulmouthed, and a great drinker. He neither sucked after intellectuals nor married money. He loved to kill bulls and lived with much passion and enjoyment."[5] In other words, *noble*. If one had to die, it was best to die in a charge, if one was the bull, or in a beautifully executed *natural*, if one was a matador, even if one's knees trembled as one took his ground.

Another parallel occurs to me here: "The bullfight has been so developed and organized," Hemingway writes, "that the bull has just time enough coming into the ring completely unfamiliar with dismounted men to learn to distrust all their artifices and reach the summit of his danger at the moment of killing."[6] It is an echo, is it not, of Frederick Henry's complaint of life when Catherine Barkley dies: "You never had time to learn. They threw you in and told you the rules and the first time they caught you off base they killed you."[7]

One might describe Hemingway's ethic of the hero as one that has been overwhelmed by its own metaphor—life as a fatal athletic event for which a certain amoral grace was required—in which morality itself was a brilliant pole-vault, an intuition, or as he puts it, "what is moral is what you feel good after and what is immoral is what you feel bad after." In much the same way Ibsen represents Hedda Gabler sacrificing human lives to her narrow concern with life as an aesthetic experience. The fumbler who cannot do things beautifully, with "emotion, courage, and sincerity," these being the desiderata of great bullfighting, cannot excuse his failures at the moment of truth by citing a vast inventory of domestic virtues elsewhere.

It is instructive to consider "The Short Happy Life of Francis Macomber" as the magnification to absurdity of Hemingway's code, its practitioners, its neophytes, its obstacles, and its totemic animals: its consistencies with respect to love, marriage, comradeship, violence, and death that are an insistent note in all his works. It is in a sense his best, worst story.

The story achieves full orchestration of all his thematic effects. It takes place on a rather expensive African safari, where a variety of animal totems, including an African cousin of the fighting bull, is readily available. The ordeal by sportsmanship is acted out; the blood-brotherhood between two men is consummated, and the bitch woman who tries to talk like a man gets her comeuppance after she has done her worst.

The unforgivable sin in the story is cowardice, "like a cold, slimy hollow." It is not fear; that is more a reflex, which Hemingway excuses in Death in the Afternoon, when he says, "To show nervousness is not shameful; only to admit it." Cowar-

dice is a failure of the will, and it implies that it was within a
man's power to choose to stand or fly in the face of danger. One
must, to be able to survive in Hemingway's robust world, face
death at least once, and with a certain finality, in order to purge
oneself of the fear that saps life of all its vigor. That Macomber
stands up to a lion is secondary to his undergoing an ordeal in
which his life is at stake and his courage challenged.

But there is an extension in "The Short Happy Life of Francis
Macomber" of the code beyond its reasonable application to
men facing great danger, to cover any and all of life's contingen-
cies. Wilson is the man with courage. He is the "white hunter,"
and more than this, he is the "white father" to Macomber.
Wilson is Macomber's sponsor, godfather, and ego–ideal. He
attempts always to steer Macomber in the right responses, to
keep him from behaving badly, and in the end, although the
lesson is lost on Macomber, Wilson teaches the correct way to
sleep with Margot Macomber—Orion and Hymen both to his
callow disciple.

Margot Macomber, like almost all of Hemingway's women,
is a generalized type. There are, roughly speaking, only two
types available to him: the first, an innocent, squawlike daydream of a woman, who clings, is loyal, loves, and almost
always perishes. The other is, as Wilson pronounces the attributes of the American woman, "the hardest, the cruelest, the
most predatory and the most attractive, and their men have
softened or gone to pieces nervously as they have hardened." [8]

Equating cowardice with castration or impotence, Hemingway finds that courage on the opposite hand will include as the
immediate byproduct of its acquisition the ability to stand
up not only to the lions of the jungle, but up to the Margot
Macombers as well. Her fortunes must rise or fall as Macomber
is brave or cowardly. The analogy, and the symbolism, are certain; the repressed half of the analogy is Macomber's inability
to satisfy his wife. To be able to kill gracefully is to be able to
make love, and Margot's going to Wilson's cot is the acting out
of that equation. It is a matter of standing up to anything in the

bush or in the bed. In this story all the latent identifications between matadors and bulls in *Death in the Afternoon* emerge in the frankly totemic use of the animal. Macomber "had not thought how the lion felt, as he got out of the car." Wilson had known "something about it and only expressed it by saying 'Damned fine lion.'" Wilson, in other words, has "eaten" the lion in the old sacramental sense as it would obtain among the Masai tribes, where to kill a lion or to drink its blood confers its virtue upon one. The buffalo becomes for Macomber the ritual objectification of the world that has threatened him, and in a fine, uncomplicated rage he stands up to the beast in the jungle. His death is, as often in Hemingway, the measure of Macomber's triumph.

Now, if we were to leave Ernest Hemingway at this point, in this world of two-dimensional heroes, the morality of the bull-ring and the safari, his work would continue to have something, by virtue of his style, and even of the simple pathos of his theme. But at its best it would survive, as much of Hemingway has survived, like a cowboy ballad which recalls only an indefinable nostalgia because somewhere Indians, buffalo, and cowboys wandered on some lone prairie. One hears its dying footfall, like the steps of a strayed American Legionnaire who has by some unaccountable mischance got lost in the Louvre. We hear it in *Across the River and into the Trees* when the headwaiter of the Gritti Palace Hotel says to the Colonel, "We were bad boys then and you were the worst of the bad boys."

But there are at least two ways in which we can understand, if not excuse, Hemingway at his most banal, and recognize qualities in his art that at their best bespeak him a writer of permanent importance. The first of these refractions is the historical milieu in which he worked; the second is his own unique adjustment to his experience within the milieu.

The war years and the 1920s have received perhaps the fullest critical treatment that any decade has been given up till now. The decade, roughly enclosing the years 1917 to 1929, is our century's showpiece, like Alfred de Musset's description of the Napoleonic era following the French Revolution—the best of times and the worst of times, as Dickens called them. World War I buried the nineteenth century in a shell-hole and with it the dignified principles of order and the bland assurances a dying century gives itself that it will continue along the same old lines.

In America, as in Europe, among the front-line intellectuals, more alert to the change than their contemporaries, arose a pattern of rejection; they could no longer speak to their elders, having nothing more in common. Moral and social values had become meaningless. The "great words," as D. H. Lawrence called them in *Lady Chatterley's Lover*, were hollow frauds. The experience of the war, the exposure to Europe effectively, as Malcolm Cowley puts it in *Exile's Return*, uprooted its more intelligent American veterans. Their roots in the American soil were destroyed, not only by the war but by the "leveling out of local and regional peculiarities" by the conformism of American industrialism, education and finally by the army itself.

In Hemingway we return in uniform to a question Americans have always considered in their fiction: the encounter with Europe. Hemingway is one of those who returned to Europe after World War I and who subjected his imagination and his moral nature to the broadening atmosphere of the European milieu. The air of postwar Europe in the 1920s was laden with the pollens of influence. Naturalism, which sang of the habitual—the peacetime squalor of the ordinary breeding the ordinary within a stable socioeconomic framework—was yielding to the exigencies of the immediate and unique experience of war and social change. Europe grown sinister, more sinister than when it frightened James's Lambert Strether, inspires Eliot's apocalyptic *The Waste Land* and Hemingway's tragedies of beautiful souls having their crowded hour in a beautiful but dangerous world—where death is the antagonist and the loved one all at once.

Young Americans had, Malcolm Cowley writes, "a thirst for abstract danger," which, when the war had brutally sated them, gave way to an extreme disillusionment and an "evaporation of words," even those which described the very virtues their exposure to danger had engendered. Hemingway describes the experience in *A Farewell to Arms*:

> I was embarrassed by the words sacred, glorious and sacrifice and the expression, in vain. . . . There were many words that you could stand to hear and finally only the names of places had dignity. . . . Abstract words such as glory, honor, courage or hallow were obscene beside the concrete names of villages, the numbers of roads, the names of rivers, the numbers of regiments and their dates.[9]

Yet wars have a way of justifying themselves to the young. They speak to the uneasy sense of invulnerability that must be put to the test, the erotic confusion between love and death, and the glamor that chaos holds in its promise of a release from the duller commitments of maturity. The young Americans who knew there was a war in Europe felt their own peaceful existences turn stagnant, and they hurled themselves into war, as Hemingway did, via the ambulance corps of France, England, and Italy.

Now Hemingway, for whatever reason he entered it, emerged from the war with the healthy conviction that it was an outrage to the human spirit. The wounds it inflicted were "unreasonable" and so were destructive of any system of values. Within this moral vacuum, it would seem ironically inevitable that the only experience worth writing about would be the experience that had destroyed him. It was a choice between an innocuous nothing, the *nada* of "A Clean Well-lighted Place," and an evil something. Thus Hemingway could write in *Death in the Afternoon* for a public which in 1932 was more amused than admiring of this archaic attitude: "The only place where you could see life and death, i.e., violent death now that the wars were over, was in the bull ring and I wanted very much to go to Spain where I could study it. I was trying to learn to write, commencing with the simplest things and one of the simplest things of all and the most fundamental is violent death." [10]

In a time of war—when it is better to yield, retreat, or to die than to enjoy a hollow victory, where courage in defeat is the best if not the only virtue one can exercise—Hemingway's almost superstitious fatalism and the heroic code are, if not admirable, at least attractive. What we cannot, even if we are willfully obtuse, understand or forgive him is his steadfast refusal to retool for peace. And the explanation is, I believe, a tragically simple one—he could not. His stoicism is not a philosophical but a psychological stoicism. His protest is not a social protest but a personal one. And he was destined to write the way he did because, by and large, he was bound to the imperatives of his nature.

We do him an injustice when we deplore his insistence on the masculine assertion, his overvaluing of courage, for the inarguable reason that for him the experience of the war was the normative, and thus the formative experience of his creative life. Preconditioned by the forces that influenced his childhood and youth—an idealized devotion to a father who taught him hunting, fishing, and a morbid belief in a cruel and malevolent fate; a hostile contempt for the mother who, with her narrow intolerant piety, seemed to embody that fate—he was peculiarly susceptible to the masculine appeal of violence. When that violence did his body and mind serious and permanent injury, he was then equally susceptible to the anodynes that violence as a thing in and for itself offered him. If ever the old and widespread superstition that only the blade or rust of the spear that wounded one could heal the wound had any plausibility, Hemingway's story makes its contribution to it.

I have generalized so far on the Hemingway hero as a two-dimensional figure, "frank, brave, simple, and easily deceived." But I have not mentioned another group of characters who cannot be relegated to the two-dimensional. Whereas Hemingway's Ole Andresons, his matadors, boxers and hunters, are not so much human as unhappy animals with interesting stimulus-response patterns, this smaller group—Nick Adams, Frederick Henry, and Jake Barnes, to name the principals—inhabit the three-dimensional world of breathing humanity.

It is truistic to hold that one of the highest achievements of a writer's craft is to create a living character. But there are not that many that one can take them as a matter of course, or easily account for them. The question is more or less an open one, and complicated by the fact that a living character may not be a great character—may, in fact, be inferior to the two-dimensional product—but he will at any rate be alive.

Hemingway creates life in a handful of his characters. Nick Adams, Jake Barnes, and Frederick Henry (these, at least, are the prime examples) measure their lives from experiences they share with their creator—experiences that range from the toy slings and invisible arrows of childhood's not-so-outrageous fortune to the artillery shell which almost killed the author on 8 July 1918, at Fossalta di Pieave in Italy.

II

It is fashionable in American criticism, when a writer exhibits an interesting set of literary characteristics, to psychoanalyze him. Several people have suggested interesting, and I think plausible reasons for Hemingway's fascination with violence, war, the bullfight, and even reasons for his style.

One critic calls attention to the fact that death as a terminal experience, an escape from the agonies of life into some peaceful sleep, has been replaced by a symbolic death in which a character suffers an injury under violent, meaningless circumstances. Such an experience destroys not the man, but his past, and separates him from the familiar and valuable world he has grown up in. When the injury is inflicted by some impersonal social force, such as that graveyard of civilized hopes, the World War, then the symbolic death becomes a criticism of society, a refusal to belong to a society which will allow such catastrophes to take place.

There is a constant in Hemingway's fiction that all the experiences men value in peacetime—the ambition to succeed, the ability to fall in love, to fall out of love, to make enemies, to hate vindictively—all are flat, cold, without value. I cite two of his stories as examples of this flattening of experience that takes place. Both of them are about the war; both of them are about soldiers who no longer have to fight, one because he has been wounded and is recovering in a hospital, the other because the war is over and he has returned to America. In a nineteenth-century novel or story such an event would be the occasion for quiet joy, for reunions with the beautiful, peaceful world. Not so in Hemingway. It is here that his ability as a stylist is superb. He is the stylist of stoicism. By the poetic addition of sound and rhythm he accomplishes certain meanings. He accomplishes ennui, the twilight sleep of death's other kingdom. His sentences are repetitious, metrically monotonous, and express a complete withdrawal of emotional content that makes the description flat, cold, withdrawn.

In the beginning of his story "In Another Country," the lines act out the numbness of pain and ennui:

> In the fall the war was always there but we did not go to it any more. It was cold in the fall in Milan and the dark came very early. Then the electric lights came on and it was pleasant along the streets looking in the windows. There was much game hanging outside the shops and the snow powdered in the fur of the foxes and the wind blew their tails. The deer hung stiff and heavy and empty.[11]

Note the rhythms that come unpleasantly close to being too regular for prose, suddenly broken. The return to death in the dead animals, the deer hung stiff and heavy and empty. The protagonist in the story has a wounded knee, and it too is stiff, heavy and empty. The prose is close to the waste land poetry of T. S. Eliot—"The Hollow Men," for example.

The story, "Soldier's Home," demonstrates another approach to detachment. A returned veteran, Krebs, can no longer interest himself in life:

> He would have liked to have a girl but he did not want to have to spend a long time getting her. He did not want to get into the intrigue and the politics. He did not want to have to do any courting. It wasn't worth it.
>
> He did not want any consequences. He did not want any consequences ever again. He wanted to live along without consequences. Because he really did not need a girl.[12]

Psychoanalysis explains this emotional detachment, the refusal to accept the normal responsibilities of life, as a defense against any kind of excitement. Because mind and body were so violated by some injury in the past, any subsequent excitement revives the original trauma. People who have been hurt by life retreat categorically from all life, because they are afraid of a repetition of the original injury. For this reason, many veterans, wounded in war, find it impossible to work at anything but the simplest tasks. They retreat into simple, primitive functions—games, mechanical occupations, fishing, the enjoyment of ritual activities. They deny themselves their higher functions—the excitements of love, argument, adventure, discovery.

It is this mood of withdrawal that Hemingway imitates in all his fiction. It is the mood that has led his uncritical public to think of him as the monosyllabic tough guy—the stereotype of the veteran, the moving picture hero, Humphrey Bogart, Jean Gabin.

In addition to the question of mood in Hemingway's fiction, psychoanalysis considers his subject matter, and his passionate interest in the images of violence: war, the bullfight, hunting. Freud, in his work "Beyond the Pleasure Principle," described the tendency of human beings to repeat painful experiences in their lives even though they consciously denied seeking such experiences. It was then observed that those who had suffered (as Hemingway suffered) a severe injury were compelled to return again and again to some mitigated version of the original injury. Such a compulsion to return to the same experience is explained as an unconscious attempt to prove that one has survived the original injury. One becomes a traumatophile, attempting always to bring the painful experience within the grasp of one's conscious control. One allows oneself, like a patient who is about to have an operation, to cast a sidelong glance at the surgeon's knife, to be able to reassure himself that he knew where his pain and injury were going to come from: thus, in Freud's term, the "repetition compulsion" works.

If the man who has suffered such a shock is a writer, he will write about it repeatedly, as Hemingway does in *A Farewell to Arms*, *For Whom the Bell Tolls*, and in innumerable short stories. Or he may in his own life discover analogues to the original violence—bullfighting or big game hunting. He will then project these experiences into his fiction. And finally, he may create a hero who can stand up to these fatalities with a courage that lies on the far side of thought, a character such as Manuel the bullfighter in "The Undefeated," for example.

There is something of this spirit of a conscious, anguished confrontation of one's painful experience of life that has been institutionalized in the existentialist philosophy of Jean Paul Sartre. Like the Hemingway hero, Sartre's conscious heroes return out of choice to the agonies they suffered. Like the Hemingway hero, the existentialist hero plays his part against a backdrop of the absurd; he sees his life as a studied, conscious performance, a game, in which one's volitional acts are crucial, self-liberating challenges to what Sartre calls "the inescapable contingency of our human condition." Like the Hemingway hero, the existentialist hero separates himself from the nostalgia that makes men love the past and the weight of tradition. One of Hemingway's characters even acquires the nausea proper to the existentialist hero, "in regard to experience that is the result of untruth or exaggeration."

To pursue one more psychoanalytic concept, I should like to

speculate on the relevance to his own death by suicide of certain literary and biographical data. Many years ago, writing about himself, Hemingway said: "Since he was a young boy he has cared greatly for fishing and shooting. If he had not spent so much time at them . . . he might have written much more. On the other hand he might have shot himself."

To this statement there is a tragic parallel, the death of Hemingway's father in 1928, by a self-inflicted bullet. Hemingway uses the incident in *For Whom the Bell Tolls*, when Robert Jordan says how sick he felt when he knew his father was a "coward." In another story, "Fathers and Sons," Nick Adams (whose role is often a very transparent mask for Hemingway himself) is with his own son, and remembers his father:

> Like all men with a faculty that surpasses human requirements, his father was very nervous. Then too, he was sentimental, and like most sentimental people, he was both cruel and abused. Also he had much bad luck, and it was not all of it his own. He had died in a trap that he had helped only a little to set, and they had all betrayed him in their various ways before he died. All sentimental people are betrayed so many times.[13]

There is, finally, poignant evidence of Hemingway's own love for his father, and his unconcealed preference for him, rather than for his mother. In a short story, "The Doctor and the Doctor's Wife," (Hemingway *père* was a doctor), Hemingway symbolically chooses his father's way of life to his mother's: "'Your mother wants you to come and see her,' the doctor said. 'I want to go with you,' Nick said." And with that the story ends.

A certain formulation suggests itself here: the concept of the ego-ideal, in this instance the one related to Hemingway's father-image. The term *ego-ideal* implies a continuous identification of oneself with others—excessively so.

III

Nick Adams is representative of those Hemingway characters who think and cannot control their thoughts. Their internal situation is like King Lear's; betrayed to his own train of thought, he cries, "O, that way madness lies; let me shun that." Hemingway reveals only the outward signs of such a struggle. Nick Adams carefully baits a hook, escapes into the ritual of fishing, cooks a can of beans, avoids a dark place in the stream, and camps in a "good place." Only gradually do we realize that the fishing and camping idyll described in a story like "Big Two-hearted River" contains terrible latencies, introduced in those whispers that are the hallmark of Hemingway's style. Over the campfire Nick remembers a friend with whom he had fished. "They never saw Hopkins again. That was a long time ago on the Black River. Nick drank the coffee, the coffee according to Hopkins. The coffee was bitter. Nick laughed. It made a good ending to the story. His mind was beginning to work. He knew he could choke it because he was tired enough." [14]

Who was Hopkins? Did he die in the war? That is outside the story. Hemingway's style is by neurotic definition, occlusive rather than illuminating. We notice the dark of Nick Adams' mind, or Jake Barnes's mind. That way madness lies.

The code hero, like Nick Adams, appears to think very little, but it is because he has no choice. He is, by design, more often than not intellectually limited, like Ole Andreson in "The Killers," or he is a cultural primitive, like the bullfighter Manuel Garcia in "The Undefeated." His personality is truncated, impoverished with regard to everything but the repetitive business of standing up to death, absorbing the body blows of fate. When Nick Adams would count the number of ways to walk into town from the army hospital, Manuel Garcia would fall asleep, or Ole Andreson would stare at the ceiling.

The psychiatric explanation just reviewed here, if it were limited in its application merely to the work of this one man, would constitute an individious criticism. It would relegate him to that select but unenviable company of unhinged geniuses whose minds have foundered in their own deep. The effects of trauma on Hemingway's experience of life find corroboration in an unexpected quarter. Emily Dickinson, whose life was measured out in coffee spoons, and whose traumatic experience was either being crossed in love, or frightened by a garter snake, anatomized the symptoms of traumatic neurosis in a single poem as deftly as Hemingway has epitomized it in a dozen stories and novels:

> After great pain a formal feeling comes—
> The Nerves sit ceremonious, like Tombs—
> The stiff Heart questions was it He, that bore,
> and Yesterday, or Centuries before?

From the start the child, or the child recalled by the adult author, must develop images of heroes, most often beginning with one's parents. The image changes as one grows older, incorporating all sorts of identities, but somewhere in the vaults of the unconscious, there is an absurd and incorruptible image toward whose likeness the child strives—the fairy tale knight in armor, the aviator in the funny-paper. In those crises of adult life when one's own psychic integrity is threatened intolerably, one regresses to that inviolable image of perfection that the child has constructed for himself.

It is not too difficult to trace in those implausible heroes of his the lineaments of Hemingway's earliest image of his father, or to see in Wilson and his neophyte Macomber the idealized relationship between Hemingway father and son. Seen thus, "The Short Happy Life of Francis Macomber" contains certain sinister latencies—puberty rites, and a sexual rivalry with a terrible woman whose favors are only rendered to those who can conquer her.

As Hemingway developed his own identity as the legendary "Papa" of his own patriarchy, to become finally the weary, wise old man of *The Old Man and the Sea*, it is normatively conceivable that he fused these roles within himself. He enveloped the full octave of his father's character—the man who taught his son to shoot and fish, who oversimplified human relations in an attempt to control them, who was baffled by a wife who rode his life like a malevolent fate, who was nervous and sentimental and finally put a bullet through his head. In the end, Hemingway's sense of his separate identity, rubbed smooth like an old coin—weakened by the subsiding of his creative powers, old age and disease—coalesced absolutely with that of his father, and the son rushed toward the death he feared along the only path he had certain knowledge of.

IV

The Sun Also Rises is, I think, Hemingway's best sustained work of fiction. Its flaws are as inconsequential as they are obvious: Brett Ashley's being built "with curves like the hull of a racing yacht," and a certain morbid preoccupation beyond the call of despair with the in-group snobbery of the noble wounded, just about sum them up.

The novel contains, on the other hand, two of the most interesting characters to come out of Hemingway's work—Jake Barnes and Robert Cohn—and with them it presents a view of life slightly more complex than what Hemingway usually suggests. The book is not so much a record of a personal agony as it is a portrait of a generation. The love relationships that, as *A Farewell to Arms* and *For Whom the Bell Tolls* attest, are not Hemingway's forte, and the anatomy of violence, which is too much his forte, are both absent. Jake's disability makes the one a practical impossibility, and the exigencies of the plot reduce the violence to a stark minimum. Hemingway's style and theme, as Philip Young describes them in *Ernest Hemingway*, "integrated and bound tight around a core of shock," are nowhere so gainfully employed as they are here. *The Sun Also Rises* moves with the intricate monotony of Ravel's *Bolero*, which as music is not so much pure feeling as it is an escape from feeling.

Carlos Baker describes the characters in *The Sun Also Rises* as "the wastelanders," the term derived, of course, from T. S. Eliot's monumental poem, which appeared in 1922. Eliot's poem is a Dantean portrait of the twentieth century, a waste land of spiritual vacuity, passionless lust, and meaningless distraction. Its central symbol is the medieval Fisher King, a syncretized Christ figure, whose nameless, sexual mutilation imposes barrenness on all the land.

There is a certain plausibility to the comparison, reinforced by oblique evidences of Hemingway's familiarity with the poem. In *A Farewell to Arms* Frederick Henry and Catherine Barkley hear a motor car honk in the street below their hotel room, and it prompts Frederick to remember Marvell's "To His Coy Mistress,"

> But at my back I always hear
> Time's winged chariot hurrying near.

In Eliot's *The Waste Land*, of course, the motor horns blow right into Marvell's poem. More than this, in *The Sun Also Rises, The Waste Land* is qualitatively invoked. It too is a hell of incomplete relationships, of impotence. Jake, the central character, is mutilated and, as Young points out, "once more The Fisher King is a man who fishes."

The circles of Dante's hell and Eliot's recurrence of myth find their parallel in the shape of the novel which brings us in a circle by limousine and taxicab to where we started from. Jake says, "I had the feeling as in a nightmare of it all being something repeated, something I had been through and that now I must go through again."

And finally the separation from spiritual grace—the "death by drowning," Eliot's symbol of baptism, the absence of "The Hanged Man" from the fortune teller's cards, Eliot's symbol for Christ—has echoes in the special embarrassment Jake Barnes and Brett feel about their religious inadequacies. "I regretted that I was such a rotten Catholic, but realized there was nothing I could do about it, at least for a while, and maybe never, but that anyway it was a grand religion," Jake thinks as he kneels in the cathedral. Brett simply dismisses her spiritual failure by saying, "I've got the wrong kind of face."

Still, we are mistaken if, in the last analysis, we read *The Sun Also Rises* as a prose *Waste Land*. If Eliot and Hemingway write *about* a waste land, it is because they lived through the same historical moment and saw pretty much the same events happen. But there is a temperamental bulkhead that divides them, as high and wide as eternity, that makes Hemingway's characters permanently incapable of acting according to Eliot's lights.

Earlier I drew an analogy between Eliot's and Hemingway's preference for the ritual act over the accidental, and I believe one can derive their differences from their choice of ritual. It is a choice between the human tragedy and the divine comedy—between the bullfight and the Mass. Eliot has his eye on the resurrection because he is religious; Hemingway keeps his eye on the crucifixion because he is not. The characters in Eliot's poem are dead to the anxieties of Hemingway's characters. The fires of lust, anger, and illusion that confine the human spirit must be extinguished, according to Eliot's belief. Hemingway's people with that rage to live that sends them into Spain would give their eyeteeth for lust, anger, and a few illusions. It is because they cannot live that they suffer. For Eliot, with his telephone line to God, the death of the body's desires invigorates the spirit. Hemingway's implicit belief is closer to D. H. Lawrence's and, as *Women in Love* and *Lady Chatterley's Lover* bear witness, to the expression of that belief: that the death of the body kills the spirit. Eliot's characters have no energies, and that is why they are in limbo. Hemingway's characters have too much energy, and that is why they are in hell. Their energies have been forbidden expression along with the great words that have become obscene. The best that can be said is that Hemingway's "wastelanders" meet Eliot's as they go in opposite directions around the same fixed point.

Jake Barnes and Brett Ashley are best understood in terms of the language and behavior of shock. They are particularly understandable in terms of *A Farewell to Arms*, which provides belatedly, since it came out after *The Sun Also Rises*, a past for Brett and Jake. The Catherine Barkley, whose long hair Frederick Henry loved, whose first young man was blown up in the war, and whose love idyll is ended by her death in childbirth, becomes the easy-virtued Brett Ashley, who will not let her hair grow, the barren mother who rages in her barrenness, and who, because she cannot be fulfilled, destroys the men who love her—a jazz age Rachel weeping for her children because they were not. *Tenente* Frederick Henry, for whom conjugal love remains a "sacred subject," becomes the Jake Barnes whose grander values have been swept away by the abomination of the war, and who is willing to settle for the little there is left. It is materially important that we understand that he is practically impotent, not incapable of passionate thought, but of passionate action, in order to understand Jake Barnes as Hemingway's symbol of the paralyzed lost generation. Jake has been crucified, not castrated.

What gives Jake magnitude and makes *The Sun Also Rises* a superior novel is that Jake is unique among Hemingway's characters in that he is a reconstructionist. *A Farewell to Arms* becomes finally a bittersweet dream, a heavenly hell of pleasant unlikelihoods, with Frederick Henry voicing his belief in the permanent vindictiveness of the gods toward lovers. It seems to be a belief which carried the day with Hemingway, since it is the one which survived. This idea finds explicit statement in *Death in the Afternoon*, where Hemingway says,

> All stories, if continued far enough, end in death . . . especially do all stories of monogamy end in death, and your man who is monogamous while he often lives most happily, dies in the most lonely fashion. There is no lonelier man in death except the suicide, than that man who has lived many years with a good wife and then outlived her. . . . If two people love each other there can be no happy end to it.[15]

The sentiment strikes, finally, an adolescent note, and begins to sound more like an excuse for polygamy, or a covert admission that Hemingway found his profoundest pleasures in the society of men, than like an elegaic praise of marriage.

Jake is tougher and more realistic. He has, in psychological terms, greater survival value. He is closer to valid stoicism than anyone else in Hemingway's fiction. Lying awake in the dark, Jake invents a philosophy of life for himself, which, although he thinks disparagingly, "will seem just as silly as all the other fine philosophies I've had," lacks the self-pitying complaint that Frederick Henry voices.

Jake accepts:

> No idea of retribution or punishment. Just exchange of values. You gave up something and got something else. Or you worked for something. You paid some way for every-thing that was any good. I paid my way into enough things that I liked, so that I had a good time. Either you paid by learning about them or by experience, or by taking chances, or by money. Enjoying living was learning to get your money's worth and knowing when you had it. You could get your money's worth. The world was a good place to buy in.[16]

Jake's spiritual wholesomeness, his role as the sanity of the novel, finds a not wholly unprepared affinity with the character of Lambert Strether in James's *The Ambassadors*. In an amusing by-play of wit between Bill Gorton and Jake Barnes, Bill says:

> "You're an expatriate. You've lost touch with the soil. You get precious. Fake European standards have ruined you. . . . You don't work. One group claims women support you. Another group claims you're impotent. . . . That's what you ought to work up into a mystery. Like Henry's bicycle."
> "It wasn't a bicycle," I said. . . .
> "I think he's a good writer, too," Bill said.[17]

The reference to "Henry's bicycle" is of course an unmis-takable allusion to the celebrated and not secret wound that

Henry James suffered in his youth. It is the wound which has furnished us with the hypothetical basis for James's own celibacy and the sexual timidities of his major characters. Elsewhere, in *The Green Hills of Africa*, we have the evidence for Hemingway's admiration for Henry James; Hemingway places James with the other lights, Mark Twain and Stephen Crane. We realize, too, in every line Hemingway writes about *his* encounter with Europe, that he loved his Paris, his Italy, his Europe, the way Henry James loved his—with the same mixture of love, fear, and contempt that is the product of American Puritanism. In this coupling of Henry James's legendary sexual trauma with Jake Barnes's real mutilation, Hemingway has performed a tour de force of bringing literature to bear upon literature.

There is, in Jake's enforced neutrality, his moral pragmatism, his role as sheet anchor to this *bateau ivre* of lost souls, a close resemblance to the refined martyrdom Lambert Strether chooses in order to remain a tower of strength for the wayward Chad and the lost Mme. de Vionnet. Knowing that if he yields to the amoral blandishments of Europe and the charms of Maria Gostrey, he will lose the power to bless their irregular relationship, he interposes himself as a sacrifice in order that these beautiful people may float easily "up the silver stream of impunity." He returns to Woollett and certain failure, the lamb of God who carries away the sins of the worldly.

The Ambassadors, no more than *The Sun Also Rises*, is not to be read as a paean to the good life. It is a monument to American Puritanism. Strether represents it at its best, just as Mamie Pocock represents it at its worst. In Strether, as it is in the war-battered Jake Barnes, Puritanism is a living force. Jake must be a witness to the good and the bad, and search for them in the tents of the unrighteous. He must test the myth of the wicked woman; he must expand the preconceptions about relationship, virtuous and vicious; he must recognize the force and quality of love; he must learn to differentiate between nominal appearances and the real existence of things. The sterile idealism of

America tends to reduce experience to geometrical abstractions, in the name of truth and righteousness. Strether's consciousness is never corrupted by this pseudo–puritanical intellectualism. He hunts down the facts without trying to reconcile them with some predetermined formulation.

The practical good of Strether's Puritanism merges imperceptibly with the magic of ritual sacrifice. The value lies in his being able, from the center of his self-denying integrity, to give moral sanction to the irregularities about him. There is something of the Indian *sadhu* about Strether, a figure of power, who gathers strength through his austerities. For him to marry Maria Gostrey would be for him, after all, to be a false messiah. Going off to Woollett to be sacrificed, even though its futility strikes us as morbid, confers nonetheless a blessing on Chad and Mme. de Vionnet. It is something of this *sadhu* quality Jake Barnes shares with Lambert Strether.

While Jake and Brett are central to *The Sun Also Rises*, Robert Cohn most interests me. I want to do something about him, organize a Citizens for Cohn, or the New Friends of Robert Cohn. Very few people have anything nice to say about him. He is messy; he stands opposite the bullfighter Pedro Romero at the corners of Hemingway's moral scheme. He is neither matador nor bull; he is an unheroic horse. Watch the bull, says Hemingway in *Death in the Afternoon*, and the horse's death will not distress you. I should prefer for a moment to keep my eye on the horse.

A peculiar ambivalence characterizes the responses of the important characters to Cohn. Ignoring Mike's flat, merciless anti-semitism, and some of Bill Gorton's comic anti-semitism, we find that Jake and Bill pay Cohn a special kindness. He puzzles Bill Gorton. "The funny thing is he's nice, too. I like him. But he's just so awful."

He puzzles Jake Barnes too, but Jake constructs a moral system around the way people treat Cohn. "I do not know how people could say such terrible things to Robert Cohn. There are people to whom you could not say insulting things. They give you a feeling that the world would be destroyed, would actually be destroyed before your eyes, if you said certain things."[18]

At the same time Jake enjoys seeing Cohn hurt. "I liked to see him hurt Cohn. I wished he would not do it, though, because afterward it made me disgusted at myself. That was morality; things that made you disgusted afterward. No, that must be immorality."[19]

What emerges here is a character who is half in, half out of literature, half in, and half out of Hemingway's intentions. The part of Cohn that does not seem part of the plan of *The Sun Also Rises* is the gratuitous contempt he draws upon himself, his faculty, as Jake observes, for "bringing out the worst in anybody"—Jake's dislike of Cohn's "look of eager, deserving expectation," when he sees Brett Ashley. This Cohn is the unassimilated Harold Loeb who still emerges fresh and clear in his book *The Way It Was.*

The part of Cohn that belongs in the novel finds its affinity with Francis Macomber, who is also "very fit," an athlete, with the same tendency to be "moulded" by women. Cohn is a Jewish Macomber who because he was not granted the opportunity of being shot in the back of the head, is destined to lead a long, unhappy life. Hemingway, if he is anti-semitic, is a part of that vast element in enlightened Christendom which believes that the Jews possess in abundance a certain set of racial characteristics: an inordinate love and respect for women and family life, a distrust of Anglo-Saxon virtues like tight-lipped fortitude and taciturnity, a tendency to feel left out and to behave masochistically for the secondary pleasure of having people feel pity.

But Cohn, like Macomber, and like Jake Barnes, and Pedro Romero, has found certain values to which he can commit himself. The trouble is that Cohn's values have not been pruned, by the war or the winnowing effect of danger, to a few manly essentials. His emotions have not been traumatized. Brett's reference to the Count, "he's one of us," has a sinister (Conradian) ring when we realize who the "us" includes. She rejects Pedro

Romero in a gesture of renunciation, like a vampire renouncing a man of flesh and blood. Its corollary is her rejection of Cohn because he is disgustingly alive. She and Jake Barnes dream of a world where there *are* grand values. Cohn has read W. H. Hudson and, all credulous, brings love and a sense of the sacred into a context where, like the other abstract words, they are obscene. The world of Jake Barnes is not an orgiastic order so much as it is an austere order that has gone beyond all vows in its renunciation of the world. Brett belongs in her way to his monastic order. She is its lay sister.

If we excuse the moral ambiguity of Barnes's act of pimping for Brett—more degraded than anything Cohn could possibly do—as an act of sympathy and renunciation, then we should be equally capable of appreciating the veniality of Cohn's offenses against the code of tightlipped resignation. As we have seen, in Hemingway's later novels, when the tightlipped resignation is all that is left of Hemingway's ethic, it turns out to be pretty thin stuff.

If, after all, we cannot help reproaching Hemingway for the imbalances he exhibits throughout his career, we must consider that the whole literary epoch in which he worked was an exhibition of imbalances. He, along with his contemporaries, was a man walking in a tilted world. His survival and his popularity obscure the fact that they all behaved strangely. They were all, for one thing, in search of instant values, and when we consider some of the alternatives—Ezra Pound dreaming of some Renaissance *magnifico* who would patronize the arts, and settling in the end for Mussolini; T. S. Eliot's warning the good citizens of Norfolk, Virginia, to watch out for city slickers and "free-thinking" Jews because they were dragging the country down in his absence—Hemingway's own lopsidedness, which was a sort of insulation around a core of lacerated nerves, has an honorable quality.

As an influence, Hemingway has drawn at least one first-rate talent into the circle of his genius. The language and moral disinterestedness of Camus' *The Stranger* find their origins in *The Sun Also Rises*. It may be that wherever and whenever the language of crisis and the behavior of men under inhuman pressures are the subject of literature, Hemingway's name and accomplishment will be invoked.   [1962]

6.

Lyrical Darwinism and the Mythical World of Faulkner's *The Hamlet*

To deal with the distasteful in the modern novel, I realize I could choose works far more eligible for discussion than *The Hamlet*. The studied squalor of James T. Farrell's *Studs Lonigan* trilogy suggests itself, or that more recent and most controversial novel of Vladimir Nabokov, *Lolita*, or the ill-fated *Lady Chatterley's Lover*. But setting aside the strictly legal question of what is offensive to normal tastes, I can only speculate on what if anything is distasteful to modern readers.

For this reason it is not so much my purpose in discussing this particular novel to exhibit the sexual and moral squalors of Faulkner's Snopeses as it is to suggest at least one way of rationalizing such material into the province of art.

To begin with, one needs to determine what is the distasteful in art. The criteria by which one decides what is or is not suitable to the work of art have a long and varied history. I do not here intend to go behind the lace curtain of smug propriety. I will deal here not with art, or with a critical public, but with literature seen as a kind of chintz loincloth designed to cover as suggestively as possible what good literature should reveal.

We find that the first concerns were by and large moral ones. Aristotle, for example, in his description of the tragic drama, finds repellant a situation in which an entirely good man, in short a saint, is brought to misfortune through no fault of his own. He finds equally repellant a situation in which a very bad man comes to good fortune through his evil machinations. As for the physically distasteful, he is permissive, disallowing scenes of violence in the drama, but allowing them in epic poetry. He found the pleasure we take in works of art in our general delight with any kind of imitation. As he puts it:

> And it is also natural for all to delight in works of imitation. The truth of this second point is shown by experience: though the objects themselves may be painful to see, we delight to view the most realistic representations of them in art, the forms, for example, of the lowest animals and of dead bodies. The explanation is to be found in a further fact: to be learning something is the greatest of pleasures, not only to the philosopher, but also the rest of mankind however small their capacity for it.[1]

As with Aristotle, so it has been with his posterity. To cover twenty centuries in about twenty seconds, one might generalize that the critic of literature has required only that if sin and evil are represented as disgusting or ridiculous, they are never represented as triumphant or noble; and as a corollary to this that virtue must always be painted better than life, and that it must win out in the end. Such an approach to what was admissible into the province of literature was postulated on some theological system that condemned vice to ugliness and calamity and, while it did not always save its heroes alive, it kept them attractive to the end.

Literature has always been extremely sensitive to any scientific or theological reordering of the universe, for such reordering demands a redefinition of the role of humanity, and describing the role of humanity is the unique province of the artist.

Whatever an age determines its role to be, human beings by some mysterious but accountable process, proceed to fulfill that role. In an age of faith human beings dedicate themselves to building temples, or to perpetual virginity, or inquisitions, or elaborate funeral rites. In an age of reason people invent watches, write counterpoint, and behave reasonably. Society organizes itself politically around a tyrant or a limited monarch, a president or a dictator.

In the last half of the nineteenth century a staggering revision of the traditional concepts of the world and man's place in it occurred. The scientific proponent of this new view of man and nature was Darwin, whose *Descent of Man* and *Origin of Species* changed overnight the concepts of special creation and providence to those of natural selection and the struggle for existence. The philosopher of evolution theory was Herbert Spencer, who insisted that the only method of human knowledge was scientific method.

The propagandists of this new world view were the artists, and a literary process evolved during this period of complete and unmitigated scientific materialism. The writer followed the scientist into the laboratory and attempted in language to perform for art what the scientist was doing for matter: to record the processes of human behavior—this struggle for existence and natural selection—with scientific detachment, relying not on inspiration but on carefully kept notebooks. The new literary movement called itself naturalism, and it claimed the dignity of a science.

Its practitioners renounced the random, and presumably inspired, inventions of their literary predecessors, who were not above insinuating their own feelings and ideas into the work. The naturalistic novelist, on the other hand, went to work like an anthropologist or a sociologist, examining mankind in the bulk. And like the sociologist or anthropologist he found his best material among those people who, without the privileges of money or culture, were born to flourish, propagate, suffer, and die under conditions that were statistically predictable. The naturalist described with as much biological accuracy as the age would permit all the homely natural functions—childbirth, disease, death, drunkenness, brutality.

Acting upon Darwinian principles, the novelist substituted for the ancient idea of Fate the factors of heredity and environ-

ment, and at the intersection of these two factors he created a
living character. It was thus possible upon real statistical evidence to write the biography of a prostitute, or a dipsomaniac,
as Zola does in *Nana* and *L'Assommoir*, whose title is the name
of a saloon in Paris and means, freely translated into English,
"The Mickey Finn."

It is a delightful irony that naturalism should have emerged
when the Victorian era, that figleaf on the body of history,
was in full tide. Sex was everywhere in mothballs, as was anything else that remotely resembled human function. Middle-
class morality was the human norm, when novelists like Zola
dragged out everything lock, stock, and barrel, and flung it
into the laps of an indignant generation. To give some idea of
how the Victorian responded to the distasteful, and what constituted the distasteful, below are quotations from two poems
by Alfred Lord Tennyson, the most outstanding apologist for
dignified repression. In "Locksley Hall Sixty Years After," he
has poor Art herself lamenting the decline of morals:

> Authors—essayist, atheist, novelist, realist, rimester, play
> your part,/Paint the mortal shame of nature with the liv-
> ing hues of art.

> Rip your brothers' vices [Snopes!] open, strip your own
> foul passions bare;/Down with Reticence, down with Rev-
> erence—forward—naked—let them stare.

> Feed the budding rose of boyhood with the drainage of
> your sewer;/Send the drain into the fountain, lest the
> stream should issue pure.

> Set the maiden fancies wallowing in the troughs of Zo-
> laism,—Forward—/Forward, ay, and backward, down-
> ward too into the abysm.

> Do your best to charm the worst, to lower the rising race
> of men;/Have we risen from out the beast, then back into
> the beast again?[2]

The answer, for the Darwinian novelists was—YES!—and
their *work* in the first flush of its novelty, in the integrity of

its practitioners, and in the midst of the spate of romantic Victorian novels whose titles are mercifully lost to us, which charmed the lives of maidens, spinsters, and retired clergymen, found an enthusiastic, if not too respectable, readership.

But the great claim of the naturalistic novel was to reform; it more often than not had, or suggested, some sort of political or social program—women's rights, child labor laws, divorce laws, free love, mixed bathing, and so on.

Naturalism lapsed, after the first thrust of its men of genius, into dreary absurdity, in which poorhouses, charity hospitals, and brothel scenes occurred as a matter of course, like bedroom scenes in Jayne Mansfield movies. In America, Theodore Dreiser represents the last significant appearance of a naturalist novelist. His *Sister Carrie*, because Caroline Meeber lived with men, found no publisher for several years after its writing. Here is Dreiser's literary credo: "Man is no more essentially just than he is unjust. He is an impulse, a will to live, a sharply reflected chemical and physical impulse in Nature, which acts or reacts as the nature of other chemical stimuli in immediate contact with him suggests or compels, and which same may be by no means as moral as we think." [3]

A philosophy of literature, like this one of Dreiser's, which proposed the intrinsic unimportance of its characters, could not—once the novelty of exotic squalor and vice wore off, for the jaded writer or his audience—survive its own principles. It had to be succeeded, and it was. Because it had expanded the realm of artistic subject matter and had freed literature from the narrow morality of sectarianism and convention, naturalism worked out its own salvation.

The naturalistic novel had all along proposed (following the line of Darwinism) that certain constants were present in human behavior—constants that were biologically and culturally inherent in all human societies everywhere. The cultural anthropologist turned in a wide circle of interest to the examination of strange folkways, religions, myths, fairy tales, ancient rites—and returned to his own immediate, contemporary culture with the conclusion that the past had never really died, that human institutions were endlessly repetitious of themselves.

Early in our own century such works as William Graham Sumner's *Folkways* and Sir James Frazer's *The Golden Bough* appeared, exhaustive studies in the universality of custom and religious practice. To the endless embarrassment of conservative protestant clergymen, Christ was ceremonially eaten and resurrected in the Fiji Islands. In short, human history was the endless translation of ancient impulses, to a new language.

For the artist, already committed to the bold investigation of the hard, cold facts of life, this lyrical aspect of Darwinism came as a great relief. The dignity of the ancient myths, and their ritual repetitiousness, reaffirmed his belief in man's heroic, tragic nature, his permanence and his doom. The artist could then presume that in the simplest, the basest, even the most sordid human action, there may be a special, formal significance, which it then becomes his task to isolate and describe.

There was no longer the need, if one wanted to find tragic dignity, to return to the past for it. Good artists know that nostalgia is the kiss of death to a living literature, and works like Tennyson's *Idylls of the King*, and the sometimes painfully inaccurate historical novels are more often than not literary antique shops. How much more exciting to isolate in the everyday commonplace lives of men and women the mythological constants, to find in one's own town the betrayals, martyrdoms, rapes, marriages and sacrifices with which epochs, religions, and harvest seasons begin and end!

The artist we credit with having been the greatest, if not the first, to launch upon this new literary adventure, is James Joyce. In *A Portrait of the Artist as a Young Man* Stephen Dedalus, his spokesman, sees himself as a "priest of the eternal imagination, transmuting the daily bread of experience into the radiant body of everlasting life." Joyce asserted the role of artist to be synonymous with that of the maker of myths. The myth is the form that otherwise meaningless, repetitive experience takes. History, as he has Stephen Dedalus say in *Ulysses*, "repeats itself

with a difference." This *Ulysses*, as Joyce conceived it, transforms the otherwise humdrum day in "dear dirty old Dublin,"
into yet another recapitulation of the original Odyssey of the
original Ulysses. Mr. Bloom, the hero of the novel, performs
in his humblest functions (and they are extremely humble,
and outrageously functional), the most profound and most traditional rites. He literally cannot sit down in a watercloset
without its becoming a Holy of Holies. He cannot pass between two other characters without their becoming Scylla and
Charybdis.

Ulysses has been described as both the culmination of naturalism and its death blow. It not only dealt with the distasteful
minute particulars of human function; it wallowed in them. It
exalted them, and what would most have distressed Tennyson,
it made them beautiful. Mr. Bloom has become, as a hero, as
important to us as Hamlet.

When we turn to America we find, under this new stimulus,
poets like T. S. Eliot and Ezra Pound dipping into Frazer to
find images for their poetry. In "Sweeney among the Nightin-
gales," one hears echoes of Greek tragedy. The novelist Conrad
Aiken writes *The Coming Forth by Day of Osiris Brown*, a novel
which had the temerity to anticipate Joyce's *Finnegans Wake*.
And finally we have the playwright Eugene O'Neill in a play
like *Mourning Becomes Electra* discovering the tragic theme of
the Greek Electra in the Civil War.

How then are we to read *The Hamlet*? We know enough
about Faulkner and his poetic beliefs to assume that, as in James
Joyce's work, the characters and actions of his novels transcend
their own local and finite identities. We know that all of Faulkner's works are structured around a central theme, and that
theme is the life and death of the South. He has created a
mythical county, Yoknapatawpha, whose seat is the town of
Jefferson, Mississippi, and its generations before and after the
Civil War. He describes the slow disintegration of the South in
the jaws of history—slavery, the economic strangling of the
South by the industrial North, the Civil War and secession, the

Emancipation and Reconstruction, the carpetbaggers, the Ku Klux Klan, and the lynch mobs, the cruelty and senseless greed of a mongrel race of predatory men who bled the country, hacked down its forests, and settled themselves in what had once been the seat of a gracious, virile, inherently aristocratic society.

Faulkner sees (to go at once to the mythological form he has imposed on this vision) the same decline and fall that the Greek poet Hesiod observed, from a golden age of men like gods, to a silver age on which sin entered, to a bronze age of fierce warriors, and an age of heroes (who fought against the Trojans), and finally an iron age, of degenerate men as we know them,

> when the father will not agree with his children. . . nor comrade with comrade; nor will brother be dear to brother. . . . There will be no favor for the man who keeps his oath or for the just or for the good but rather men will praise the evil doer and his violent dealing. . . . Envy, foul mouthed, delighting in evil, with scowling face, will go along with wretched men one and all.[4]

Now there are certain hazards to going into a perfectly good work of art with an eye for its mythical backgrounds. For one thing, one runs the risk of losing the particular in the general. This is a risk that both artist and reader run. For another thing, one may try to stretch the work of art over one particular myth, and have thereby to rationalize much that will not fit. This is the reader's lookout. The writer's vision is plastic, flexible, and once he sets his mind to a mythical event, all its many corollaries must inevitably cry for admission.

The Hamlet records the moment in the disintegration of the South when all the heroes and demigods are gone from the land. Frenchman's Bend reflects a glory that was. The best have died in the War between the States; the remainder preserve certain decencies, certain amenities, but these are negative virtues which cannot withstand the positive malevolence of the Snopeses. The Snopeses are a mysterious tribe. They do not so much destroy the hamlet as the hamlet in its decline calls them into being. They are like the horsemen of the apocalypse who emerge out of chaos. They are, so to speak, the scourge of god, "men with eyes like stagnant water, or agate, axe blades or new plow-points, like black glass in uncooked dough."

Book 1, "Flem," could be subtitled "The Coming of the Snopeses." The hamlet yields to the Snopeses under the threat of fire, the stiff, terrible, loveless man who burns barns. He is a cold genius of defiance, like Lucifer, or old Satan, to whom Faulkner likens him in that strange epilogue in Hell at the end of the second book, "Eula."

It is in Book 2 that the mythological referents of *The Hamlet* assert themselves without ambiguity, and it is these referents that redeem the novel from its picayune squalors and corruptions. Faulkner calls Eula Venus, the goddess of love, and her would-be lover, the schoolteacher Labove, sees her prophetically, married like Venus to a "crippled Vulcan," who has bought her, but who is himself a "dwarf, a gnome, without glands or desire"—in short, Flem Snopes.

We are meeting here the myth of Venus and Vulcan in its purest form, but here, as in Joyce, we "must look for them, [these divinities] not among the gods but among men." Nor is this the Venus of classical sculpture, all white marble and in the best of taste. This is a Venus reduced to her elemental terms, as the Greeks conceived of her when she was a living force, a goddess of fertility, unlimited sexuality, married to an impotent fool in order that she might all the more freely give herself to all men. Faulkner conceives of her as James Joyce conceived the heroine Molly Bloom, in *Ulysses*; her breasts and her rump are her most salient features. As Joyce describes her: "Adiposterior female hemispheres redolent of milk and honey and of excretory sanguine and seminal warmth . . . expressive of mute immutable mature animality."[5] So Eula is The Great Mother. She gives herself to and is impregnated by the strongest of her suitors.

Flem Snopes, the Vulcan of this divine couple, is more complex in his mythical identity. Vulcan is the crippled, ill-favored and impotent blacksmith of the gods. He is traditionally the fool of the gods, but he was also their banker. He worked in precious metals. His identification with the devil, however, brings up two other possibilities connected with the Snopeses gaining possession of the land.

The Greek divinity who shares honors with Venus as a fertility goddess is the goddess Demeter, the Roman Ceres. When her daughter Persephone was stolen by the god of the Underworld, Dis—or Pluto—the god of wealth, the lord of the dead, the land was made barren, there were no crops, and men starved. In both these mythological figures we have attributes and actions that suit the symbolic actions of *The Hamlet*. Flem Snopes has stolen, in Eula, the life of the land.

Regarding Book 3—"The Long Summer"—I should like to concentrate on the shooting of Houston, and what one of the Snopeses calls with lighthearted accuracy "the stock-diddling" of the idiot Snopes, Ike.

To take the least sensational of the two events in the "long summer" first, we find that Mink Snopes shares with his cousin Flem the possession of the overripe, elemental female, "the fierce, simple cave of a lioness." But Mink is a variation on the theme of the possession of the South by the Snopeses. Unlike his cousin, who is impotent, Mink (and his name gives him away) is the Snopes who will people this land with his seed that his wife describes as "rank poison." If Flem Snopes is cold and avaricious, Mink Snopes is hot and homicidal. They represent extremes in the periodic table of poisonous elements that is the Snopes clan.

No self-respecting divinity is without her bestial equivalent; more often than not, when one looks for an animal that is emblematic of a fertility goddess, that animal will turn out to be a cow. At one point or another the Egyptian goddess Isis replaced her human head with the head of a cow, and was so worshipped. In Greek mythology at least one of Zeus's mistresses was changed into a cow—the heifer Io; and when Homer wanted to praise a goddess's eyes he referred to them as *bou-sopa*—"cow-eyed." In India, similarly, the consort of Shiva, the mother earth herself, takes animal form as a cow. It becomes a regular occurrence in all religions that the god or goddess worshipped has some more convenient, totemic form—an animal that one may then worship, sacrifice, eat, or as with Ike Snopes, make love to. In that relationship which I assume to be unspeakable and distasteful to most of us, Ike is enacting the degraded equivalent of an already-degraded ritual being enacted by his cousin Flem.

It seems to me also that, in terms of this descent from human form to animal of the fertility goddess, a third step is worked out. After Lump is dissuaded from selling admissions to see this prodigy, the cow is butchered (sacrificed) and Ike is consoled with a wooden replica of the cow, a doll. This too is a step in the descent of a divinity from her incarnate self to her animal substitute, and finally to a replica of that animal, an image, like an Easter lamb in the form of a cake, or a wooden toy. "The battered wooden effigy of a cow, such as children receive on Christmas."

In the last book of *The Hamlet*, Flem Snopes, having cornered in a manner of speaking all the females, proceeds on a grand scale to gather all the wealth into his hands. The spotted horses are demonic animals, wicked, intractable—symbolic, in their wild, spotted state, and their overrunning the countryside, spreading the blight upon the land. In the iconography of Catholicism, spotted things are inherently evil. The spotted leopard, for example, represents Satan himself. Immaculate means "without spot"—thus, without sin.

Throughout *The Hamlet* there is one person who seems to hold out against the malevolence of the Snopeses. This is the salesman, Ratliff, who appears at all times the detached, melancholy, sometimes amused observer, capable of the full range of human emotions. It is his fall, tempted by the hint of buried treasure, that completes the degradation of Frenchman's Bend. Thus, for Faulkner, the realistic southern observer—a naturalistic figure—must succumb to the power of myth and lyricism. In Ratliff's fall is the rise of the Snopes myth.

[1968]

7.

William Faulkner
and the Runaway Slave

One is left, when one reads about the black in William Faulkner, with the feeling that Faulkner is not describing human beings but ritual objects, which, when correctly used, bring good fortune, and when profaned, disaster. "They are better than we are," says Isaac McCaslin in "The Bear"; they have the virtues of "endurance, pity and tolerance and forbearance and fidelity and love of children."[1] But the superiority is dangerous; it is above the homely bill of human rights. And their virtues seem better suited to household gods, or that anagram of god, the dog, than they are to the complexities of the human spirit.

By virtue of this exemption of the black from humanity, Faulkner's attitude to the question of bondage or freedom, and more recently, to integration or segregation, seems not to reflect on his moral integrity. His morality in this connection is archaic; we cannot accept the ground of its being and yet it shows itself worthy of our trust.

In addition to the fact that, in our heterodox, secularized culture, the ritual control of nature (which had formerly enjoyed serious acceptance), can legitimately appear in our fiction as an improvisation, we can invoke Faulkner's known predilection for relating classical mythology to nonmythical events in order to adduce to his using the black as ritual object.

In *The Hamlet*, for example, Faulkner plays out in the best syncretistic fashion the combined myths of Venus and Vulcan, the metamorphosis of Juno, and the *Nibelungenlied*. Eula, the bride of Flem Snopes, is

> . . . one blind seed of the spendthrift Olympian ejacula-
> tion . . . she would transform the very wooden desks and
> benches themselves into a grove of Venus . . . she would sit
> on the sunny steps and eat like one of the unchaste and per-
> haps even anonymously pregnant immortals eating bread
> of Paradise on a sunwise slope of Olympus . . . what
> Brunhilde, what Rhinemaiden on what spurious river-
> rock of papier mache, what Helen returned to what topless
> and shoddy Argos, waiting for no one.[2]

And Flem Snopes is ". . . a dwarf, a gnome, without glands or desire . . . the crippled Vulcan to that Venus, who would not possess her but own her by the single strength which power gave, the dead power of money, wealth, gewgaws, baubles, as he might own."[3]

In the bestial equivalent of the goddess, the cow to which Ike Snopes pays court, Faulkner sees the ox-eyed Juno. "Within the mild, enormous moist and pupilless globes he sees himself in twin miniatures mirrored by the inscrutable abstraction: one with that which Juno might have looked out with, he watched himself contemplating what those who looked at Juno saw."[4]

I should like, then, to transfer this feeling of Faulkner's for the mythical experience to two stories, "Was," and "Dry Sep-tember," which exhibit not the avatars of Olympus, but their despised surrogate, the black, in his role as ritual object. It is, moreover, an exhibition of the vicissitudes to which this role has been subjected—vicissitudes which may serve to expand our understanding of the myth Faulkner has drawn from the his-tory of the South.

"Was" is a comic rondo whose comic element lies in the rigidity of its action, in the absolutely determined nature of the chase, flight and pursuit, pursuit and flight, in a rustic counter-point of hound and fox, clown and clowness, lady and squire.

The white men in the story are characterized by their ob-sessive fear of women and marriage; the white woman, on the other hand, is equally desperate for a man in marriage. And to accomplish her ends she appeals to the mutual sympathies of Tomey's Turl and Tennie, the slaves, who are unabashedly intent on one another, and who help her in what is only *apparently* an unsuccessful attempt to entangle the man she wants.

"Dry September" takes its title from a time of drought, an annual occurrence in the deep South. In the dry, parching weather, out of her own discontent, a spinster, Miss Minnie Cooper, complains of a black—a significant decrescendo of accusations—"attacked, insulted, frightened." A man named Plunkett leads a lynch mob which kills the black and drops him into an abandoned, bottomless vat. Plunkett returns to his "neat new house," where his wife has waited up for him. He flings her aside and goes to the door, where, "with his body pressed against the dusty screen he stood panting. There was no movement, no sounds, not even an insect. The dark world seemed to lie stricken beneath the cold moon and the lidless stars."[5]

Minnie Cooper's character is relegated to the indifferent pronoun "she." Her life and habits and her one blighted romance with an unimpassioned lover are as regular and predictable as the life cycle of the housefly. The lynching restores her momentarily as the center of morbid attention, but the moment ends in hysteria, as Plunkett's ends in despair.

The affinities between the two stories seem at first glance to be very slight, unless, as sometimes happens, we unconsciously recognize symmetrical oppositions as identical. Good-natured tolerance has changed to a cold, joyless hatred; accomplices have become antagonists.

But both stories share, to begin with, the same ritual expectancy that attends the habitual. In "Was," "about twice a year" Tomey's Turl runs off to "hang around Mr. Hubert's girl, Tennie."[6] Buck must then put on his necktie and risk his single state to bring the slave back. In "Dry September" the circumstances are more grimly familiar to us. They amount to what is still, in the deep South, a folkway, more honored in the breach than in the observance. When a white woman is "attacked, insulted, or frightened" by a black, a lynch mob takes up another kind of necktie and goes on a more fateful pursuit. Thus there is in both stories a pursuit of the black, and an attempt on the one hand to prevent and on the other to punish a sexually motivated transgression.

When we consider the chief actors in both stories, we find once more that similarities outweigh differences. Minnie Cooper is Sophonsiba without a plantation. Both are desperate spinsters for whom the age of marriage has struck without a wedding bell. Miss Sophonsiba

> came down the stairs. Her hair was roached under a lace cape; she had on her Sunday dress and beads and a red ribbon round her throat and a little nigger girl carrying her fan . . . and he remembered how one time his grandmother and his father were talking . . . and his grandmother said that Miss Sophonsiba had matured into a fine looking woman once. Maybe she had.[7]

Minnie Cooper is

> thirty eight or thirty nine. She lived in a small frame house with her invalid mother and a thin, sallow, unflagging aunt. . . . Against that background Minne's bright dresses, her idle and empty days, had a quality of furious unreality. She went out in the evenings only with women now, neighbours, to the moving pictures. . . . Men did not follow her with their eyes any more.[8]

Uncle Buck and Plunkett are both solitaries, misogynists for whom the chase holds all the pleasures their natures know. Uncle Buck's pursuit of Tomey's Turl is the pursuit of the cleverer fox, and the same hunting terms describe it. Plunkett, going after Will Mayes, brooks no moral debate. "Figure out, hell!" he answers the barber. "All that're with me get up from there."[9]

But the resemblance between Will Mayes and Tomey's Turl lies below personality. Both men are objects, like animals possessed of a single, fixed quality that identifies them. In "Was,"

Tomey's Turl as property has to be rounded up; in "Dry September," Will Mayes, as vermin, has to be destroyed.

These parallel considerations have so far revealed only a nostalgic contrast between the old and the new, an apology for the antebellum South, where—even if slavery was an abstract evil—it was also a modus vivendi, capable of tolerance and fair play within its framework. It was a world, like the world Yeats dreams of, "where all's accustomed, ceremonious." In these terms the two stories accomplish respectively sentimental yearning for the past and a horror of the disinterested present where Minnie Cooper must molder silently and secretly and Plunkett hunt in the streets of the town and Will Mayes lack a master's protection. They illustrate statements like the one Bertram Doyle quotes in his *Etiquette of Race Relations in the South*: "'In Southern Society, before the Civil War,'" says Sumner, "'whites and blacks had formed habits of action and feeling toward each other. They lived in peace and concord, and each grew up in ways that were traditional and customary.'" [10]

But Faulkner's vision being mythical and ritualistic, we must look beyond sociology, where a more fearful symmetry awaits us. Evident still in the white folklore of the black and latent in Faulkner's myth of the South before and after the Civil War is a persistent undercurrent of belief about the nature of the black. It appears reduced to satire in Aldous Huxley's *Brave New World*, in which all the pleasure at the "feelies" (Huxley's extension of cinematic realism) is the experience of a black's embracing a blond white woman in an airplane. It is a belief in the extraordinary sexual potency of the black, and with it the assumption that his potency renders him incapable of higher functions and drives him to illicit acts of lust, accompanied, if necessary, by violence.

Seen as an animal, the black derives from this identification the secondary advantage of being thought superhumanly virile. But it has become a psychological necessity that the white man deny this quality as an admirable one, and that he further treat its possessor as his racial or cultural inferior. Psychoanalysis sees our present civilization as one that is founded upon our sacrifice of the unrestrained sexual impulse in favor of its total repression. Habits of industry and thrift have replaced a tropical *dolce far niente*, and our ascription of unbounded fecundity to the teeming poor and the backward brown-skinned nations below the equator, constitutes a sociological pun in which the lower functions are relegated to the lower classes. In this present connection it is Jung who provides the clearest description of the unconscious attitude of the white toward the non-white races. He writes: "When with Europeans it is a vagabond or a criminal, with Americans it is a Negro or an Indian which represents the individual's own repressed sexual personality and the one considered inferior." [11]

Mythology and ritual appear, in the light of psychology, to record the systematic ascription of these vital sexual impulses to appropriate bestial or human agents and their proclivities. The elevation or degradation of these agents depends on the extent to which the impulses are condoned or repressed in any given human society.

How, we may ask, are the actions in these stories compatible with what we know of genuine ritual? To what extent do they represent universal, timeless aims?

Sir James Frazer, in *The Golden Bough*, derives a unifying principle from his vast consideration of an ancient and primitive ritual. The genesis of his exploration is the cult of the priest-assassin of the sanctuary of Diana at Nemi, whose sacred tenure lay in his ability to outfly his pursuers and defeat his would-be successor. His life was a perpetual vigil. But in both life and death he served the goddess of fertility, for both these states were symbolic aspects of the natural cycle. [12]

But extending beyond this and any other formal *cultus* Frazer discerned the timeless association between marriage and fertility, between the male power to conceive and the female power to bring forth and the survival of the tribe. In its formal, ritual expression, a god or goddess was postulated who granted or withheld the fruit of the earth or the conditions of rain or sun which nurtured them. A ritual object then, human or animal or both, was invested with the attributes of a deity, in whose generative vitality lay the expectation of plenty, and in whose death lay the hope of renewed life. The ritual techniques employed, as the thirteen volumes of the unabridged work bear witness, are various, and many times obscure as to their own significance.

Out of Frazer's study certain elements appear which are germane to a study of Faulkner's use of the black as ritual object. The slave-owning societies of the ancient world could and did understand the idea of a slave as an intelligent chattel and could in their religious practices conceive of him as the logical *substitute* for a human being. In archaic times kings and priests were normally considered to be semidivine, the consorts, usually, of the goddess who ensured the prosperity and continuation of the tribe. When age or infirmity threatened to overcome this vessel of the godhead, he was sacrificed, in order that the god might not languish, and a new king was appointed in his place. In order to prove his virility the king, or the candidate for kingship, had often to run literally a footrace for his office, and just as literally, to run for his life.[13]

But the vicissitudes of this ritual pursuit and sacrifice were all downward. As the institutions of kingship and priesthood grew more substantial, as they drew further off in time and fervor from their tribal origins, the tragic cycle of their roles was assigned to the social outcast or the slave who was utterly expendable, and in these terminal rites substituted for his betters.

Thus the so-called King of the Woods of the sanctuary of Diana was by prescription a runaway slave who had eluded capture, had broken off a branch of the sacred tree and slain his predecessor in single combat. Later on even the dignity of priesthood is denied the fugitive slave, and what had been a ceremony of great moment becomes a superstitious expedient or a completely secularized travesty on the original ceremony. An Athenian custom, for example, in which "a number of degraded and useless beings" were maintained at public expense, to be sacrificed in the event of a public calamity, is far removed from the myth of the dying god. Finally the moment comes, as Frazer records it, when "the divine character of the animal or man is forgotten and he comes to be regarded merely as an ordinary victim. . . . Thus the killing of a god may sometimes come to be confounded with the execution of a criminal." [14]

Still, that sense of godhead persists; Frazer observes it in connection with the Roman Saturnalia, with the mingling of servitude and privilege in the slave, when master and slave exchange their roles, and the one took liberties for which in any other season he might suffer torture or even death. [15]

It is also interesting to observe within the context of "Dry September" that in the special magic of rainmaking, a slave, or a black animal, cat or goat, was thrown into a pool of water as an act of homeopathic magic to induce the black rainclouds to release their waters. [16]

Considering the framework of primitive and ancient ritual, can we now assign a formal role to the black as ritual object, trace within the stories those elements that can be properly described as ritual, and account historically for the shift from the comic action of "Was" to the tragic action of "Dry September"?

Slavery, we might hypothesize, was not, for Faulkner, in itself the great Sin of the South, as some have suggested; it was only sinful (in the antique sense of ritual pollution) as it ignored, or abused, or failed to recognize the black for what he was—in effect, the Luck of the South. His slave status was augmented by the fact that when he excelled in those animal virtues of potency, his "love of children," his ability to reproduce his kind, he became a talisman, possessed of extraordinary powers that perhaps hearken back to the fact that some slaves were in fact workers of magic, whose *jujus* and incantations duly impressed their white owners.

The emancipation and the Civil War become for Faulkner analogous to the enforced conversion of the pagan to Christianity. For the animistic pagan, the wild men of the woods, the dark satyrs of their orgiastic faiths, were a benevolent, fructifying principle of nature. The conversion to an austere, self-mortifying Christianity led to a reordered view of these natural forces. The satyr embodied the same principle of fertility all too well—he became the devil. So the liberated slave, manumitted from his accustomed role, became a frightening, anarchistic embodiment of brute sensuality.

"Was" and "Dry September" are fertility rites described at two widely separated historical moments, differing in their forms but without a difference in their aims or in the nature of the celebrants. The first story accomplishes its ends because it accurately recognizes the correct means to those ends. The second, disinherited by time and custom from the pristine ritual, has distorted the original order of the service. Returning to its own roots in search of its lost vitality, the modern South finds only dusty death. The comic Saturnalia of paganism has been replaced by the tragic sacrifice of the Crucifixion.

Bertram Doyle describes the privileges the slave enjoyed, which, though not sanctioned by any calendar feast, can be described as Saturnalian, in that they apply particularly to the functions most intimately concerned with fertility. Commenting on the extraordinary privileges the slave enjoyed in servitude, Doyle describes the marriage of house slaves as being the most remarkable. Both the bride and bridegroom as well as the attendants were decked out in the best jewels and finery belonging to the master and mistress. "The entire occasion was a solemn one, being entirely devoid of absurdities, and as solemn and imposing as were the same rites when partaken by whites." [17]

Or, again, an aged black mammy or uncle who, like Uncle Remus, had won the love of a whole generation of children, was held in veneration.

> Certain of the old slaves, especially on the plantation, were addressed as "uncle," usually with the Christian name. Next to "mammy" this title perhaps represented the highest respect paid to a slave by white persons. . . . These old

men are always giving the master advice, too; and tell with
all oracular dignity whether the moon is just right to plant
the different kinds of grain, or when to give the corn the
last ploughing. . . .[18]

The blacks, Tomey's Turl and Will Mayes, are, in Faulkner's
white Southerner's world, the ritual objects, the slave-priests
who serve the goddesses of the woods and fields, and to whom
the attributes of animality and sexual potency adhere. Will
Mayes is, like the priest of the Sacred Grove at Nemi, a night
watchman. And Tomey's Turl's main duty is to maintain the
hunting equipment of the McCaslins. He is also precisely equa-
ted, in the parallel chases of the fox by the hounds and Tomey's
Turl by Buck, with an animal.

Their invocation as fertility objects in connection with the
white principles in both stories has its basis in the contrapuntal
flight of Uncle Buck from Sophonsiba's antique charms in
"Was," and Minnie Cooper's enforced spinsterhood and Plunkett's brutal rejection of his wife in "Dry September." The
sexual indifference of the white men in both stories, the low
level of libidinal energy, the outright aversion to marriage of
Buck and Buddy and Hubert Beauchamp and Plunkett, are
contrasted with the manifest sexuality of Tomey's Turl and the
assumed potencies of Will Mayes. The white men in both
stories are the principals for whom the slave substitute works
his *mana*. The sexual indifference of the men, even the "dryness"
that symbolizes sterility, brings sharply to mind the nightmare
T. S. Eliot envisions in *The Waste Land*.

Sophonsiba and Minnie Cooper are Dianas in decay. Their
virginities have staled into mawkishness and sterility. But their
differences comprise the alternate workings-out of the two
stories. In "Was" there is a complicity between the fugitive slave
and the languishing goddess. They make common cause against
celibacy, and the potent success of the one promises magically
the success of the other. Tomey's Turl is pursuing Tennie; Sibby
is pursuing Buck. She becomes, goddesslike, the guarantor of

Tomey's Turl's success, by helping him escape capture. And he pronounces her attributes in terms that are a literal paraphrase of the attributes of a rustic Demeter or Artemis.

> "Huh," Tomey's Turl said again. "I got more protection than whut Mr. Hubert got even." He rose to his feet. "I gonter tell you something to remember: anytime you wants to git something done, from hoeing out a crop or getting married, just get the women-folk to working on it. Then all you needs to do is set down and wait. You remember that."[19]

His own powers are considerable. "Was" also invokes the magic of divination by cards, and the fateful dealing of the hand of stud which gives Tennie to him is done by the runaway.

There would seem to be a single flaw in the fact that in spite of her complicity with Tomey's Turl, Sophonsiba loses Buck. But because, as I suggest, we are working with ritual, which is repetitive, and with Faulkner, who is devious, we must check the genealogy of the teller of the story against what we know about the McCaslins, and Isaac McCaslin in particular. The story is told—as we suspect from the introduction of Isaac McCaslin in "Was" and discover with certainty in "The Bear"—by the son of Uncle Buck and Sophonsiba.

In "Dry September" the ritual elements are even more pronounced. The portentous has been added to the human actions in the movements of the moon. All through the story the peregrine moon follows the action. The lynchers leave in the "bloody September twilight . . . below the east was a rumor of the twice-waxed moon." Before the capture of the black "the wan hemorrhage of the moon increased. It heaved above the ridge, silvering the air, the dust, so that they seemed to breathe, live, in a bowl of molten lead." When the black is killed, the moon spurns the event, going higher, "riding high and clear of the dust at last."[20] And finally the moon is at its last position in the midnight sky, at its remote zenith, when Plunkett stands in his doorway panting for breath.

Minnie Cooper's lunar identity is denied her in her barrenness, and her barrenness is visited upon the town, dying in the hot, airless, dusty night. Her attempt to reawaken men's sexual interest in her is renewed, but it is only morbid, summed up in the words of one of the barbers: "You reckon he really done it to her?"[21]

But as with the goddess so with the tribe. They have lost touch with their own mysteries. Plunkett and his followers have lost their natural spiritual heritages. They are incapable of the acts of love and the pursuits of peace. They pursue, instead, its negation, hatred. Plunkett's only positive accomplishment is that he had "commanded troops at the front in France and had been decorated for valor."[22]

The opposite of procreating is killing. For Plunkett the concern for Minnie Cooper is secondary to his hatred for the black. Elsewhere Faulkner writes about the hunter's "loving the life he spills" and in "The Bear" makes the killing of the bear an act that is not without love and identification with the victim. But for this hatred, the sacrifice of Will Mayes, the black animal, to the rain-giving moon, might have a certain grim plausibility. But no rain falls; Minnie Cooper's moment declines into hysteria, and Plunkett casts his wife aside. The causes of a pollution, as the *Oedipus* and *Antigone* tell us, cannot legislate its expulsion. The correct ritual, the only way to renew the barren land under the "cold moon," involves other rites than the blood sacrifice committed in hate. The moon rejects it. And Minnie Cooper and Plunkett, the representatives of Southern womanhood and manhood, are travesties on their old identities. [1963]

8.

Caliban on Prospero:
A Psychoanalytic Study on the Novel
Seize the Day, by Saul Bellow

Saul Bellow's novel *Seize the Day* represents an extraordinary contribution to the relationship between father and son as a theme in fiction.[1] The father-son relationship is an area of experience which the artist shares to a larger degree than he does any other kind of experience with the cultural historian, the moral philosopher, and more recently with the psychologist, particularly the psychoanalyst.

The relationship has always been the nuclear symbol for the artist-mythologist when he attempts to place himself or his race within its proper *Weltanschauung*. Time, in literature, defines itself as the recurrent clashing of generations. The vicissitudes of Oedipus, from the unloved infant to the reigning parricide, seem to appoint the equally tragic alternatives for all posterity to explore. The most superficial inspection, from Oedipus to old Karamazov, must convince us that what makes the relationship so apt a symbol for the historical process is that one quality it shares in equal intensity with both literature and history—unceasing conflict with atonement at the end. As for the atonement between the father and the son in whom he is well-pleased, it is in actuality a pious wish, in literature a posthumous reconciliation more formative of a religious belief than a real human relationship.

Within any given epoch conditions arise which determine the outcomes of these conflicts, and certain historical periods seem to be entirely exempt from viewing the conflict as tragic.

In these periods arise situations such as are dealt with in the theater of Plautus in which *iuvenis* outwits and conquers *senex*, or in the Restoration theater in which spindle-shanks is, as Northrop Frye suggests in his essay "The Structure of Comedy," essentially comic.

It is, I suppose, in those situations where life turns back upon itself and breaks where it should begin, that the tragic, historical significance of the father-son relationship occurs. One thing seems fairly certain—that literature abounds more in those situations in which David destroys Absalom, and Rustum, Sohrab, than those in which Theseus succeeds Aegeus and Prince Hal, King Henry—and more often than not denies the biological truism of youth succeeding age. It represents instead the efforts of an innately hostile father, who by force of sheer vitality, or by the inertia of his established position, reverses the flow of progress and overshadows the son.

Recently, new elements have been introduced into the literature of such conflicts. Their nature has been subtilized, introverted. The question has retreated from the palpable borders of physical survival or of moral superiority to the most elemental of all bases—the natural psychological ambivalence inherent in the relationships between fathers and sons, the recognition that with all the manifest good will in the world fathers and sons are more often than not mutually destructive entities. Not that the psychological ambivalence has not always existed, but now it has come forward to claim its right as the central subject, with the older, more public issues as mere corroborative appendages.

The old public battlefields—the promethean rebellion of the more spiritual son against the harsh fact of the brutal repressive father, the desertion of the family *business* in favor of the personal *vocation*, the preference for the kingdom of love over the safe-deposit vaults of Mammon, the whole flight from gross reality—no longer offer a sound footing for waging the conflict. Fathers and sons are no longer warring socioeconomic or cultural entities. When the artist follows the psychologist into the green-room of family relations where the masks of character are laid aside, he finds not oppositions but strange complicities. Love and hate and all the acts of the conscious will are a part of the public pantomime. The moral content of the struggle becomes a rational fiction. The real pathos grows from the artist's ability to construct his characters from their non-volitional bases, and to be able to translate their mute appeals for help or understanding, or their inchoate threatenings into an intuitively coherent language of significant character traits and forms of action. He must, in order to grasp the whole of his theme, make the ultimate commitment and postulate, as Dostoevsky does, an unconscious—the things "which a man is afraid to tell even to himself." The impulse to make this commitment arises, of course, from our having accepted in the other, nonaesthetic quadrants of our lives, certain psychological data as our guide to the understanding of ourselves, data which Freudian psychoanalysis has systematized into a science. From having been mildly concerned with the psychologically accurate components of a literary work of art, the artist has come to insist that they be accurate, and that psychological inaccuracy puts as heavy a tax on probability as the miraculous.

The psychoanalyst Otto Fenichel defines the new entente between the artist and the psychologist:

> It is in no way true that in discussing events of human life one has to choose between the vivid, intuitive description of an artist and the detached abstractedness of a scientist thinking only quantitatively. It is not necessary and not permissible to lose feeling when feeling is investigated scientifically. Freud once stated that it was not his fault that his case histories gave the impression of a novel.[2]

Freud himself appears to have been aware that a new subject for literature was emerging from the psychoanalytic recognition of neuroses and character traits as products of the conflict between inward strivings and environmental frustrations. We might object that "Sophocles long ago had heard it on the Aegean," but it is Freud's original contribution that he brought the recognition up to full consciousness. He has written, in effect, an addendum to Aristotle's *Poetics*, a rational guide to the composition of a work of art. In a posthumously published essay he deals directly with the drama.

> If religion, character, and social drama differ from one another, chiefly with respect to the arena in which the action takes place, from which the suffering has its origin, we may now follow the drama to still another arena where it becomes the psychological drama. For it is within the soul of the hero himself that there takes place an anguished struggle between impulses, a struggle which must end, not with the downfall of the hero but with that of one of the contending impulses, in other words, with a renunciation. . . .
>
> The psychological drama becomes the psychopathological when the source of the suffering which we are to share and from which we are to derive pleasure is no longer a conflict between two almost equally conscious motivations, but one between conscious and repressed ones. Here the precondition for enjoyment is that the spectator shall also be neurotic. For it is only to him that the release, and, to a certain extent, the conscious recognition of the repressed motivation can afford pleasure instead (as in the non-neurotic whose repression is counterbalanced by the original force of the repression) of merely making for unacceptance. . . . It is only in the neurotic that such a struggle exists as can become the subject for drama.[3]

I should like to consider, with what I trust is neurotic sensibility, Saul Bellow's *Seize the Day* as a novel in which the character and the action of the central figure, Tommy Wilhelm, are determined by and represent the neurotic conflict between instinctual cravings and outwardly determined frustrations. The conflict between father and son is central to the novel, but its repressed content is latent throughout until the last moment, when, as Freud describes it, "the repression is shattered." The novel is interesting, too, in that without deserting the psychoanalytic point of view one can apprehend in the action certain cultural implications. When I finished reading *Seize the Day* I was struck by what appeared to me to be the premeditated delineations of the character and psychopathology of Tommy Wilhelm. But I was equally struck by the unpremeditated affinities of both Tommy Wilhelm and his father with Kafka father and son as they appear in Kafka's "Letter to His Father." It is this affinity that suggests an extension of the neurotic problem—the outwardly determined frustration which is the product not of a single cultural milieu, but of an encounter between two conflicting milieus.

Kafka, writing in the cosmopolitan city of Prague, lives, in the "Letter to His Father," in a psychological ghetto, stoning himself with marvelous, and I think semiconscious, irony, for the heresies of sensitivity, physical infirmity, and cultural breadth in the presence of the father whose insensitivity, brutality, and intolerance Kafka praises as the virtues of a patriarch. In the "Letter" we see in its most acute form what must invariably take place within any cultural minority: the transitional generation arrested as Kafka says, "without forebears or progeny," between the microcosm and the macrocosm. In Kafka's case, because he was both a neurotic and an artist, we see him draining his genius white to justify his father's ways to himself, at the mercy of repressed infantile fantasies in which the father must be conciliated at all costs. The family situation which we can infer from Kafka's writings is typical of Jewish culture in its struggle to survive. The patriarch dies a hard death, adapting himself to the urban wilderness by shedding his Yahwistic dignity in favor of a religious concern for business. And the matriarch, whose only weapon against the hostile, un-Jewish environment, against perhaps a now predatory father, is tenderness and submission, teaches these questionable virtues to her overprotected, breast-loving children. Kafka himself describes it:

> Mother unconsciously played the part of a beater during a hunt. Even if your method of upbringing might in some unlikely case have set me on my own feet by means of producing defiance, dislike, or even hate in me, Mother can-

celled that out again by kindness . . . and I was again
driven back into your orbit . . . one could always get protection from her, but only in relation to you.[4]

In *Seize the Day* when his father forgets the date of his wife's
death, Tommy Wilhelm, who has asked the question disingenuously, thinks bitterly, "what year was it! As though he
didn't know the year, the month, the day, the very hour of his
mother's death" (p. 27).

Kafka wrote to his father about his father's Judaism:

> Later, as a boy, I could not understand how with the insig-
> nificant scrap of Judaism you yourself possess, you could
> reproach me for not (if for no more than the sake of piety,
> as you put it) making an effort to cling to a similar insig-
> nificant scrap. . . . And so there was the religious material
> that was handed on to me, to which may be added at most
> the outstretched hand pointing to "the sons of the mil-
> lionaire Fuchs," who were in the synagogue with their fa-
> ther at the high holidays.[5]

Tommy Wilhelm "often prayed in his own manner. He did
not go to the synagogue but he would occasionally perform
certain devotions, according to his feelings. Now he reflected,
In Dad's eyes I am the wrong kind of Jew. He doesn't like the
way I act. Only he is the right kind of Jew" (p. 87).

Kafka describes to his father the answer he gave him when
the son asked his father for sexual advice.

> It is not easy to judge the answer you gave me then; on the
> one hand, there was after all, something staggeringly frank,
> in a manner of speaking, primeval about it. . . . But its
> real meaning, which sank into my mind even then, but
> only much later came partly to the surface of my con-
> sciousness, was this: what you were advising me to do
> was, after all, in your opinion at that time, the filthiest
> thing possible. . . . The main thing was . . . that you re-
> mained outside your own advice, a married man, a pure
> man, exalted above these things.[6]

Similarly when Wilhelm asks his father for advice, the old man's impulse is to degrade the son in his own eyes. One of Wilhelm's numerous failures was in his job as a salesman. Dr. Adler asks him why he left the job.

> "Since you have to talk and can't let it alone, tell the truth. Was there a scandal—a woman?"
> Wilhelm fiercely defended himself. "No, Dad, there wasn't any woman. I told you how it was."
> "Maybe it was a man, then," the old man said wickedly [p. 51].

Kafka's father reproached his children, Kafka wrote, "for living in peace and quiet, warmth and abundance, lacking for nothing, thanks to your hard work. I think here of remarks that must positively have worn grooves in my brain, like: 'when I was only seven I had to push the barrow from village to village.'"[7]

Wilhelm's father angrily tells his son why he is a success. "'Yes. Because of hard work. I was not self-indulgent, not lazy. My old man sold dry goods in Williamsburg. We were nothing, do you understand? I knew I couldn't waste my chances'" (p. 50).

These are parallels only between Kafka's autobiographical letter and *Seize the Day*, and they exhibit a cultural frame of reference, dramatically abnormalized, within which one can consider the work of either writer. But when we turn to comparisons between *Seize the Day* and Kafka's fiction we are aware of just a pivotal connection—the mutilated relationship between sons and fathers. Kafka's gray Petrouchka-like protagonist and his two-dimensional, expressionistic backgrounds expand into the extremely dimensionalized Tommy Wilhelm and his crowded hour on upper Broadway. But the psychic conflict is identical, and the outcome, while it would not be one Kafka would have chosen, is at least Kafkan.

The desolation of Tommy Wilhelm is a very carefully determined event whose determinants are only explainable in psychoanalytic terms, and whose aesthetic achievement is only valid if we accept the somewhat invidious precondition for enjoyment Freud proposes. In Kafka the neurotic is in the artist, not in the work. The work itself is delivered over, in a manner of speaking, to the controlled insanity of Kafka's world; the interpretive potential is manifold. In *Seize the Day* the neurotic is in the work—and the interpretive potential is singular, a matter of reconciling the events in the novel to the character of Tommy Wilhelm, of explaining the manifest in terms of the repressed.

The day Saul Bellow seizes on which to describe Tommy Wilhelm is the day of one of Wilhelm's many undoings, distinguished from the rest only by the lyric, and poetically desirable revelation purchased at the price of everything he owns.

On the day in question Wilhelm has been refused money and love by his father; his wife badgers him for more money; the bogus psychologist Dr. Tamkin has power of attorney over Wilhelm's remaining funds, which have presumably been invested in lard and rye futures. The lard and rye fall; Wilhelm is wiped out, and Tamkin disappears. Wilhelm's reaction to these misadventures is best described as despair, tempered at the very outset by resignation, neurotic fatalism.

> But at the same time, since there were depths in Wilhelm not unsuspected by himself, he received a suggestion from some remote element in his thoughts that the business of life, the real business—to carry his peculiar burden, to feel shame and impotence, to taste these quelled tears—the only important business, the highest business, was being done. Maybe the making of mistakes expressed the very purpose of his life and the essence of his being here. Maybe he was supposed to make them and suffer from them and suffer from them on this earth. . . .
>
> How had this happened . . . how had his Hollywood career begun? It was not because of Maurice Venice, who turned out to be a pimp. It was because Wilhelm himself was ripe for the mistake. His marriage too had been like

that. Through such decisions somehow his life had taken form. And so, from the moment when he tasted the peculiar flavor of fatality in Dr. Tamkin, he could no longer keep back the money [p. 58].

The broadest psychoanalytic category within which Tommy Wilhelm operates is that of the moral masochist, the victim, for whom suffering is a modus vivendi, a means of self-justification. This aspect of Tommy Wilhelm is the most explicitly realized level of his character. But it deserves closer study as the basis for other, more subtle elements in the novel. The person to whom Wilhelm is masochistically attached is, of course, his father, Dr. Adler, before whom he exhibits his helplessness. And it is equally apparent, even to Wilhelm, that, with individual differences, the other figures on whose mercy he throws himself are in a declining series, fathers—Maurice Venice, the Rojax Corporation, Tamkin, Mr. Perls, and Mr. Rappaport. He even appreciates the masochistic commitment when, in considering old Rappaport's devotion to Theodore Roosevelt, he thinks, "Ah, what people are! He is almost not with us, and his life is nearly gone, but T. R. once yelled at him, so he loves him. I guess it is love, too" (p. 103).

What determined Wilhelm's fixation on this all-powerful father in the past is supplied in the novel to the extent that we can reconstruct his childhood—the love and protection of his mother and the stern, sadistic disciplinarianism of his father— followed by his mother's death at the moment of his first failure in Hollywood. The death of one parent, in fact, any intimate bereavement, induces a retreat from adult dependence on the surviving parent. Dr. Adler was pressed, willy-nilly, into service as the mother in addition to his role as the father. But Dr. Adler's tyrannical, uncompromising character has anticipated what might in Wilhelm's life have been a momentary lapse from effectiveness into fixed regressive patterns, has rendered his son incapable of independence. In this sense, a psychoanalytic irony enters into the description of the relationship between father and son, in that the doctor's forthright disgust with his son's weaknesses is a disgust with a situation of which he himself is the author. There is more truth than Dr. Adler is aware of in his "What a Wilky he had given to the world!" But we can reasonably argue Wilhelm is not always unsuccessful. He has assumed adult responsibilities over twenty years of his life, and until the ultimate day of his latest failure, he has not invoked his father's help. However, we must consider that as a neurotic personality, Wilhelm is not completely *hors de combat*; he is crippled, not dead, and his ego, besieged from without and betrayed from within, is still in command. He knows a hawk from a handsaw.

What the day of the novel exhibits is the phenomenon known as traumatophilia. The neurotic calendar is crowded with grotesque anniversaries, the observance of which offer a certain relief to the mechanism of repression, worn out in the service of the ego. The consciousness must be allowed from time to time to participate in the unconscious strivings of the individual, as Sandor Ferenczi suggests, to "equalize" the effects of the original painful experience throughout the psyche. It is the return of the repressed. In Wilhelm it is the masochistic necessity to fail, to be destroyed at the hands of the punishing father, in order, under the terms of the moral masochistic commitment, to retain his love, and, in less obvious ways, to memorialize certain events in the past.

What might save Wilhelm from a complete debacle on this particular day would be his insistence that Tamkin withdraw from the market before the lard and rye drop. Tamkin agrees reluctantly to pull out, but Wilhelm then allows his money to ride. Certain fatalities intervene and paralyze his will. The first and most apparent is his father's cold, overt hostility, and the passionate review of the past that has taken place in Wilhelm's mind in the morning. A second recollection involves Wilhelm's distress that his mother's grave has been vandalized, and that his father cannot remember the date of her death. With this renewed grief over his mother's death Wilhelm's old dependence returns, displaced now to his dependence on Tamkin. "Poor Mother! How I disappointed her," he thinks, as he comes down for breakfast. And his next act unconsciously reveals the renewal of his own bereavement. He returns, as Otto Fenichel suggests that bereaved people return, to an oral phase of his development.[8] Wilhelm must suckle. "He turned to the Coca-Cola machine. He swallowed hard at the Coke bottle and coughed over it, but he ignored his coughing, for he was still thinking, his eyes upcast and his lips closed behind his hand" (p. 15). It is a caricatured representation of the nursing child.

An external contribution to the significance of the day appears in the form of an actual anniversary. The month is late September, and it is, as old Rappaport reminds Wilhelm, the eve of *Yom Kippur*, the Jewish holiday immediately following the Jewish New Year. *Yom Kippur* is the Day of Atonement for the Jews, when one makes formal acknowledgment for one's sins. *Yiskor*, which falls on *Yom Kippur*, is the service at which one remembers and prays for the dead. "Well, you better hurry up if you expect to say *Yiskor* for your parents," old Rappaport tells Wilhelm (p. 86). And Wilhelm remembers his mother's burial, and his father's indifference, and his having paid for having prayers sung for her. A moment later he allows Tamkin to let their combined investment ride to its loss.

I propose now to deal with Wilhelm's moral masochism, its causes and symptoms and contributions to his traits of character. Freud's first concept of the masochistic personality—the moral masochist specifically, to differentiate him from the sexual masochist, for whom sexual perversion is the outward enacting of his drive—was based on an intrapersonal conflict. The original sadistic impulse directed at the parent, recoiled to become parentally derived superego, which commanded certain self-sacrifices as the penalty for aggressive fantasies. Thus Freud conceived of Dostoevsky's psychic epilepsy and gambling mania as a self-determined punishment for having willed the father's death. From this concept arises the accepted notion that self-degradation is simply the mirror image of hate. But though this concept falls short of explaining the dramatic conflict in Wilhelm's character, it required coordination rather than replacement. Part of Wilhelm's character (his gambling almost immediately suggests itself) is explained, but the concept does not completely explain his relationship with his father, although, as we shall see, it makes finally a major contribution to the end of the novel.

Bernhard Berliner in his essay, "On Some Psychodynamics of Masochism," while accepting Freud's motivational basis for masochism (guilt, need for punishment) describes moral masochism, not as a pathological way of hating, but as a "pathological way of love." It is not, as Freud described it, an intrapersonal problem, but one involving an interpersonal relationship. "In all cases the disturbance of the interpersonal relationship leads to and is maintained by a peculiar character formation. Masochism is a character neurosis."[9] The subject

> relives and re-enacts in interpersonal relations a submissive devotion to and need for love of a hating or rejecting love-object, . . . originally a parent or a preferred sibling or some other unfriendly person of his childhood, and who lives in his superego. It is the superego that keeps the original situation alive through transference to any suitable person or set of circumstances in later age.[10]

The history of masochists reveals accompanying the unhappiness of childhood an abnormal need for oral satisfaction. In contrast to the more normal adjustment to dislike (the giving-up of the hating object) the person represses the hatred and in adulthood submissively accepts the cruelty as love. "Simultaneously he represses any hostile reaction against the loved object because that also would cause its loss. . . . Masochism is the hate or sadism of the object reflected in the libido of the subject."[11] It is not, Berliner insists, an instinct, like love or sadism, but is a "neurotic solution" to a "conflict between manifestations of those two instincts."

The moral masochist exhibits "the servility of the beaten dog," with the human awareness that suffering enhances one's own value. "Suffering has come to mean being worthy of love. This narcissistic position fails in reality in that one must continually work out the old trauma." And, "The deeper underlying motivation of this unhappiness is the wish to please a hating parent, or to placate or ingratiate himself with the parent by being unhappy, by failing, or, in other cases, by being helpless or stupid. It is the wish to be loved by the parent who hates or depreciates."[12] Guilt, in the moral masochist, is not a reaction to sadistic impulses on the child's part, but stems from the oral need for love from the punishing parent who has engendered the guilt; the masochist adopts the parent's view of himself as wrong and the parent as right. He "makes himself the whipping boy for the benefit of a sadistic parent. In adult proportion, any external reality or fate may take the form of this parent."[13]

If the moral masochist is aggressive it is "an intensified bid for affection, in which the suffering gives him a claim for being loved, and also for prestige and domination. . . . He welcomes being hurt, not because it makes him right above others. . . . Making someone sorry, by self-sabotage, is intended both to hurt the love-object and make it concerned for the subject."[14]

Unconsciously the masochist tries—unsuccessfully, because the love-object is beyond "magic" control—to deny and libidinize the hatred and sadism of the love-object by making aggressive demands on it, as if love and punishment were causally connected.[15]

The ultimate sacrifice of the moral masochist to the love-object accounts for his greatest paradox, his perverse refusal to "please" the parent in any rational sense of the word. The masochist identifies himself with the hating love-object. He turns against himself, not his own sadism but the sadism of the parent. His guilt becomes the guilt the hating parent should feel if his cruelties are unjust. Since the parent cannot be wrong, the child must then feel guilty for him. He must be the bad child who deserves such chastisement. Turned against the world, these perversely "good" actions can be criminal, a psychopathic flouting of the law. "To accommodate a hating person he may make himself as unlovable as he feels that parent wants him to be. He may deny his good qualities, or his intelligence, often to pseudo-imbecility. . . . He is stigmatized with unwantedness and displays his stigma as his bid for affection." [16] As a person the moral masochist has a weak ego, is dependent and love-seeking, and forms, because of his oral fixation, strong transferences. Unlike the anal-sadistic, compulsive neurotic, who punishes himself for hating, the masochist wants only to gain love. As Berliner differentiates between them: "The compulsive neurotic is paying imaginary debts, not knowing what the real debt was; the masochist is presenting an old, unpaid bill for affection." [17]

Using this as our point of departure, let us reenter the world of Tommy Wilhelm. On this day of days his whole personality has been given over to an exhibition of his neurotic symptoms. And the external world obliges by offering him a realistic basis for such an exhibition. Systematically and seriatim the more-or-less loved objects from his present punish him—his father, his estranged wife, and Tamkin. Their betrayals evoke the memories of earlier betrayals and humiliations, finding their ultimate source in the original mistreatment by his father. To illustrate in a single example the relation between his masochistic submission to the father and the oral nature of the masochism, I will take up one of the leitmotifs of Wilhelm's thoughts.

Thinking indignantly about his father's self-love, Wilhelm recalls from his college literature course the line, "love that well which thou must leave ere long," from Shakespeare's sonnet 73. "At first he thought it referred to his father, but then he understood that it was for himself, rather. *He* should love that well. 'This thou perceivest, which makes thy love more strong'" (p. 12). The memory of this line reminds him of the anthology (Leider and Lovett's *British Poetry and Prose*) and with it another poem he loved—"Lycidas," the line he remembers being "Sunk though he be beneath the wat'ry floor."

Later in the course of the morning, when, arising from his argument with his father, he has decided that it is his "peculiar burden to feel shame and impotence," the lines from "Lycidas" again return, this time coupled with a line from Shelley's "Ode to the West Wind," "that dirge of the dying year." The line is "I fall upon the thorns of life! I bleed!"

> And though he has raised himself above Mr. Perls and his father because they adored money, still they were called to act energetically and this was better than to yell and cry, pray and beg, poke and blunder and go by fits and starts and fall upon the thorns of life. And finally sink beneath that watery floor—would that be tough luck, or would it be good riddance? [p. 56].

The fourth poem comes to Wilhelm when Tamkin reminds him that he was an actor. Wilhelm remembers a job he had as a film extra. He had to blow a bagpipe. He "blew and blew and not a sound came out. . . . He fell sick with the flu after that and still suffered sometimes from chest weakness."

Margaret nursed him.

> They had had two rooms of furniture which was later seized. She sat on the bed and read to him. . . .

> Come then, Sorrow!
> Sweetest Sorrow!
> Like an own babe I nurse thee on my breast!

> Why did he remember that? Why? [p. 89].

Of the four fragments the line from the sonnet is the one Wilhelm most immediately apprehends. Throughout the day Wilhelm's thoughts about his father's age and imminent death undergo revealing vicissitudes. He excuses his father, at the same time, for ignoring the fact that he himself must also die.

But his most moving thought is what his father's death will mean for him.

"'When he dies, I'll be robbed, like. I'll have no more father. . . . Of course, of course, I love him. My father. My mother—' As he said this there was a great pull at the very center of his soul. When a fish strikes the line you feel the live force in your hand" (p. 92). His feelings about his father are in apposition to the sonnet in which the older man calls attention to his approaching death, not to arouse compassion, but to impress the younger man (presumably the sonnet is addressed to a young man) that he faces a great loss.

Even if we disallow the homoerotic nature of Shakespeare's sonnet and its bearing on Wilhelm's feeling about his father, we find, in the line from "Lycidas," an overdetermination of the homoerotic element, and in its combination with the line from Shelley's poem (the cruelty with which Shelley's father treated him, Shelley's doctrine of nonviolence, and his actual drowning reinforce the line of poetry) a willingness to be the sacrificial victim. Wilhelm has "fallen on the thorns of life," and the prospect of sinking beneath the ocean's watery floor is not such a distressing one. It is consistent with Wilhelm's masochistic character that the line has come to mean for him the return to the womb, the death instinct that is a component of masochism. Implicit, too, in the context of the novel, the lines suggest that achievement of superiority which is the bitter consolation of the victim, although Wilhelm makes an ironic distinction between his superiority to Mr. Perls and his father, and his abjection.

The fourth poem, the lullaby, and its autobiographical context, stand in relation to the first three as symptom stands to repressed aim. The sonnet names the object of Wilhelm's masochistic strivings; "Lycidas" and the "Ode to the West Wind" describe the wished-for torment and oblivion, falling on the thorns and sinking. The lullaby and its context indicate the mental and physical character-components of the masochist.

The suckling dependence of the moral masochist is symbolically described here as well as the frustrations that accompany deprivation. Wilhelm's orality has expressed itself in character-formation in that he has been attracted to acting, speech being an acceptable oral survival. But his career as an actor was a failure, and the memory of Hollywood that returns to him returns him also to the roots of the failure. He is blowing a false bagpipe, "blew and blew, and not a sound came out." Bagpipe as breast and sound as milk are perfect correlatives. Wilhelm is "sucking a dry teat." He has lot his mother, who, because of his peculiar needs, epitomized the only generosity he can ever know. From his father, to whom he has attached himself, he can only draw the sour milk of sorrow, the masochistic substitute for real nourishment. His wife, Margaret, also figures here, nursing him, as Wilhelm's immediate substitute for his mother, but along with his father equally unsatisfactory. Sorrow—"Like an own babe I nurse thee on my breast!"—is Wilhelm's baby. The thought of his mother drives him to the Coke machine; the ill-treatment of his father compels him to eat not only his own breakfast, but a large part of his father's. Denied any overt love on his father's part, Wilhelm works out a primitive solution: he eats from his father's plate.

"Wilhelm understood he was being put on notice and did not express his opinion. He ate and ate. He did not hurry but kept putting food on his plate until he had gone through the muffins and his father's strawberries and then some pieces of bacon that were left" (p. 42).

Another element remains to be explained in connection with the last poem Wilhelm remembers. It is his "chest weakness" which has never left him, the sense of suffocation he feels at critical moments during the day, especially at those moments when his father or his wife is either rejecting him or making demands on him. Both are situations which cause anxiety connected with oral fixation. The one, the father's refusal, involves a denial of nourishment, a traumatic weaning; the other, Margaret's sadistic demands for money, is a projection of Wilhelm's own insistent need on to the woman. The flow is reversed; the woman drains the man. For the orally fixated man, orgastic discharge perverts the unconsciously infantile relationship between himself and the woman. "'Well, Dad, she hates me. I feel she's strangling me. I can't catch my breath. She just has fixed herself on me to kill me. She can do it at long distance. One of these days I'll be struck down by suffocation or apoplexy because of her. I just can't catch my breath.'" (p. 48).

Throughout the day Wilhelm suffocates in the presence of his tormentors. But this is not so much a "chest weakness" as it is a conversion hysteria, Wilhelm's repressed ideas expressing themselves in physical symptoms. Respiratory disorders are frequently associated with acute anxieties, centering mainly, according to Otto Fenichel, around "the repressed idea of castration," and the "reaction to separation from the mother."[18] Wilhelm has reason to fear both; his sense of suffocation is induced by both. A further insight into the hysterical nature of his behavior is afforded by the correlation of his dramatic acting out of the strangulation, and the fantasy he has woven about Margaret. "'Strange, Father? I'll show you what she's like.' Wilhelm took hold of his broad throat with brown-stained fingers and bitten nails and began to choke himself" (p. 48). (Note even the "brown-stained fingers" and the "bitten nails," the additional stigmata of Wilhelm's oral frustrations.) Fenichel identifies "irrational emotional reactions" as analogues to hysterical attacks. They serve to "reactivate infantile types of object relationships" when some associatively connected experience occurs. They involve an hysterical introversion, a turning from reality to fantasy.

> However, hysterical "acting" is not only "introversion" but is directed toward an audience. It is an attempt to induce others to participate in the daydreaming, probably to obtain some reassurance against anxiety and guilt feelings

(or to evoke punishment for the same reason). . . . It is an attempt to return from introversion to reality, a kind of travesty of the process underlying artistic productivity.[19]

When Wilhelm turns from his father to find a kinder father, his choice of object is determined for him by the same orality that governs his relations with his father. But with this difference, that as a singular individual his biological father must frustrate any preconceived fantasy on Wilhelm's part as to what his father should be to him. Wilhelm's masochistic submission to Dr. Adler represents the extent of his compromise. This is not so when he is free to exercise his fantasy and find in the real world the father who suits him. Dr. Tamkin (and Bellow invests him with a comic-grotesque unreality), is the answer to Wilhelm's dreams, and I will limit discussion of him at this point to his appearance in Wilhelm's fantasy-life.

In his retreat to orality, Wilhelm returns to the infantile belief in the omnipotent parent, who grants in return for doglike trust and acceptance full protection and endless beneficence. Wilhelm describes himself when he describes his beloved dog Scissors to his father: "He's an Australian sheep dog. They usually have one blank or whitish eye which gives a misleading look, but they're the gentlest dogs and have unusual delicacy about eating or talking" (p. 47). Tamkin is magic; he reads Wilhelm's mind. He is what Fenichel calls a "magic helper," whose relationship with Wilhelm, Karl Abraham describes in these terms: "Some people (oral suckling types) are dominated by the belief that there will always be some kind person—a representative of the mother, of course—to care for them and to give them everything they need. This optimistic belief condemns them to inactivity."[20]

As Wilhelm thinks about him: "That the doctor cared about him pleased him. This was what he craved, that someone should care about him, wish him well" (p. 73).

I have considered so far those qualities in Tommy Wilhelm which represent him as a willing sacrifice to fate, and indeed this would seem to be the only side of Tommy Wilhelm to consider. His last appearance, all alone beweeping his outcast state at the bier of a stranger, would seem to be his last and most satisfying submission to the austere, intractable father-image which dominates his being.

But in allowing this as the basis for *Seize the Day* we are ignoring an important portion of the statement I had considered axiomatic to the enjoyment of psychological literature: that the struggle within the soul of the hero "must end, not with the downfall of the hero, but with that of one of the contending impulses, in other words, with a renunciation."

Tommy Wilhelm's downfall, at the end of the novel, is not a downfall in the acute singular sense of the word as in classical tragedy. In the timeless world of Wilhelm's psyche the downfall has been a fait accompli almost from the beginning. The failure in the stock market is its latest and most vivid instance. Likewise the act of renunciation, the outcome of an inner conflict between opposing impulses, has taken place before, and now finds its perfect expression and, on an emotive level, recognizes itself beside the old man's coffin.

> "Oh, Father, what do I ask of you? What'll I do about the kids—Tommy, Paul? My children. And Olive? My dear! Why, why, why—you must protect me against that devil, who wants my life. If you want it, then kill me. Take it, take it, take it from me. . . ."
>
> The flowers and lights fused ecstatically in Wilhelm's blind, wet eyes; the heavy, sea-like music came up to his ears. It poured into him where he had hidden himself in the center of the crowd by the great and happy oblivion of tears. He heard it, and sank deeper than sorrow, through torn sobs and cries toward the consummation of his heart's ultimate need [p. 118].

The symphonic orchestration of such an ending must presuppose something beside an unchecked drift toward submission. There must be a crisis, a conflict, symphonic in its nature. At one point, before this resolution has been achieved, the brasses must have risen up against the violins and been, not without a struggle, silenced.

In dealing with the character of Tommy Wilhelm at its furthest remove from effective, mature activity, I have isolated the level of regression descriptive of such abject helplessness, the position of the infant at its mother's breast. But there are no "pure" strains of orality past actual infancy; while Wilhelm is denied, perhaps permanently, any successful adult accomplishment—the masculine self-sufficiency and self-esteem, the ability to have good relationships and pursue realistic rather than fantastic schemes for survival—his helplessness is more the helplessness of a strong man caged than a weak man at liberty. To see him otherwise is to deny him his quality as a protagonist, and to dismiss him as Freud dismisses the "full-blown and strange neurosis. . . . We call the physician and deem the person in question unsuitable as a stage figure."[21]

What I must deal with now are those traits of character and neurotic symptoms that belong, in psychoanalysis, to the oral and anal-sadistic types of regression. To this aspect of Wilhelm's personality such concepts as Freud's original theory of masochism are more germane. We will deal with tendencies in which, although it is repressed, aggressive hostility takes the place of submissive exhibitions of suffering. Every phase of a child's development has its erotic and aggressive subdivisions. At the mother's breast the mouth is the pleasurable organ and suckling the means to that pleasure. With its first teeth, and the experience of weaning, come the first feelings of deprivation and frustration. The so-called biting stage sets in, in which the infant displays ambivalent feelings toward objects, compounded of aggressions against them and a wish to eat them. The withheld breast becomes an enemy to be taken by force. The old complicities of mother and child become a battle between the hungry infant and the alien world. At the same time another source of pleasure and aggression supervenes in the form of the anal period. The feces, the first objective products of the body, become a source of pleasure in their retention or elimination and, for the same reason, a source of power and aggression.

Because of the inauguration at a very early age of the discipline of bowel training and the overt disapproval of the infantile pleasure in fecal play, anal eroticism is regularly repressed. In its place appear the aggressive qualities connected with bowel discipline—the "stool pedantry" Sandor Ferenczi describes. To these pregenital sources of pleasure and power, psychoanalysis attributes a whole system of orifice psychology. Good suckling and good weaning, good evacuation and good discipline are thought to constitute the basis for good work habits and good character traits in the mature human being. If, for a multiplicity of reasons, one or any of these stages was accompanied by a frustration or trauma, or if it offered a great deal of satisfaction, or if the stage following brought with it pain instead of pleasure, a fixation takes place. Anal-oral fixations survive in adult life as character traits and neurotic symptoms. But because the mouth can still retain its primacy as a pleasurable orifice—as in eating and speaking and kissing, these functions need not undergo repression to the same extent as the anal component of infantile sexuality.

Psychoanalysis has long observed the connection between the emphasis on the discipline of anal drives and the character of Western culture. William Menninger observes that "our own emphasis on production, value to time, material possessions, wealth and power, is evidence of what might be called an 'anal phase' of civilization."[22] From this observed connection psychoanalysis has been able to describe the variations in character and the neurotic behavior of the adult in terms of fixations and anxieties related to various stages of sexual development. Otto Fenichel describes the relationship. "The prevalence of anal character formation in modern times and the 'drive to become wealthy' present a particularly good field for the investigation of the relation between social influence and instinctual structure."[23]

Tommy Wilhelm's aggressions are more inhibited, necessarily, than his masochistic bids for love. As distorted as they are, his gestures of submission achieve a certain level of completion. His aggressions are literally choked off, turned aside, or rendered as opposites of themselves.

Dr. Adler lives in his tight, tidy, old man's world of money saved. He has gone into his old age retaining everything, "a fine old scientist, clean and immaculate" (p. 12). His entire philosophy of life is costive, parsimonious. Love means expenditure and he cannot give it. His anal-sadism reveals itself in his cruelty to Wilhelm; his coarse suggestion that perhaps it was not a woman who caused Wilhelm's failure in his job, but a man, and his repeated injunction to his son, "I want nobody on my back. Get off!" are graphic revelations of the doctor's own anal preoccupation. "Concentrate on real troubles—fatal sicknesses, accidents" (p. 55).

Poor Wilhelm can only lumber after his father in an apelike distortion of the thrifty anal character. He has accepted the economic objectives of society, but he recognizes them as a form of cruelty, intimately connected in this case with his father. He is incapable of accomplishing the socially acceptable anal traits, the thrift and industry and self-discipline that distinguish his father. He cannot "retain" money; his retentions like so many of his other traits, are at an infantile level. His principal character trait is his messiness, his dirt, the barely acceptable substitute for feces.

> A faint grime was left by his fingers on the white of the egg after he had picked away the shell. Dr. Adler saw it with silent repugnance. . . . The doctor couldn't bear Wilky's dirty habits. Only once,—and never again, he swore—had he visited his room. Wilhelm, in pajamas and stockings had sat on his bed, drinking gin from a coffee mug and rooting for the Dodgers on television. . . . The smell of dirty clothes was outrageous [p. 36].

His playing the stock market is, like his gin rummy, a form of gambling, in which he contrives to lose. Freud, in his "Dostoevsky and Parricide," describes the act of gambling as a compulsive, repetitive act, in which the anal-sadistic hostilities towards a parent are displaced to the gaming table. To make a "killing" at the table (or in the market) is to kill a hated object. But Wilhelm's aggressions are characterized by their abortive quality. He commits, instead, financial suicide.[24] "For the last few weeks Wilhelm had played gin almost nightly, but yesterday he had felt that he couldn't afford to lose any more. He had never won. Not once." (p. 7). His pockets are full of "little packets of pills, and crushed cigarette butts and strings of cellophane," and pennies. His hatred of "the world's business" represents merely a diversion from aggressions directed against his father, for whom a large income is the mark of success. "Holy money! Beautiful money! It was getting so that people were feeble minded about everything except money. While if you didn't have it you were a dummy, a dummy!" (p. 36). Wilhelm's speech patterns are interesting as they reveal his oral-anal sadism. He is given to violent, explosive, scatalogical utterances, in which anal function has been displaced upward. "In certain neurotics," writes Karl Abraham, "speaking is used to express the entire range of instinctual trends . . . every kind of bodily evacuation, including fertilization."[25]

> Too much of the world's business done. Too much falsity.
> He had various words to express the effect this had on him.
> Chicken! Unclean! Congestion! he exclaimed in his heart.
> Rat race! Phony! Murder! Play the game! Baggers! [p. 17].

But Wilhelm exhibits even more pronounced symptoms of repressed hostility, which translate themselves into tics, involuntary physical gestures, which reveal in an abstract movement of the body a repressed impulse. Rage, or sexual excitement, or grief are represented by a gesture. They are, says Fenichel, "an archaic means of communication."[26]

> But Dr. Adler was thinking, why the devil can't he stand
> still when we're talking? He's either hoisting his pants up
> and down by the pockets or jittering with his feet. A regu-
> lar mountain of tics he's getting to be . . .

> Unaware of anything odd in his doing it, for he did it all
> the time, Wilhelm had pinched out the coal of his cigarette
> and dropped the butt in his pocket, where there were many
> more. And as he gazed at his father the little finger of his
> right hand began to twitch and tremble [p. 28].

Wilhelm also stammers, a "slight thickness in his speech,"
especially when he speaks to his father. In this too he reveals his
concealed hostilities, the death wish. Stuttering is "exacerbated
in the presence of prominent or authoritative persons, that is, of
paternal figures against whom the hostility is most intense. . . .
Speaking means the uttering of obscene, especially anal words,
and, second, an aggressive act directed against the listener."[27]

The most direct form of aggression on Wilhelm's part appears as its opposite, as a reaction formation to Wilhelm's death-
wish. It appears as Wilhelm's fear of giving pain and his preoccupation with his father's death. He remembers explaining to
his mother why he does not want to study medicine. "I can't
bear hospitals," he tells her. "Besides, I might make a mistake
and hurt someone or even kill a patient. I couldn't stand that"
(p. 16). He is obsessed with the thought that all his father thinks
about is his own death.

> And not only is death on his mind but through money he
> forces me to think about it, too. It gives him power over
> me. He forces me that way, he himself, and then he's sore.
> If he was poor, I could care for him and show it. The way I
> *could* care, too, if I only had a chance. He'd see how much
> love and respect I had in me. It would make him a different
> man too. He'd put his hands on me and give me his bless-
> ing [p. 57].

It is out of these elements, which we have considered as
being to the highest degree ambivalent expressions of love and
hate—a wish to preserve, a wish for an omnipotent father and a
paranoid fear of an omnipotent father—that we can construct
the unconscious process by which Wilhelm comes to his act of
renunciation.

When Wilhelm looks at the dead man he sees what his soul has wanted to see all during the terrible day; he sees his father dead. He sees, too, his own death, mirrored in the face of the gray-haired, "proper" looking, but not aged man before him. It is here that the renunciation proper to the psychological drama takes place. Wilhelm gives up his death wish against the father and accepts, but without the masochistic insistence that characterized his earlier courtship of paternal cruelty, his own role as victim.

A few minutes before this he has been standing over the body of his father stretched out on a table in the massage room of the hotel, "the thighs weak, the muscles of the arms had fallen, his throat was creased." He makes a last plea to his father for help, which will include not only money, but understanding. The father, as impatient with his suffering as he is with his dependence, sends him away with an old man's curse. "'Go away from me now. It's torture for me to look at you, you slob!' cried Dr. Adler. Wilhelm's blood rose up madly, in anger equal to his father's but then it sank down and left him helplessly captive to misery" (p. 110).

The dead man in his coffin is the symbolic fulfillment of two alternatives—the wish to destroy the hated father and the wish to be destroyed. In giving up his death-wish Wilhelm passes through what amounts to a phylogenetic process by which he is reconciled to his living father. The theme of *Totem and Taboo* is recapitulated here and extended beyond the suggestion that the only good fathers are dead fathers. Karl Abraham writes:

> The results of psychoanalysis justify us in coming to the conclusion that it is only when he thinks of him as a dead person, or wishes him to be so, that the son elevates his father to the level of a sun-god. These death fantasies give expression to impulses of hate, hostility and jealously on the part of the son. They rob the father of his power so that he is in reality helpless and harmless. An omniscient power is then subsequently granted him as a compensation.[28]

But Wilhelm goes beyond this cycle of death and apotheosis. He has accepted Tamkin's existentialism; he no longer wishes for his father's death, can give up his helpless hatred, and with it, his equally hopeless love for this degraded, fragmented man of money.

The broadest cultural implications of *Seize the Day* involve the father's representing symbolically the sadistic, profit-seeking culture, and the son's willingness to be destroyed by it rather than share its heartless infamy, or fight against it.

That this cathartic experience will mark a new beginning for Wilhelm in a fatherless world would be a vain, Dickensian assumption. When we return *Seize the Day* to its coherences as art, its momentary solution is what must satisfy us. That moment of rest, like that moment in Joyce's *Ulysses* when Bloom and Stephen almost recognize their relationship, in which Tommy Wilhelm sees the futilities of his love-hate relationship with his father, is perhaps to be followed by the imperative *da capo* of his neurotic servitude.

Dr. Tamkin, the psychologist, is a problem.

He is a palpable fraud; the realistic hyperbole that envelopes him is hazardous to the realism of the novel. He abuses Wilhelm's confidence and loses his money for him, and yet he is wise, accurate psychologically, and responsible for Wilhelm's final enlightenment. He discusses the "guilt-aggression cycle" (p. 64), as if he had been reading Menninger's essay on character derivatives from the anal phase. He is aware of the relationship between counting as a sadistic activity and killing. He explains the market to Wilhelm in these terms (p. 69). "You have an obsessed look on your face" (p. 57), he tells Wilhelm, who could easily have had an obsessed look on his face, having immediately before been thinking about his father's death. "You have lots of guilt in you."

A transference appears to have been effected. Tamkin has been "treating" Wilhelm "secretly," and Wilhelm has responded to this paternal benevolence by finding himself able to remember his past with more clarity than ever before, "the poems he used to read" (p. 12). More significantly, the sadistic homosexual phrase his father had used has shifted to Wilhelm's dependence on Tamkin. "And Wilhelm realized that he was on Tamkin's back. It made him feel that he had virtually left the ground [a dream symbol for erection] and was riding upon the other man. He was in the air. It was for Tamkin to take the steps" (p. 96).

And Tamkin's advice is irreproachable; it enters the fabric of Wilhelm's mind as his vision of the authentic life. About his marriage Tamkin says,

> "Why do you let her make you suffer so? It defeats the original object in leaving her. Don't play her game. Now, Wilhelm, I'm trying to do you some good. I want to tell you, don't marry suffering. Some people do. They get married to it, and sleep and eat together, just as husband and wife. If they go with joy, they think it's adultery" [p. 98].

" 'This time,' thinks Wilhelm, 'the faker knows what he's talking about. . . . The real universe. That's the present moment. The past is no good to us. The future is full of anxiety. Only the present is real—the here and now. Seize the day'" (p. 66).

I can only speculate on Tamkin's formal function in the novel, and my speculation leads me invariably beyond the bounds of the novel itself. I conceive of literary psychoanalysis as a truncated form of psychoanalysis. One does not willingly knock on the door of the artist's life. But I can only see in the character of Tamkin—beyond of course his simpler level of function in Seize the Day—an ironic portrait of a psychoanalyst and his patient, even to the fact that the patient gives all he has in order to discover the unprofitable truth about himself. There is much to be said, if we accept this supposition, for the representation of the psychoanalyst as a figure of fun, whom even the patient can think of as being part faker. He combines areas of experience which have hitherto only been combined in comedy—the excremental with the spiritual (Freud's *ecclesia super cloacam*), the facts of life with the fantasies of love—his solemn and costly considerations of the trivia have added to the repertory of *The New Yorker* and *Punch* cartoonist what law and medicine added to the art of Hogarth and Daumier. But whatever Tamkin's extraordinary functions in *Seize the Day* may be, I cannot object to his presence. He is an accessory to the understanding of the novel.   [1962]

III ᔟ

ON EUROPEAN
LITERATURE

9.

D. H. Lawrence:
The Forms of Sexual Hunger

The years 1911–13 were crucial years in Lawrence's life; they saw his mother's death, and the publication of his first novels, *The White Peacock*, *The Trespasser*, and *Sons and Lovers*. They saw his flight with Frieda Weekley. We must bear in mind as we read these early stories of fierce, murderous struggles between unequally matched men, the deaths of mothers, and the sudden sexual attractions between men and women, that Lawrence in his own life was pursuing similar adventures and suffering a real bereavement. There is an important correlation between his life and his art, of which his art is the chronicle.

The end of *Sons and Lovers* describes Paul Morel forced to a choice between a dead mother and the lights of the living town, between the "drift toward death" and life, the *thanatos* and the *eros* instincts. The one implies a lapse into the permanent role of the unproductive, bereaved son; the other, the assumption of a new role, the aggressive, productive husband. Paul Morel walks toward the town.

It is unfortunate for Lawrence, as indeed it is for any artist, that his nature cannot imitate his art, so that with the aesthetically satisfying resolution of his novel there could also take place the psychologically satisfying resolution of his neurosis. *Sons and Lovers* and "The Prussian Officer" as works of art are, so to speak, the imitations of a release from the Oedipal ties. They imply not so much a rejection of the mother as the life-saving impulse on Lawrence's part to throw his lot in with the father—the aggressive, virile principle that could allow him in a moment to become artist, husband, no longer son. In his life in the world, Lawrence, like James Joyce at the conclusion of *A Portrait of the Artist as a Young Man*, calls not upon his mother but upon his father to "stand him now and ever in good stead."

What Lawrence's works will demonstrate from this point forward, with almost mathematical economy, are the steps by which the elemental situation of *Sons and Lovers* transformed itself into its polar opposite.

As a corollary to the repressed, unappeased homoerotic sexual aims in the modern man, Ferenczi describes the displacement of this "sexual hunger" to an abnormal dedication to heterosexual drives. "I quite seriously believe that the men of today are one and all obsessively heterosexual as the result of this affective displacement; in order to free themselves from men, they become the slaves of women."[1]

Lawrence's acknowledgement of this slavery, to the extent that he could be objective about it, is explicit in a letter he wrote to Katherine Mansfield, a letter in which his friend John Middleton Murry figures, as he will figure in *Women in Love*, as a whipping boy for Lawrence. The date is 1918.

> I send you the Jung book. . . . Beware of it—this mother-incest idea can become an obsession. But it seems to me there is this much truth in it; that at certain periods the man has a desire and a tendency to return unto the woman, make her his goal and his end, find his justification in her. In this way he casts himself as it were into her womb, and she, the Magna Mater, receives him with gratification. This is a kind of incest. It seems to me it is what Jack does to you, and what repels and fascinates you. I have done it, and now struggle with all my might to get out. In a way Frieda is the devouring mother. . . . But Frieda says I am antediluvian in my positive attitude. I do think a woman must yield some sort of precedence to a man, and he must take this precedence. I do think men must go ahead absolutely in front of their women, without turning around to ask for permission or approval from their women. Consequently the women must follow as it were unquestioningly.[2]

The Jung book is undoubtedly *The Psychology of the Uncon-scious*, translated in 1916. Chapter 6, "The Battle for Deliv-erance from the Mother," must have riven Lawrence's prophetic soul with its appositeness to his own situation. Two things strike us in this letter to Katherine Mansfield: one is his now almost calm acceptance, via Jung, of the devouring mother im-age; the other is his strenuous orientation, already noted in "The Prussian Officer," but now in connection with his own marriage, toward the father's less sensitive, more masterful at-titude toward women. A certain pathos breathes through the letter; Lawrence's walking in front of his woman sounds more like a program than a natural gesture. But it perpetuates at least the outward forms that Lawrence described when he wrote about Nottinghamshire coal miners walking out with their wives and cronies on a day off.

In his attempts to exorcise the Ave Maria of *Sons and Lovers* from his work, Lawrence, the artist, practiced continual gemi-nation upon himself. He consigns his hyperintellectual, hyper-sensitive personality at times to the spokesman for his cultus, from whence he sings the mindless man from the top of his intellect, or else to the enemies of instinct, the Gerald Criches and Clifford Chatterleys. His other self, patterned after the father ideal, he fashions into the gamekeepers, miners, and artisans.

The marvelous fortuity that made Lawrence's extempore marriage to Frieda Weekley a final relationship owes its perma-nence to the fact that, in addition to her intrinsic beauty and intelligence, her situation was designed to be irresistibly appeal-ing to him. Like Clara Dawes in *Sons and Lovers*, she has de-scribed herself as having been, until Lawrence's advent, "un-awakened." Older than Lawrence, with three children, with none of the restraints associated with the "woman of impec-cable moral purity," married to a man who was bound to be "injured" and who, moreover, stood, as Lawrence's professor, in loco parentis, she fulfills, like a fairy-tale princess, an ex-traordinary array of conditions. Even her social status, superior to Lawrence's, provided a distorted recapitulation of the marriage of Lawrence's well-bred mother to an underbred miner. In all these instances, Lawrence, so far as his art was concerned, was making autobiographical points around which his ideas could rally.

It is not that his life relates to his writing in a *post hoc ergo propter hoc* sense, but that the same unconscious sources fed both the actions of his fiction and the events of his life. His marriage as a totality of conscious and unconscious motivations was to provide Lawrence with the physical body of his symbolism. The miners of *Sons and Lovers* now forsake their naturalistic degradation to become the dark, underground, threatening, sensual male principle. And the well-bred lady, the bourgeois mother of *Sons and Lovers*, becomes the passive, unawakened female principle, whose perceptions the man must waken. It is as if, with extraordinary luck, Oedipus had fled from Thebes to Corinth to marry his foster mother Merope.

In his flight from his filial bondage Lawrence was trying to escape "the grey disease," as he called it, of mental consciousness. The imagery in which he envelops it, as for example in criticizing Marcel Proust, involves masturbation, which, like Swift's scatology, aroused his ultimate disgust. I equate Lawrence's rejection of mental consciousness with his rejection of his old incest fixation on his mother. The object of the original masturbation fantasy is, Freud insists, the mother herself. For Lawrence, in sexual relations an understanding between minds constituted a very real incest, implicit in the act of *knowing* someone sexually. To the psychologist, Dr. Trigant Burrow, Lawrence wrote:

> Do you know somebody who said: *on connait les femmes, ou on les aime; il n'y a pas de milieu?* It's French, but I'm not sure it isn't true. I'm not sure if a mental relation with a woman doesn't make it impossible to love her. To kow the *mind* of a woman is to end in hating her. Love means the precognitive flow—neither strictly has a mind—It is the honest state before the apple.[3]

He provides, for the puritan temperament, a handbook for sinners. In *Women in Love,* for example, the characters of Gerald Crich and Gudrun are the more terrible for representing to him the forcibly controlled desires of his own psyche. There lies between them, as he puts it, an "obscene recognition," and he flies from it into synthetic yogic philosophies and cultural primitivism. It is a flight from the mother in the mind to the father in the blood.

Lawrence Durrell, in his novel *Balthazar,* has one of his characters describe Lawrence as a man with a "habit of building a Taj Majal around anything as simple as a good f—k."[4] Nothing could be further from the truth. The same unconscious processes we have described in other contexts manifest themselves here as well.

The sexual descriptions in Lawrence's novels contain always the imagery of what is recognizable as coitus anxiety, which implies a neurotic regression to some prior state, before the genitals have assumed primacy as the sexual organ par excellence, when for the child the pleasurable organ is the mouth, which does not give but receives through suckling. The orally dependent infant, for whom all orifices in fantasy satisfy oral (sucking) needs, fears the giving of himself in an orgasm. His own hunger, which he attributes as well to the object of his desire, the nursing mother, threatens to devour him. The neurotic Oedipal man, for whom the nursing situation was the paradisal one, equates orgasm with loss and withdraws in horror from a mother image that is more predator than nurse. The clinical descriptions are consistently those of death; violent, explosive annihilation; and mutilation.[5]

Lawrence explores the full octave of this experience, from violent, prolonged torment on the edge of orgasm to complete annihilation and nirvana. But bliss is never certain. In his novel *The Rainbow,* which, like Mann's *Buddenbrooks,* crosses through three generations, Lawrence takes up the marriage of Will and Anna Brangwen and finally the relationship between the daughter, Ursula, and her lover Skrebensky. In both we are aware of both the desire for, and the dread of, coitus. We are aware also of the tremendous overvaluation of the woman and the unconscious incestuous content latent in it, manifesting itself in the pleasurable intellectual experience of shame, which in *The Rainbow* is almost Byronic in its unabashed intensity.

That the experiences represent Lawrence's could be deduced from his repeated and idiosyncratic handling of them, experiences so personal as to be unique, even if we doubted Frieda Lawrence's statement that the "inner relationship [between Ursula and Skrebensky] is Lawrence's and mine."[6] The first relationship is between Anna and Will Brangwen:

> He [Brangwen] had always, all his life, had a secret dread of Absolute Beauty. It had always been like a fetish to him, something to fear, really. For it was immoral and against mankind. . . .
>
> But now he had given way, and with infinite sensual violence gave himself to the realization of this supreme, immoral, Absolute Beauty, in the body of woman. . . .
>
> But still the thing terrified him. Awful and threatening it was, dangerous to a degree, even whilst he gave himself to it. . . . All the shameful, natural and unnatural acts of sensual voluptuousness which he and the woman partook of together, created together, they had their heavy beauty and their delight. Shame, what was it? It was part of extreme delight.[7]

In the relationship between Ursula and Skrebensky the anxieties take the upper hand, and the pleasurable sense of shame is absent. The imagery is wholly that of destruction, fear of being devoured combining with castration anxiety, a fear of the *vagina dentata* of the virgin:

> . . . his heart melted in fear from the fierce, beaked, harpy's kiss. . . . The fight, the struggle for consummation was terrible. It lasted till it was agony in his soul, till he succumbed, till he gave way as if dead. . . . He felt as if the knife were being pushed into his already dead body. . . . He felt, if ever he must see her again, his bones must be broken, his body crushed, obliterated for ever. . . .[8]

Even, in his frenzy, he sought for her mouth with his mouth, though it was like putting his face into some awful death. She yielded to him, and he pressed himself upon her in extremity, his soul groaning over and over ["Let me come, let me come"].[9]

A horrible sickness gripped him, as if his legs were really cut away, and he could not move, but remained a crippled trunk, dependent, worthless. The ghastly sense of help-lessness, as if he were a mere figure that did not exist vi-tally, made him mad, beside himself. . . . After each con-tact his mad dependence on her was deepened. . . . He felt himself a mere attribute of her.[10]

Women in Love presents ostensibly two men and two women whose relationships are respectively desirable and undesirable. Gerald Crich, the blond man of power, was conceived of by Lawrence as a composite figure, derived from a mine operator in the Midlands coal regions and Lawrence's friend Middleton Murry. Gudrun, Gerald's mistress, is Katherine Mansfield.[11] The character of Rupert Birkin is presumably Lawrence him-self. But if we accept this separation of identities we deny the continuity of Lawrence's self-description, and his ubiquity in sexual relationships whose common denominator is the anxiety manifested above. From Birkin's own actions we suspect that his search for "polarity" and "otherness" and the "ultraphallic" emerges from the fear of the intrauterine absorption that his friend Gerald seeks. On the strength of Gerald's actions and his resemblance to other earlier characters in Lawrence's work (the Prussian officer comes to mind), I would maintain that Gerald is psychically closer to Lawrence than Birkin—that Gerald is Lawrence's practical involvement in the world, and Birkin merely, perhaps totally, his dialectic personified.

Gerald Crich, like Paul Morel, comes to a woman for relief: Paul after his mother's death, the other after his father's. Gerald's experience is a curious mixture:

And she [Gudrun], she was the great bath of life, he wor-shipped her. Mother and substance of all life she was. And he, child and man, received of her and was made whole. His pure body was almost killed. But the miraculous, soft effluence of her breast suffused over him, over his seared, damaged brain, like a healing lymph, like a soft, soothing flow of life itself, perfect as if he were bathed in the womb again. . . . Like a child at the breast he cleaved intensely to her, and she could not put him away.[12]

It is between Gerald and Gudrun that the obscene mental recognition of their mutual sensuality occurs, the "shame" that with Will Brangwen "was a part of extreme delight." And now in this extravagant image the coitus is transformed into a nursing fantasy in which the brain, in an exotic placement of orgastic relief, is put to sleep at the breast of the mother, the man becomes infant.

In *Aaron's Rod*, Aaron Sisson, one of Lawrence's composite selves, is sick unto death for having surrendered himself to a woman. "'I felt it—I felt it go, inside me, the minute I gave in to her. It's perhaps killed me,'" he tells his friend Lilly.[13] Lawrence's women destroy with the power of love. They draw men to them, only to destroy them. In *Aaron's Rod* they are not beaked predators; they are constrictors.

Josephine Hay, the *belle dame* of Aaron's delirium, is an undeveloped version of the Gudrun of *Women in Love*. She is the artist woman, sexually attractive and intellectually aware. She does not fulfill herself sexually at the man's expense but is herself sexually disinherited, Lilith, not Eve. Lawrence envelops her in serpent imagery, describes her licking her "rather full, dry lips with the rapid tip of her tongue. It was an odd movement, suggesting a snake's flicker."[14]

For Lawrence, as for Yeats, there is something deathly about the woman in whom physical beauty and clarity of mind are combined. It is a confusion of genres that a beautiful woman, a silent artifact, should have opinions, destructive foibles, a will. Lawrence treats the woman artist as she appears in Josephine and Gudrun as a sexual monster. He equates the "will," that ultimate term of opprobrium when he applies it to the unsubmissive woman, with the conscious act of creation, reserving it on the physical plane for the man's aggressive phallicism and on the intellectual plane for the artist's shaping spirit. In either case the exercise of the will is the male function. In the female it becomes the harpy's beak, the snake's flicker.

In Josephine the full import of the snake is unrealized. Lawrence's maternal women, those who destroy with the power of love rather than the power of negation, are constrictors, women like Anna Brangwen, the sacred pythoness of *The Rainbow*, and Lottie of *Aaron's Rod*. With these women he dwells not on the snake's flicker but on its heavy coils, its crushed, flat look, and its tenacity: "[Aaron] had a certain horror of her [Lottie]. The strange liquid sound of her appeal seemed to him like the swaying of a serpent which mesmerizes the fated, helpless bird. She clasped her arms around him, she drew him to her, she half roused his passion." [15]

The imagery of destruction that inheres in Lawrence's description of sexuality is a reminder of the "catastrophe theory" Ferenczi describes: "Many neurotics unconsciously regard coitus as an activity which either directly or subsequently is calculated to endanger life or limb, and in particular to damage the genital organ, i.e., an act in which are combined gratification and severe anxiety." [16] Lawrence swings continually in his novels between the nirvana imagery of "being given in peace" and the recoil from it. It is an endless cycle of Oedipal and anti-Oedipal impulses.

Even in *Lady Chatterley's Lover*, in which finally the Son of Woman is brought to bliss, the gamekeeper Mellors, in his catalogue of women, recalls to mind the harpy's beak, this time displaced below: "She sort of got harder and harder to bring off, and she'd sort of tear at me down there, as if it were a beak tearing at me." [17]

As time went on Lawrence consolidated this recoil from the orgasm into a synthetic philosophy derived mainly from yogic quietism. Thus he justified it in terms of the conservation of vital energy. *The Plumed Serpent*, Lawrence's novel about Mexico, describes the sexual relations between the Englishwoman Kate and the Indian Don Cipriano: "When, in their love, it came back on her, the seething, electric female ecstasy, which knows such spasms of delirium, he recoiled from her. . . . By a dark and powerful instinct he drew away from her as soon as this desire rose again in her. . . . She could not know him." [18]

The character of Cipriano is perhaps a clue to the strategy Lawrence had recourse to. He belongs to the dark, mindless instinctive order of beings with whom Lawrence identified the father. To this figure Lawrence imputed an attribute of virility which often qualifies the appeal of his protagonists—their high indifference to the woman's sexual enjoyment. It becomes increasingly more pronounced in Lawrence's later works and can only be interpreted as an unconscious equation between orgasm and annihilation or, again, between orgasm and castration. In the father there is security from the woman. The son, the server of woman, is always in danger.

It is impossible within this context to overlook the innumerable allusions in Lawrence's fiction, letters, and essays to Christ's passion, crucifixion, and resurrection—allusions that culminate, finally, in *The Man Who Died*. But, in terms of the castration anxiety that terrifies his characters, it is perhaps more in connection with the mutilations of Attis and Osiris than with Christ that the messianic theme in Lawrence becomes understandable. For Lawrence is the martyrologist of the sexual experience in all his works, from *Sons and Lovers* to *Lady Chatterley's Lover*. We have seen, in *Sons and Lovers*, how Paul Morel, in resigning from his manhood's rivalry with Baxter Dawes and returning to his childhood's dependence on his mother, achieves power over "their three fates" as the prize for his renunciation. We see, in *Lady Chatterley's Lover*, the gulf Lawrence sets between the gamekeeper and the mutilated Clifford, with his "queer, craven idolatry" of Constance and his lapse into a perverse childhood under the care of Mrs. Bolton, "the Magna Mater." We have seen throughout Lawrence's work his revulsion from the role of the "server of woman," and its agonizing alternatives. But it is not until we adopt the vantage point of *The Man Who Died* that the mythical formulaton becomes clear.

On the one hand, the Jesus who survives his crucifixion reviews the life-denying tenets of his doctrines with regret. He sees himself as the dupe of his female followers, the Son of Woman, and not the Son of Man. He meets, in Mary Magdalen, the possessive, self-conscious adoration of a woman determined to grovel at the feet of a messiah who conforms to her own epicene vision. Her virtue is the virtue of the reformed prostitute who despises what she used most to enjoy. She therefore worships the ascetic Christ to the chagrin of the man in him. He has become the apotheosis of castration.

On the other hand, he accomplishes his regeneration as a man (his cry, "I am risen!" describes a phallic, synecdochic resurrection) in the arms of the priestess of Isis. Her acceptance of him is free of the mental, personal relationship he has known with Magdalen. She allows him to become the virile Christ, absolved of the recognitions so fatal to his manhood.

I read *The Man Who Died*, coming as it does so close in time to the composition of *Lady Chatterley's Lover*, as the spiritual abstract of that novel, its anagogic level made explicit. In *The Man Who Died* Lawrence has an eschatological fling at the antinatural doctrines of Christianity. In *Lady Chatterley's Lover* he extends the theme and tilts against the dark, satanic windmills of our own century's mechanistic civilization.

Clifford Chatterley, like Christ before he repudiated himself or, if you please, Attis irredeemably mutilated, is the castrate par excellence, the apotheosis of industrialism, "queer and rapacious and civilized with broad shoulders and no real legs." He is full of sage platonisms and contemptuous of the flesh. His sister-in-law, Hilda, who like Magdalen has had her lovers and destroyed them in her service, now despises sex and admires Clifford because he has none.

But it is the gamekeeper Mellors who runs the gamut from the crucified Jesus to the coming forth by day of the phallic

Osiris. He is, when he first appears, in a touch-me-not stage of resurrection, on the margin of life. Like the farmhouse in which Christ recovers, the gamekeeper's cottage lies between some spiritual Calvary and Jerusalem, between the great dead pile of Wragby Hall and the squalors of Tevershall. Constance Chatterley's coming about to an acceptance of the impersonal nature of her sexual communion with the gamekeeper as a thing indifferent to the individual communicant has its analogue in the shift from the ascetic Christ to the risen Osiris. In her complete subjection lies his peace.   [1962]

10.

Freedom and Immortality: Notes from the Dostoevskian Underground

The poet William Butler Yeats distinguishes, in one of his essays, between the straight line and the curve as the difference between man's thought and the "winding of Nature." But he separates what we have come to think of as the intellective process, the poet from the rational thinker. "The straight line," he says, "is the mark of saint or sage. I think that we who are poets or artists, not being permitted to shoot beyond the tangible, must go from desire to weariness and so to desire again, and live but from the moment when vision comes to our weariness like terrible lightnings in the humility of the brutes." [1]

What Yeats is here explaining is that feeling all "forthright men," as Dostoevsky would call them, have—that the poet is somehow looking squint-eyed at a reality which appears to them to be also forthright. He appears to ignore what looks like the shortest distance between two points. Like Moses he casts down his prophetic staff, and it becomes a serpent with its tail in its mouth.

It is not only on aesthetic grounds that the poet forsakes the straight and narrow path to the palace of wisdom, curved lines being more graceful than straight lines, but in the interest of wisdom itself. The poet trades on a concept of mind and intelligence in which reason is only an inconspicuous room in a rambling palace which, like Bluebeard's castle, is full of dark underground cellars with skeletons in every cupboard, and (so forthright men are apt to think) with bats in the belfry. The poet assumes that what baffles the rational mind speaks more or less plainly to the intuitive, and that in this dialogue between poetry and mind, reason is more apt than not to be a troublesome intruder.

The history of Dostoevsky's reputation, and the continuing events of which his works are and continue to be prophetic, bear eloquent witness to the assertion I have made. His first appearance in Russian letters divided Russia like the advent of Jesus in Jerusalem; he was alternatively praised as a selfless saint and blamed as an exhibitionistic trickster. After his death he was honored for his benevolence, his piety, his respect for the Czar, and his morality. Today in Soviet Russia, since the passing of the Stalinist regime which could not quite forgive him for denouncing from the grave their not-so-crystal palace, he is described as "one of the greatest *word* artists of all countries and people," a description which rather coyly ignores his subject matter.

But most significantly, Dostoevsky is honored by the world not for his piety, which was heretical, nor his humanity, which was distempered by cruelty, nor for his morality, which was morbid, but for those traits which most repelled his first readers and which still repel the doctrinaire Marxists of his own Russia: his meticulous and savagely accurate analyses of human motivations back, as the underground man would say, to their first and largely selfish causes. It is this psychological honesty which so intrigued and at the same time confused the immense intellect of Sigmund Freud. As a man who loved poetry, he loved and understood the winding circles of Dostoevsky's mind; as a dedicated man of science he was disappointed that Dostoevsky, as Freud thought, turned his back on freedom. He wrote:

> After the most violent struggles to reconcile the instinctual demands of the individual with the claims of the community, he landed in the retrograde position of submission both to temporal and spiritual authority, of veneration both for the Tsar and the God of the Christians, and of

a narrow Russian nationalism—a position which lesser
minds have reached with smaller effort. . . . Dostoevsky
threw away the chance of becoming a teacher and liberator
of humanity and made himself one with their gaolers.
The future of human civilization will have little to thank
him for.[2]

William Butler Yeats would say merely that Freud was ask-
ing Dostoevsky to leave the ranks of poet and pursue the
straight line of the sage, that Freud was forgetting that on the
curved surface of the natural world the shortest distance between two points is a curved line.

There is no essential quarrel between the two: Dostoevsky as
artist represents reality as he finds it; Freud tries to make that
reality instrumental to our well-being. But both men embody
a humanism vast enough to contain all history, a humanism
which supports our thirst for freedom, and defines that freedom as the possession of one's own unfettered consciousness,
for better or for worse.

I should like for the moment to describe an unpoetic circle
around the works of Dostoevsky and to consider the issues of
freedom and immortality as we meet them, now in this man,
now in that, in the past, and in the present.

Thomas Mann's novel *The Magic Mountain*, written at a time
equidistant between the publication of *The Brothers Karamazov*
in which "The Grand Inquisitor" appears, and our own historical moment, will serve as a perfect point of departure. For as a
novel it constitutes among other things a history of Western
thought, embodied in a series of characters who all together
form what might be called a periodic table of world views. The
two I am interested in here are Herr Naphta and Lodovico Settembrini. These two constitute an absolute antagonism of
views, and their arguments are all the more poignant in that
they meet on the eve of World War I, when all ideas were overwhelmed in chaos.

One of these characters the reader will recognize from Dostoevsky's works; the other may very well be the reader himself.

Naphta is the more complex of the two, a frightening and implausible combination of elements unified only in their representing all that is suppressive and authoritarian in human society. He was born an orthodox Jew, the son of a ritual slaughterer of animals. Left an orphan when his father was crucified in an anti-semitic uprising, he became a neophyte in the ranks of the Jesuits. A devout Roman Catholic, he equates world Communism with Catholicism, as two streams which must ultimately join. Both despise the middleman who makes money on time and the labors of others, and both exalt the tiller of the soil. Their quarrel is therefore a theological quibble.

Naphta's opponent, Settembrini, is a liberal, a child of the Italian *Risorgimento*, the champion of democracy, reform, and tolerance, and the amenities of middle-class life. He is in constant correspondence with the international agents of enlightenment in Geneva, Switzerland. He is the avowed enemy of the Catholic Church and of Communism.

Both men are passionate in their devotion to freedom, the one in the name of the soul and spiritual progress to the city of God, the other in the name of the body and material progress to an earthly paradise, the perfect state.

Settembrini states his argument thus:

> "You see, through the space of countless ages, life developing from the infusorium up to man: how can you doubt then that man has yet before him endless possibilities of development? And in the sphere of the higher mathematics, if you would rest your case thereon, then follow your cycle from perfection to perfection, and, from the teaching of our eighteenth century, learn that man was originally good, happy, and without sin, that social errors have corrupted and perverted him, and that he can, and will once more become good, happy, and sinless, by dint of labour upon his social structure."[3]

To which Naphta replies:

> " . . . any system of pains and penalties which is not based upon belief in a hereafter is simply a bestial stupidity. And

as for the degradation of humanity, the history of its course is precisely synchronous with the growth of the bourgeois spirit. Renaissance, age of enlightenment, the natural sciences and economics of the nineteenth century have left nothing undone or untaught which could forward this degradation. Modern astronomy, for example, has converted the earth, the centre of the All, the lofty theatre of the struggle between God and the Devil for the possession of a creature burningly coveted by each, into an indifferent little planet, and thus . . . put an end to the majestic cosmic position of man." [And further:] "your individualism . . . is defective. It is a confession of weakness. It corrects its pagan State morality by the admixture of a little Christianity, a little 'rights of man,' a little so-called liberty. . . ."

Philanthropy, Mann adds, "would eliminate from life all its stern and mortal traits; it would castrate life, as would the determinism of its so-called science. But determinism would never succeed in doing away with the conception of guilt."[4]

When Naphta praises the "simple fact of death" for being responsible for the greatest in architecture, painting, sculpture, music and poetry, Settembrini is reminded that he is preparing for "an international congress for the promotion of cremation . . . a model crematorium would be exhibited, planned in accordance with the latest researches and experiments." And Mann momentarily concludes that

individualism belonged, singly and solely, in the realm of the religious and mystical, in the so-called "morally chaotic All." And this morality of Herr Settembrini's, what was it, what did it want? It was life-bound, and thus entirely utilitarian; it was pathetically unheroic. Its end and aim was to make men grow old and happy, rich and comfortable—and that was all there was to it. And this Philistine philosophy, this gospel of work and reason, served Herr Settembrini as an ethical system . . . the sheerest and shabbiest bourgeoisiedom.[5]

Can there not be heard behind this debate the despairing cry of the Underground man when he has left off running after

Liza, "Which is better—cheap happiness or exalted suffering?" It is a cry which has echoed ever since Dostoevsky uttered it. Even Thomas Mann, although he will not accept Naphta's extreme position, cannot help making Settembrini slightly ridiculous, a little, as he puts it, like an organ grinder. "Herr Settembrini ate [his salami] with tears in his eyes. He is a patriot, you must know, a democratic patriot. He has consecrated his burgher's pike on the altar of humanity, so that salami may be taxed at the Brenner frontier."[6]

Why is it that philanthropy and material progress have always drawn catcalls from the artist? Why is the artist, if he is worth anything, always a man poised, as it were, between the Devil and the bourgeoisie, ready if necessary to die for freedom, but not to enjoy its material advantages? Why does the feeling persist that there is something ultimately degrading about the products of a secular enlightenment which, while it opens broad vistas of material progress, closes firmly the gates of heaven?

We are habituated to the thought that science is a bright light shining in a dark corner and that the nineteenth century which saw the beginnings of technological progress and the rise of Darwinism had at last cleared the way for a world whose social organization (and in a rational society all the rest would follow) would rest securely on the firm biological foundations that Darwin proposed, freed of all the dark superstitions and metaphysical absurdities to which mankind had hitherto been committed. Crime was a disease of poverty, and economic and environmental changes would bring with them a golden age of innocence, freedom from crime and vice and guilt, and the burden of sin, which Christianity insisted was our inheritance, would fall from our shoulders, because it had never been there to begin with.

Raskolnikov's best friend, in Dostoevsky's *Crime and Punishment*, gives a party to which his student friends come. There is a fierce argument; what did the young men who came to Razumihin's party argue about? Where did Raskolnikov get his idea for the article he wrote on crime, and for the crime itself? We know from small clues, names, bits of jargon, ideas, both within the novel itself and scattered elsewhere in other novels and in the journal, *A Writer's Diary*, which Dostoevsky published serially. The names, among others, of Fourier and Auguste Comte occur in this context. These men proposed social systems which would eliminate economic competition and would, under utopian conditions, develop what Herr Settembrini in *The Magic Mountain* calls the fruits of Enlightenment, "personality, freedom and the rights of man." For Fourier misery and vice sprang from the unnatural restraints that society placed upon the passions, which were naturally harmonious and good. August Comte's "scientific positivism" similarly proposed constructing a society according to the discoverable laws of what he called "social physics," or sociology, the science of human society, the political, moral and economic behavior of men. The scientific measures of man were the twin sciences of human behavior, physiology (which presumably accounted for the activities of the brain) and sociology. There is, significantly, a complete opposition to what Comte called "illusory psychology, the last phase of theology," because it "pretended to discover the laws of the human mind by contemplating it in itself." The new man, the product of Comte's system, would be incapable of thinking unscientifically, or of being religious. The reader's familiarity with Mark Twain's *A Connecticut Yankee in King Arthur's Court* will facilitate recognition of a classical encounter between the Comtean man and the benighted Europe that Comte wished to reform. It is perhaps material to this theme to point out that Comte himself, lost in his own dream, evolved a paranoid religion of humanity, in which he and his young mistress were to be prophet and priestess.

In the new order, freed from the theological stigma of primal guilt, and the necessity for earning one's bread by the sweat of one's brow, the figure of Christ underwent a curious transformation. Dostoevsky records a memoir of his friend Bielinsky, an ardent socialist.

"But do you know," he screamed one evening, "do you know it is impossible to charge man with sins, to burden him with debts and turning the other cheek, when society is organized so meanly that man cannot help but perpetrate villanies; when economically he has been brought to villainy, and that it is silly and cruel to demand from man that, which, by the very laws of nature, he is impotent to perform even if he wished to. . . . Believe me, naive man, [Dostoevsky himself], that your Christ, if he were born in our time, would be a most imperceptible and ordinary man; in the presence of contemporary science . . . he would be effaced."

"Oh, no," interposed Bielinsky's friend . . . "Oh no! If Christ were to appear in our day he would join the movement and lead it . . ."

"Yes of course, yes," conceded Bielinsky. "Precisely! He would join the socialists and follow them."[7]

The very symbol of all this philosophical rotarianism was what was to be the first World's Fair, Century 20 in today's terms, but being Victorian, it called itself, "The First International Exposition of Art, Science, Industry and Manufacture." It was, as a contemporary writer summed it up, "a unique form of cross-world communication, celebrating equally the industrial revolution's advances in technology, and the smug, Victorian conviction that theirs was the best of all possible worlds." The Crystal Palace itself was a magnificently ugly structure of glass and steel, utterly transparent in the full sense of the word.

But beneath this bright optimistic surface flowing gaily toward the future, there runs a cold, dark, deep counter-current, which holds this ideal of progress in abomination as cheap, destructive, and inhuman—the ant-heap. It is a current which has not ceased to run; it surfaced in Huxley's *Brave New World*, and Orwell's *1984*. It is a current which, in the name of freedom, has resisted the urgings both of fatalistic theology and scientific determinism. In the ancient world the Greeks, oppressed on the one hand by the absolute domination of man by the gods of

Egypt and Persia, and repelled by the mere savagery of the barbarians to the north, discovered the middle world of human existence, in which men have learned to take the responsibility for their own actions and to endure the full range of human experience, as we see it in the tragic drama of Sophocles and Aeschylus, upon their own responsibilities.

And in the midst of the cheerful progressivism of the late nineteenth century we are confronted by the image of this titanic figure of Dostoevsky, brushing away the picture of progress with a wave of his hand, and not too clean a hand at that, and showing us in its place the disorderly, suffering, guiltridden world that has been, is and will be, perhaps until time or the human race has ended. And most amazingly, this man who looked beyond the childlike faith of the nineteenth century in the efficacy of its science, into the more considered skepticism of the twentieth century, did so with all the trappings of orthodox Christianity upon him. "The Popular Truth! The Truth of God!" was his battle cry, and the battleground was the question of man's "greatest advantage," one's own free, unfettered choice, one's essential freedom.

I am hard put to sort out of Dostoevsky's writings the elements that bear rational consideration, for without doubting his wisdom as a profound thinker, we find everywhere in his statements that touch of madness, of private obsession, of epileptic enthusiasm, which upsets our sense of the division between the rational and the irrational. As the psychologist and philosopher he saw things true; as the artist he overstates the truth, until it looks like fantasy. Reading Dostoevsky is sometimes like reading Freud's collected works printed in black letter, or translated into Church Slavonic with medieval wood engravings.

But then Thomas Mann's Dostoevskian character Naphta offers us this comfort: "The normal, since time was, lived on the achievements of the abnormal. Men consciously and voluntarily descended into disease and madness in search of knowledge, which acquired by fanaticism would lead back to health." [8]

What is wrong with the meliorism of Dostoevsky's time? Why does it not answer the needs of freedom? For Dostoevsky on one level at least, it was the reduction by science of humanity to the level of an intelligent animal—*Homo sapiens*, as opposed to the theological Adam Caedmon, the man made in God's image. It is as Dostoevsky propounds it, an imponderable, grasped intuitively if it is to be grasped at all. His refusal to accept his role as insect is what motivates our underground man who refuses as he puts it, to be a piano key, an exhibit in a behaviorist's classroom.

The argument runs along these lines: to be an animal, healthy, happy, well-fed, innocent, is to be unselfconscious. And to lose one's consciousness of self is to sell one's humanity for a mess of pottage.

In Dostoevsky's world of real human beings there is true individuality, responsibility, self-determination, the ability to distinguish between right and wrong. The inhuman doctrine of scientific causation deprives mankind of its highest attribute— virtuous action in the teeth of temptation.

But as an artist (and as Freud would insist, as a neurotic), Dostoevsky is more interested in the corollary to virtue—its antithesis—crime and vice. Crime is the collapse of the moral system, but a moral system in decay, he insists, is better than a scientifically disinfected world, in which there is no crime, and as Ivan Karamazov cries, "Everything is permitted."

Again and again in Dostoevsky that medieval paradox emerges, that spectacle of the arch-criminal being led to fire or the axe as tenderly as if he were the pope coming to be consecrated—the degree of compassion awarded each according to the degree of repentance he had manifested.

For Dostoevsky suffering was the bitter medicine that kept humanity awake as humanity. And suffering itself was a kind of insomnia of the conscience as a result of sin. Having scientifically disproved the existence of the kingdom of heaven, the least mankind could do was to remind itself that it had forever lost it. To become a piano key was to lapse into animal inanity, in which all sins were venial. Threatened by the smug assertions of the natural scientist that all the mysteries of the human spirit were ultimately knowable, the underground man retires into his burrow, defying the scientist to predict his next move.

In Russia there arose a sect that worshipped Judas Iscariot above all the other disciples for, they maintained, it was he who had by his gross criminal act in which he sacrificed both soul and body, brought about the death and resurrection of Christ.

Being human demands above all things a belief in the life of something like a soul, and its existence separate from the body. I remember once looking through an old, dreadfully outdated geology book, and coming across those divisions in geological ages: from the Cenozoic Period in whose latest division (50,000 B.C.) the author of the work goes to a period roughly equatable with the dawn of religion and labels it the Psychozoic—the Age of the Soul—a distinction more theological than geological, for that time in the history of the human race when religious impulses began to stir, and human beings knew death and transcended it. The book dated from Dostoevsky's own times and constitutes a touching attempt to reconcile science with religion.

To postulate a humanity in whose name Nature itself must be brought under control, it was necessary for Dostoevsky to postulate spiritual origins and a spiritual goal, a religious instinct which apprehended—although dimly—divinity at the beginning and the end of the natural world. But paradoxically, there is involved in a such a concept a disparagement of the things of this world.

Through his works there runs continually the refrain—childlike, dangerous—that everything must be important or nothing is important. It is Hamlet's cry when he considers Claudius' lecheries and debauches, and his own emotional underground (there is much of Hamlet in Dostoevsky's *Notes from the Underground*): "What is a man/If his chief good and market of his time/Be but to sleep and feed?/A beast, no more." And Dostoevsky echoes Hamlet—and paraphrases Hamlet's own concern for his immortal soul.

Ivan Karamazov, the brother who cannot believe in God, and whose story, "The Grand Inquisitor," reflects his torment, tells his brother, "'I only know that suffering exists, that everything passes away and equals out. But if there is no virtue . . . [that is if there is no God] Everything is lawful.'"[9]

In refusing to trust his moral being or his freedom to mere human agencies, Dostoevsky is doing something much more important for us than affirming the existence of God or the immortality of the soul. His distrust of humanity, his refusal to believe in disinterested brotherly love, stems from his having discovered out of his own dark impulses a psychology before which the rational sociology of Auguste Comte and the theories of Fourier were child's toys. Out of his own nature he could draw the cruel imperative that drove Napoleon to master Europe, and whose figure was in the nineteenth century, and still is, the type and symbol of paranoid insanity. And again he could find within himself those epileptics, criminals, and idiots whose sacrifices and sufferings within his novels come close to the image of Christ. To suffer is to apprehend an eternity beyond suffering. In short, Dostoevsky could find everything in his psychology except utopia.

In three bold strokes, Dostoevsky in *Notes from the Underground* anticipates Freud's revolutionary anatomy of the mind, with its consciousness divided from itself, the ego struggling to repress instincts which will not brook delay or decency.

> Every man has reminiscences which he would not tell to every one, but only to his friends. He has other matters in his mind which he would not reveal even to his friends, but only to himself, and that in secret. But there are other things which a man is afraid to tell even to himself, and every decent man has a number of such things stored away in his mind. The more decent he is, the greater the number of such things in his mind.[10]

It is through his descent into this underworld of his psyche that the underground man attains to whatever freedom he is capable of. It is his pathological honesty that allows him to see that his Christlike wish to be slapped in the face arises from a contemptible self-interest, a wish to "grovel in the mud," in an ecstasy of degradation. It is his honesty which allows him to recognize that he is playing a Napoleonic role with the prostitute, that he is incapable of love, which he defines as a "struggle," in which the stronger tyrannizes over the weaker. The clerk is incapable of relinquishing that self-interest that makes his own free decision to do good something less than a virtuous deed. He cannot purge himself of his own shame, see the divine in himself which will allow him to accept the pure love of the prostitute. So he *must* reject her because the ground of his acceptance is false. He pursues her when the possibility of finding her is cut off; his contrition and his despair measure the distance humanity is from salvation, but they also measure his freedom. Such a perverse interpretation of freedom is made more acceptable by calling to mind the underground man's own manifesto: "If reason drives a man to formulate himself on the edge of chaos, then he will go mad to escape reason."

Oscar Wilde's life and writing, in spite of what seems to be an abyss of culture between them, bears certain affinities with Dostoevsky's; both men contained within them those devils of cruelty and self-destruction, and the sense of personal tragedy.

> There are two kinds of artist; one brings answers and the other questions. We have to know whether one belongs to those who cannot answer or to those who question; for the kind which questions is never that which answers. There are works which wait and which one does not understand for a long time; the reason is that they bring answers to questions which have not yet been raised; for the question often arises a terribly long time after the answer.[11]

It may be that Dostoevsky is one of those whose works are bringing answers to questions which our own age has raised. It may be that his assertion that there is a tragic drama of human existence, that its dignity must be played out against the backdrop of the spirit, or else it is as meaningless as the life-cycle of the housefly and equally expendable, is in some way an answer to the statement of a Russian commissar that "as soon as man has vanquished nature religion becomes superfluous; thereupon the sense of the tragic shall vanish from our lives."

Man's sense of the tragic relates ultimately to his sense of his own importance, and his importance in the eyes of some cosmic spectator. I once speculated, in a macabre train of thought, what it would take to make the war criminal Eichmann a tragic hero, and I could not go beyond the medieval formula (which is Dostoevsky's) that he could achieve tragic stature if he acknowledged his crimes as his own free choice of evil in defiance of a power higher than the state. Eichmann's degradation lies in his having become an insect in the service of his anthill. In that respect he is, and the Germany he served, a rather horrid reflection of some of the better run, sanitary states now thriving in the world. Germany's fate is not tragic. It is, as Dostoevsky would see it (as he saw the Inquisition, the religions of statism, and the dogmatic church), the fate of a nation which has committed the ultimate heresy of worshipping itself.

I do not believe in immortality with too much conviction. As for God I can only quote Mae West's play *Diamond Lil*; when asked about God, Lil answers in her most suggestive delivery, "I've never met the gentleman." I know that Dostoevsky says something important about tragedy and freedom, and when pressed for explanation I take refuge in the insights of psychology, as it describes the evolution of the self from all that is not the self. Pain and suffering, sacrifice and choice, the resistance of authority, whether it be parental, social, religious, or even the warring oppositions in oneself, awaken the self to a sharper definition of itself than any of the soft blandishments of a unanimous mediocre utopia.

Dostoevsky's world may appear too harsh, too arbitrarily astringent for our tastes; and Freud is correct in his assertion that much of the nobility in Dostoevsky's sufferers is perverse pleasure disguised as the tragic muse. Yet Freud himself does not, as some suppose, encourage belief that the hallmark of mental health is the integration of the individual within his society. One of the reasons that psychoanalysis is anathema to totalitarian and dogmatic societies and religious beliefs is the stress psychoanalysis places upon the individual who, if he is strong, will emancipate himself from a sick society to live by his own lights. Dostoevsky represents the other side of the coin, a man who, without the ministrations of a healer (whom he no doubt would have despised) chose to live in his own darkness rather than lose himself in the anthill.

The poet Yeats, with whom I began here, said that "True immortality is the full and entire possession of oneself for one single moment." We can, I think, substitute the word *freedom* for *immortality* without losing the sense of truth conveyed.

[1960]

11.

Freudian Criticism:
Frank O'Connor as Paradigm

The status of psychoanalytic criticism in the canon of respectable critical disciplines is no longer open to argument. But its origins as the love child of medical science and one of medicine's most original geniuses make its application to art seem merely a furthering of what medical science denounced to begin with as a miscegenation of disciplines. There seem to be two opposing feelings among those who consider psychoanalysis in relation to art. The first and simplest of these feelings is that a little bit of psychoanalysis goes a long way, and the other is that, if one is going to use just a little bit of psychoanalysis, he might just as well not use it at all. I do not sense in either camp, non-Freudian or Freudian, the tendency to relax. Among the non-Freudians, who condemn by omission, the feeling seems to be that if one gives in to psychoanalytic criticism none of their daughters, Emma, Jane Eyre, Becky Sharp, or even Maisie, will be safe in their beds. The Freudians, on the other hand, confront themselves with what seems to be an imponderable problem, the transfer of the immense equipment of both theoretical and practical psychoanalysis on a professional basis into the field of criticism, without a too clearly defined notion of how it is to be applied. A recent and excellent publication of psychoanalytic essays, the volume *Art and Psychoanalysis* edited by William Phillips, contains many caveats against the too shallow prospecting in the unconscious of the erstwhile Freudian.[1]

Before I undertake the practical job of analyzing a story by Frank O'Connor, I should like to discuss some of the problems the psychoanalytic critic faces.

The first I would call the problem of the amateur. Setting aside the embarrassment one must necessarily feel at using without a license the materials of a licensed profession, I mean, by the amateur, the critic who renounces the final aim of psychoanalysis, which is after all not criticism but cure. Psychoanalysis in criticism, used undiluted, is an *aqua regia*; it effects no less than the reduction of literature to a limited number of pre-literary elements, and the reduction of all human motives to their first cause in some primordial family situation. So that one is always a little uncomfortable when an analyst speaks about art; the inevitable note of patronage creeps in—as why should it not, when the basic assumption is that the unconscious libido sleeps at art's roots? His view of art makes of it a Palladian corridor of endless instances of the same act—a continuous sublimation or degradation of a limited number of eternal verities.

In capable hands—in Ella Sharpe's, for example—the tragedy of *King Lear* becomes a tragedy of bowel control, a fantasy from Shakespeare's anal period.[2] The loose riotous knights, which Goneril and Regan deplore, are his feces, and his several daughters and sons-in-law represent aspects of the parent image. Such an analysis is comparable to Kenneth Burke's interpretation of *The Rime of the Ancient Mariner* as Coleridge's coming to terms with the monkey on his back.[3] We are astounded by the skill displayed in either case, but we ask, also, where has the poem gone? The discipline in each interpretation is not criticism but psychotherapy directed at the artist.

The consideration of a more or less aesthetically perfect work at these depths has the unfortunate effect of yielding as its end product, not the explicated work, but the protoplasmic material of its origin. One has thrown out the baby with the birth trauma.

Another unfortunate result of the too professional analysis

of the work of art is that the psychoanalytic critic has come to be regarded as an intellectual maggot whose proper meat is the diseased portions of whatever work he considers. This, the saprophytic function of psychoanalytic criticism, Lionel Trilling has dealt with capably in his essays "Freud and Literature" and "Art and Neurosis." Deprecating the Wound and the Bow concept of Edmund Wilson, Trilling dissociates the creative act from the materials it deals with. The artist, he maintains, is not only not mentally ill, but "possesses mental capabilities and psychic tone far superior to the normal man. . . . For, still granting that the poet is uniquely neurotic, what is surely not neurotic, what indeed suggests nothing but health, is his power of using his neuroticism." [4]

My feeling then is that psychoanalysis must be used with some caution—a caution more suited to the amateur than to the professional—in order, not to preserve the work of art, which is after all in no danger, but to preserve the critic, who would peep and psychoanalyze upon his mother's grave, from the temptation to ditch the aesthetic altogether, and with it the concept of the work of art. I propose then, in connection with literature, a lesser role for psychoanalytic criticism as a lay technique. From having been mildly interested in the psychological components of a work of art, the generality of readers is coming to insist that they be accurate; and inaccuracy puts as much of a tax on their sense of probability as gods from machines and other miraculous and melodramatic devices. The insistence arises from our having accepted in the other nonaesthetic quadrants of our lives certain psychological data as a guide to our understanding of ourselves. As individuals we are now psychologically interesting. Hamlet's Players, and their explicit play, "The Mouse Trap," are the outmoded external drama. The real dramatic interest has shifted to Hamlet. Not that the Elizabethan mirror is shattered, but that the inner life is spectral and cannot see itself too clearly in a mirror. The psychological accuracy of an action is the new decorum.

T. S. Eliot punctiliously ignores this fact when he writes about *Hamlet*.

> The artistic "inevitability" lies in the complete adequacy of the external to the emotion; and this is precisely what is deficient in *Hamlet*. Hamlet (the man) is dominated by an emotion which is inexpressible, because it is in excess of the facts as they appear. And the supposed identity of Hamlet with his author is genuine to this point: that Hamlet's bafflement at the absence of an objective equivalent to his feelings is a prolongation of the bafflement of his creator in the face of his artistic problem.[5]

Here Eliot is standing on the threshold of critical possibilities across which Freud has already walked.

> When [to quote from one of Freud's case histories] there is a mesalliance between an affect and its ideational content . . . a layman will say that the affect is too great for the occasion—that it is exaggerated—and that consequently the inference following . . . is false. On the contrary, the physician says: No. The affect is justified. . . . But it belongs to another content which is unknown (unconscious), and which requires to be looked for.[6]

To the extent that this "unknown" can be formulated and known through psychoanalytic method, artistic inevitability can be established (or reestablished in those works of art which appear to be deficient in it). Hamlet's "excess of emotion" becomes "adequate" once the source of these affects is revealed. And the unformulated, feeling response of the spectator of the tragedy finds critical justification on a rational basis.

At its best, then, psychological criticism should constitute a bureau of tragic or comic weights and measures, testing in the work of art for the organic, psychologically valid material. If the material contains fortuities for the sake of some aesthetic or formal purpose, then psychological criticism should betray the ersatz the way Solomon's bee betrayed Sheba's paper rose. Its amateur function should be analytic rather than reductive and therapeutic. It should recognize that the psychological background for a work of art constitutes, so to speak, its energy, but not its form, to which it is the parent.

In connection with the primacy of the work of art over its components, another problem arises. It is the question (whose resolution implies radical differences in technique) of prototype or archetype, imago, or archimago. Freud or Jung? Again the dilemma is confusing to the amateur. On the one hand Freudian criticism is full of grim warnings about attempting the interpretation of a work of art without a closely integrated knowledge of the artist. Ernst Kris, writing in *Art and Psychoanalysis*, is resolute on this point.[7] Is psychoanalytic criticism essentially biography, acquired at first hand or hypothesized from the work? But if Freud makes too much of the specific provenance of the work of art, the Jungians, on the other hand, seem to ignore it completely in the grandiose structure of their psychology.

I prefer to believe that Jung at his best is a Freudian and a very good one. He serves also the good purpose of standing as a caveat to the Freudians against their tendency toward the provincial. Born out of the same psychological egg, Freud has contracted the human condition into a very dense, finite sphere of causes, while Jung has expanded the human psyche into a nebula stretching light years of thought back to the Magdalenians, even back to the protozoans. In their bearing toward literature the one suffers the cramp of meanness; the other, the vagueness of dispersion. At his worst the Freudian is a hairsplitter; the Jungian is a sleepwalker.

Assuredly the artist's life is of unique importance in the work of art. But if we reject the notion that the etiology of the work lies always in some obscure hurt, or in some complex substitutive or restitutive process that is the exclusive peculiarity of one artist, then we can to a certain extent discount as critically unimportant the unknown or unknowable event in the artist's biography. And, if the worst comes to the worst, we can advance in the presumption that he *had* a life and that it was more or less like our own. What we have come to realize, with Freud, is that the standard, the commonplace experience in the artist's arsenal of available and valuable experiences is ultimately more important than the rare and the extraordinary experience.

As an example of such an experience and the attitude toward it that is almost absurdly typical of the modern sensibility, I should like to quote an excerpt from Volume 1 of Ernest Jones's *Life and Works of Sigmund Freud.* Jones is describing two of the most important events in Freud's early life. He writes:

> On the journey from Leipzig to Vienna a year later, Freud had occasion to see his mother naked: an awesome fact which forty years later he related in a letter to [Wilhelm] Fliess—but in Latin! . . .
>
> Darker problems arose when it dawned on him that some man was even more intimate with his mother than he was. Before he was two years old, for the second time another baby was on the way, and soon visibly so.
>
> Jealousy of the intruder, and anger for whoever had seduced his mother into such an unfaithful proceeding, were inevitable. Discarding his knowledge of the sleeping conditions in the house, he rejected the unbearable thought that the nefarious person could be his beloved and perfect father. It was early days to grapple with the inevitable problem of reality![8]

The tone is melodramatic, almost Dickensian; the material is utterly banal—the combination mock-heroic. Yet, considering the edifice—or, for a moment to be cynical, the *industry*—this vision, seen through the eyes of genius, has raised, one must allow, the tone as completely fitted to the situation. It is compatible with the new decorum.

With an artist like Kafka it is almost essential that we consider domestic trifles before we attempt to come to any full understanding of his work. He does not seem to perform what was the time-honored function of the artist—to squeeze the universal into the local and finite dramatic situation—the tacit recognition of the correspondence between the macrocosm and the microcosm. Instead, he expands the local, the finite—in his case the family situation—into the universal. Kafka Senior is not our Father Which Art in Heaven, but our Father Which Art in Heaven is Kafka the local haberdasher. In any but post–Freudian eyes this magnification might seem contemptible, the reduction absurd. But depth psychology has opened new vistas for the artist; and Kafka's vision has the validity of a coat described from inside out, in terms of seams, selvage, lining, and stains.

A further question remains of the artist's complicity in this psychoanalysis of art. To what extent is he conscious of his use of his insights in the depths? Is his work improved, damaged, or merely changed by the conscious use of psychoanalytic recognition? I feel that here the present need for psychological criticism is most justified. Stimulated by the fresh realities that have always lain like ancient cities beneath the naturalistic surface, the modern artist has set himself the task of exploring his unconscious. But he has not reckoned on the oxymoronic nature of darkness visible. It is not only Eros who vanishes when Psyche holds her candle to him; Psyche herself shrinks from illumination. The subject matter of the artist changes; the psychological energy and the disguises it wears maintain the same unconscious-conscious relationship. Sandor Ferenczi's description of the nature of symbol makes the relationship clear. "A substitutive, illustrative replacement," he says, "becomes the expression for something hidden. . . ." It occurs when the "more important member of the equation is repressed. Then the true symbol evolves."[9] The writer must pursue his unconscious bents in blindness. The recognition of the psychological correctness of the work must of necessity be an *a posteriori* function of the critic.

In fact the writer cannot win. Ignorance of Freud's Higher Laws is no excuse for flouting them. Indeed it is more damning. And, on the other hand, any conscious tampering with the unconscious, like the attempts of some benighted Boeotian to give poor dear Oedipus traveling directions to Thebes, merely makes him late for those marvelous appointments of his with Fate.

By way of illustrative material I became interested a few months back in two stories by the Irish writer Frank O'Connor—the one, "My Oedipus Complex," written later (1952) for *The New Yorker*, the other, "Judas," written earlier (1948). "My Oedipus Complex" is a Freudian *jeu d'esprit*, a kind of talking *id* story. Its comedy derives from the five-year-old child's innocently calling the turns in his Oedipal relationship with his mother. The father returns from the war and the boy assumes that the mother resents the interloper as much as he does. When the mother and the father both reject the child, the boy is crushed by the betrayal. Finally the mother has a second child; the father in his turn is made to take second place; and he and the son make common cause.

> After a while it came to me what he was mad about. It was his turn now. After turning me out of the big bed he had been turned out himself. Mother had no consideration now for anyone but that poisonous pup, Sonny. I couldn't help feeling sorry for Father. I had been through it all myself, and even at that age I was magnanimous. I began to stroke him down and say "There! There!" He wasn't exactly responsive.
>   "Aren't you asleep either?" he snarled.
>   "Ah, come on and put your arm around us, can't you?" I said, and he did, in a sort of way. Gingerly, I suppose, is how you'd describe it. He was very bony but better than nothing.[10]

It is obvious that in this story O'Connor is playing with some very simple counters, very conscious of the comic possibilities of Freud considered along broad, almost slapstick lines.

In his other story, "Judas," something very different happens. Again the overall effect is comic, but now in the profounder sense of the word; "Judas" is the comedy of the Oedipus complex, exploring the relationship and its ramifications, and resolving them.

In "Judas," Jerry, the young man, lives alone with his widowed mother. Being an only child, he explains, he "never knocked around the way the other fellows did." Finally, he falls for a girl, a nurse, whom he describes as a "well-educated, superior girl." He is shy of the girl and at the same time torn in his loyalty to his mother. He feels himself to be corrupt, unworthy of the girl. "Several times she asked me in, but I was too nervous. I knew I'd lose my head, break the china, use some dirty word, and then go home and cut my throat." Finally, wandering, desperate, he meets her in the street. She begins to understand his feelings about her. But in explaining her own position, and in trying to put him at his ease, she refers casually to her experiences with other young men in times past. Jerry's reaction is shock. "This was worse than appalling. This was a nightmare. Kitty, whom I had thought so angelic talking in cold blood about 'spooning' with fellows all over the house." [11] He composes himself, finally, to accept her paradoxical behavior; and then, since it is late, he goes home to his mother feeling extremely guilty.

With his mother, who has waited up for him, he is short to the point of brutality. But later on, in the middle of the night, overcome by remorse he wakes her to apologize, only to burst into tears and have her fold him in her arms.

"Judas," while it obviously deals with what is an extension of the same material that informs "My Oedipus Complex," seems to move structurally along lines dictated less by a sense of psychological determination than by a conscious artistic impulse. Yet I should like to suggest that "Judas," in respect to the psychological—that is, the unconscious—determination of its movement, is more directed than the playfully worked out Oedipal scheme of "My Oedipus Complex."

As Freud describes the Oedipal relationships, he proposes hypothetically that at some point in his prehistory (before any systematic memory formation takes place), the child has imagined for himself a situation in which he is his mother's sole support and companion—a situation that can come about in actuality if the father dies. Added to this is the image unconsciously retained and treasured, of the mother as one's first and only love, the ideal.

After a certain point the child consciously realizes that his mother cannot become, for many reasons (because the father has, after all, prior claims and threatens to maintain them, because the mother herself rejects him, and because society frowns on it) an object of his sexual love in reality. With this realization, and with the growing awareness of the world about him, he finds other objects with whom he can, with the permission and even the approval of himself and the world, explore the possibilities of mutual sexual attraction.

But still, especially if the original Oedipal involvement is reinforced by circumstances and so survives childhood, there is an unconscious clinging to the mother image, and this clinging constitutes one of the normal and some of the abnormal factors in the determination of the young man's choice of woman. It is a choice whose governing polarities are the contradictory ones of the incestuous fixation on the mother image and the incest barrier which forbids it.

What will the girl like the girl who married dear old dad be like? First of all, and most important, she will be pure, not a "doll" like the loose girls that Jerry Moynihan's friends go around with. The social equivalent of purity, being a "well-educated, superior girl," may represent this condition. She must also be sexually unattainable, a condition that makes the relationship almost impossible unless it ends in marriage. Another determinant, more remote, is the chosen woman's identification with something like the maternal function. Can she cook (very often waitresses are fatally attractive) or is she motherly toward the young or the infirm? Wealth is a good substitute for the ability to mother. Nurses are proverbially attractive and usually to men who are under their care.

As for the man, one can draw certain inferences about him. He is apt, because of his unconscious preference for the pure maternal image, to keep himself aloof, purer than his friends.

He is apt, too, to make a profound distinction, which is actually only a distinction between the obverse and reverse, between women who are sexually sophisticated or downright promiscuous, and the sort of girl one marries to keep company with. For the one he has a fear, tempered with a guilty desire, for the other a guilty desire tempered with fear. As one of those endearing, inspired informants of Havelock Ellis, those gourmets of sensuality, describes it,

> . . . owing to the impressions of early youth, woman (even if we feel contempt for her in theory) is placed above us, on a certain pedestal, as an almost sacred being. . . . Now sensuality and sexual desire are considered as rather vulgar, and a little dirty, even ridiculous and degrading, not to say bestial. The woman who enjoys it, is therefore, rather like a profaned altar.[12]

More obscurely, the son has mixed feelings about his mother, or for that matter, anyone's mother. Between the lines of his overt affection one can read a certain hostility and resentment. It is an impatience, compounded of guilty desire, and a frustration which defines itself consciously as an accusation of the mother for making one's own love-life impossible. In the repression of this hostility, the tendency is to turn it against oneself, to contemplate, instead of murder, suicide.

How does "Judas" fulfill these disinterested conditions? The comic side of the story deals with Jerry Moynihan's suicidal despair at being unable to establish an understanding relationship with the girl, Kitty, and his shock at finding out that she is more experienced in the ways of love than he thought. Because he feels his degraded feelings of lust make her avoid him, he attributes her avoiding him to the maternal virtue of purity. But the irony of the situation is heightened by his discovery that she is not so innocent. The discovery is not a comfort but a positive cause for alarm.

Thus the dilemma defines itself; Kitty must be both like and yet different from the mother, and Jerry must be both the innocent child, and not be the innocent child. What precipitates the overt hostility toward the mother in contrast to the comic suicidal despair that precedes it (the story is littered with razors and penknives) is in effect the rejection of the mother brought about by his success with another woman, who can be a valid successor to his mother. Kitty, by being bold, has given him courage. She is cross with her own mother and sees her clearly. She accepts Jerry with the correct mixture of boldness and modesty, and so his mother must finally move aside.

Curious about the genesis of both these stories, I wrote to Frank O'Connor and received a thoughtfully considered reply, the gist of which I quote.

About the story ["Judas"] I don't believe when I wrote it that I was even aware that it dealt with an Oedipal situation. Of course I had the same sort of intense attachment to my mother, but the chap in the story is not me. . . . The nurse on the other hand is almost a straight portrait of my first girl, and she *is* a nurse and she *was* superior. I certainly hadn't read Freud, and if I knew the term it was in the way I now talk about getting to first base without ever having seen a baseball match and ignorant of what a base looks like.

Naturally when I wrote "My Oedipus Complex" I knew Freud very well, and was taking pride in my iconoclasm. I always maintain that every chap who has an attractive mother and hasn't fallen in love with her and planned to murder his dad is missing one of the best things in life.

[1959]

Notes

NOTES TO CHAPTER I

1. Friedrich Nietzsche, *Beyond Good and Evil*, trans. Walter Kauffmann (New York: Vintage Books, 1966), p. 13.

2. Erik Erikson, *Childhood and Society* (New York: Norton, 1950), pp. 250 ff.

3. Friedrich Nietzsche, *"Ecce Homo" and "The Birth of Tragedy,"* trans. Clifton Fadiman (New York: Modern Library, 1927), pp. 279–80.

4. One observes with considerable frequency the portrayal in modern fiction of the psychoanalyst as charlatan, the flimflam man who in some way or other discredits himself as seer. Perhaps the tradition is as old as Sophocles' Tiresias whom Oedipus mocks for being blind. Mann's Dr. Krokowski is an analyst who dabbles in necromancy; Bellow's Dr. Tamkin dabbles in futures on Wall Street, and elsewhere (in *Herzog*) another analyst qualifies his good advice with private lust. The inventory grows with every new publisher's list. It is irony's last stand.

5. Phyllis Greenacre, *Swift and Carroll: A Psychoanalytic Study of Two Lives* (New York: International Universities Press, 1955), p. 27.

6. Thomas Mann, *Death in Venice*, trans. H. T. Lowe-Porter (New York: Vintage Books, 1963), p. 46.

7. "Death is the mother of beauty," says Wallace Stevens. The terrible implications of the line seem to touch the core of the tragic emotion. Even a casual review of those works that represent highwater marks in the careers of genius— "Lycidas," *Hamlet*, *In Memoriam*, the great Odes of Keats, *Sons and Lovers*, *To the Lighthouse*—would suggest that the capacity for great grief enlarges the capacity for more intense creativity, that great artists are greater for suffering great losses, and that the magical, necromantic recovery of lost loved objects is the occluded subject of works whose form is not necessarily that of tragedy. It would suggest further that our sense of the tragic would normally include our terror and pity for the poet who has had to undergo this ordeal. The Romantic elision of art and artist, reinforced by the psychoanalytic insight, renders Keats' Odes and *Sons and Lovers* "tragic," in a peculiarly modern sense, which includes, although we dare not confess it, a willingness to conceive of the artist himself as the tragic protagonist. Certainly the modern artist tends increasingly to encourage this confusion. Psychoanalytic theory suggests the final grim note that creativity originates in an oral-sadistic matrix, that a work of art is the residue of a cannibal-feast in

257

which the dead or missing have been orally incorporated. Joyce sugests this in both *Ulysses* and *Finnegans Wake*—"Ghoul, corpsechewer," cries Stephen's mourning conscience. *Finnegans Wake* is of course just that, and includes the cannibalizing of the dead.

8. Nietzsche, *Beyond Good and Evil*, p. 233.

9. Otto Rank, *Beyond Psychology* (Camden, N.J.: Haddon craftsmen, 1941), pp. 282–83.

10. Arthur Schopenhauer, *The World as Will and Representation*, trans. E. F. J. Payne (Indian Hills, Col.: Falcon Wing Press, 1958), 1:193–94 *et passim*. Schopenhauer's discussion of madness and genius anticipates our own expanded view of this relationship between passion and judgment, i.e., that sanity is a corked bottle of volatile emotions, and that leakage betrays itself in little mini-psychotic episodes that are physically manifested in gestures. Freud's *The Psychopathology of Everyday Life* is an exploration of this conception.

11. Ezra Pound, in an essay on Brancusi, speaks of works of art which "attract by a resembling unlikeness." In his search for "primary forms" and "absolute rhythms," he makes the same demands of artistic processes that psychoanalysis does.

12. Edward S. Tauber and Maurice R. Green, *Prelogical Experience* (New York: Basic Books, 1959), pp. 45–46.

13. Friedrich Nietzsche, *Thus Spake Zarathustra*, trans. Thomas Common (New York: Gordon Press, 1974), p. x.

14. Ella Freedman Sharpe, *Collected Papers on Psychoanalysis* (London: Hogarth Press, 1950), p. 252 *et passim*.

15. Sigmund Freud, *Collected Papers*, trans. Joan Riviere (London: Hogarth Press and Inst. of Psycho-analysis, 1950), 5: 247 ff.

16. Sharpe, *Collected Papers*, p. 261.

17. Norman Mailer, *Miami and the Siege of Chicago* (Cleveland: World Pub. Co., 1969), pp. 91–92.

18. Jean Dubuffet in "Notes and Comments," *The New Yorker*, 16 June 1973, pp. 28 ff. "For me, insanity is supersanity," he [Dubuffet] said. "The normal is psychotic—a collective psychosis. Normal means lack of imagination, lack of creativity." I quote this excerpt, not because it *is* the definitive statement, but because it has the ring of contemporaneity by virtue of its being an *overstatement* of the modern artist's position, an elaboration on Schopenhauer's covert respect for madness and perhaps an atavistic awe inherent in human society for the deviant. R. D. Laing has put it more sensibly in *The Divided Self*.

19. Anton Ehrenzweig, *The Psychoanalysis of Artistic Vision and Hearing* (London: Routledge and Kegan Paul, 1953), pp. 71 ff.

20. Once more, Joyce's *Ulysses* and *Finnegans Wake* are, because of my limited familiarity with other languages, my major examples, to which I could add Saul Bellow's *Herzog*, and Philip Roth's *Portnoy's Complaint*. There is ample reason to classify Ibsen as a tragicomic dramatist and an intuitive psychoanalyst. *Ghosts* and *Hedda Gabler*, given the proper actors, the lighting and other deceptions normal to the theater, excite our tears and fears. But Ibsen, read or played in cold blood, is about as detached from the tragic fates of Oswald and Hedda as Ben Jonson would be from the downfalls of Volpone and Mosca. What dies on Ibsen's stage is not so much a richly endowed human being, but an item of human obtuseness that might formerly have been regarded as a heroic, virtuous, or tragic quality.

NOTES TO CHAPTER 2

1. Samuel Daniel, *A Defence of Rhyme*, in *Criticism: The Major Texts*, ed. Walter Jackson Bate (New York: Harcourt, Brace, 1952), p. 109.
2. Source of D. W.'s citation of William James not located by eds.
3. Uncited quotation by D. W. Eds. assume from Sandor Ferenczi.
4. Sandor Ferenczi, *Sex in Psychoanalysis*, trans. Ernest Jones (New York: Dover Publications, 1956), pp. 234–35.

NOTES TO CHAPTER 3

1. Ernest Hemingway, *The Torrents of Spring*, in *The Hemingway Reader*, ed. Charles Poore (New York: Charles Scribner's Sons, 1953), pp. 62–63.
2. Stephen Crane, *The Red Badge of Courage*, ed. Sculley Bradley et al. (New York: W. W. Norton and Co., Inc., 1962), p. 90. All subsequent references to this edition will appear in the text.
3. Philip Young, *Ernest Hemingway* (New York: Rinehart, 1952), p. 162.
4. Charles Fenton, *The Apprenticeship of Ernest Hemingway* (New York: Farrar, Straus & Young, 1954), p. 56.
5. John Berryman, *Stephen Crane* (New York: William Sloane Assoc. 1950), p. 218.
6. Ibid., p. 222.
7. Robert Wooster Stallman, "Notes toward an Analysis of *The Red Badge of Courage*," in *The Red Badge of Courage*, ed. S. Bradley, pp. 248–54.
8. Stephen Crane, "Letter to John N. Hilliard," *Academy*, 59 (11 August 1900):116.
9. Berryman, *Stephen Crane*, pp. 6–9.
10. Ibid., p. 306.
11. Ibid., pp. 288–89.
12. Ibid., pp. 86–88.
13. Ovid, *Metamorphoses*, 8:188.
14. W. H. Frink, *Morbid Fears and Compulsions* (New York: Moffat, Yard and Co., 1918), p. 153.
15. Berryman, *Stephen Crane*, pp. 279–80.
16. Ibid., p. 78.
17. Sigmund Freud, "Thoughts for the Times on War and Death," *Collected Papers* (London: Hogarth Press, 1955), 4:288–317.
18. Otto Fenichel, *The Psychoanalytic Theory of Neurosis* (New York: W. W. Norton and Co., Inc., 1945), p. 56.
19. Ibid., p. 364.
20. Ibid., p. 484.
21. Gregory Zilboorg, "Fear of Death," *Psychoanalytic Quarterly* 12 (October 1943):474.
22. Abram Kardiner and Herbert Spiegel, *War Stress and Neurotic Illness* (New York: Paul B. Hoeber, Inc., 1947), p. 208.
23. Zilboorg, "Fear of Death," pp. 474–75.

24. Young, *Ernest Hemingway*, p. 26.

25. Stephen Crane, *"Maggie" and Other Stories*, ed. Austin McC. Fox (New York, 1960), p. 285. All subsequent references to these stories will appear in the text.

NOTES TO CHAPTER 4

1. Lionel Trilling, "Manners, Morals, and the Novel," *The Liberal Imagination* (New York: Doubleday, n.d.), p. 207.

2. *Sherwood Anderson's Memoirs* (New York: Harcourt, Brace, 1942), p. 116.

3. Ibid., p. 212.

4. Sherwood Anderson, *Winesburg, Ohio* (New York: Viking Press, 1963), p. 87.

5. Trilling, "Sherwood Anderson," *The Liberal Imagination*, pp. 27–28.

6. Anderson, *Winesburg, Ohio*, p. 168.

7. *Sherwood Anderson's Memoirs*, pp. 247–48.

8. Sherwood Anderson, *Poor White* (New York: Viking Press, 1967), pp. 36, 44.

9. Ibid., p. 44.

10. Ibid., pp. 60–62.

11. Ibid., p. 94.

12. Ibid., p. 112.

13. Ibid., p. 49.

14. Ibid., p. 180.

15. Ibid., p. 262.

16. *Sherwood Anderson's Memoirs*, pp. 168–69.

17. Anderson, *Poor White*, p. 34.

18. Ibid., p. 29.

19. Ibid., pp. 279–80.

20. Ibid., p. 318.

21. Ibid., pp. 346–47.

22. Ibid., p. 360.

23. *Sherwood Anderson's Memoirs*, pp. 212, 247.

24. Ibid., p. 48.

25. Ibid., p. 114.

26. Otto Fenichel, *The Psychoanalytical Theory of Neurosis* (New York: W. W. Norton and Co., 1945), p. 89.

27. *Sherwood Anderson's Memoirs*, p. 506.

28. Ibid., p. 79.

29. Paul Rosenfeld, ed., *The Sherwood Anderson Reader* (Boston: Houghton Mifflin Co., 1947), p. 25.

30. Ibid., pp. 253–54.

31. Ibid., p. 131.

32. Ibid., p. 152.

NOTES TO CHAPTER 5

1. Ernest Hemingway, *A Farewell to Arms* (New York: Charles Scribner's Sons, 1969), p. 178.

2. Ibid., pp. 249, 327.

3. Ernest Hemingway, *Across the River and into the Trees* (New York: Charles Scribner's Sons, 1950), p. 71.

4. Ernest Hemingway, *Death in the Afternoon* (Middlesex: Penguin Books, n.d.), p. 58.

5. Ibid., p. 80.

6. Ibid., p. 102.

7. Hemingway, *A Farewell to Arms*, p. 327.

8. Ernest Hemingway, "The Short Happy Life of Francis Macomber," in *The Short Stories* (New York: Charles Scribner's Sons, 1953), p. 8.

9. Hemingway, *A Farewell to Arms*, p. 184.

10. Hemingway, *Death in the Afternoon*, p. 6.

11. Hemingway, *The Short Stories*, p. 267.

12. Ibid., p. 147.

13. Ibid., pp. 489–90.

14. Ibid., p. 217.

15. Hemingway, *Death in the Afternoon*, p. 116.

16. Ernest Hemingway, *The Sun Also Rises* (New York: Charles Scribner's Sons, 1954), p. 148.

17. Ibid., pp. 115–16.

18. Ibid., p. 49.

19. Ibid., pp. 148–49.

NOTES TO CHAPTER 6

1. Aristotle, *The Poetics*, Hamilton Fyfe, ed. (London: Heinemann, 1967), 4:2–4.

2. Tennyson, "Locksley Hall Sixty Years After," in *The Poetical Works of Tennyson* (London: Oxford University Press, 1962), 11:139–48.

3. Theodore Dreiser, *Hey, Rub-a-Dub-Dub!* (London: Constable, 1931), p. 179.

4. *Works and Days of Hesiod*, in *The Homeric Hymns and Homerica*, Hugh G. Evelyn-White, trans. (London: Heinemann, 1967), 11:182–84, 190–92, 195–96.

5. James Joyce, *Ulysses* (New York: Random House, 1961), p. 734.

NOTES TO CHAPTER 7

1. William Faulkner, *Go Down, Moses* (New York: Modern Library, 1955), pp. 295–96.

2. William Faulkner, *The Hamlet* (New York: Vintage, 1964), pp. 149, 115, 124.

3. Ibid., p. 119.
4. Ibid., pp. 184–85.
5. William Faulkner, *Selected Short Stories* (New York: Modern Library, 1962), pp. 62, 77.
6. Faulkner, *Go Down, Moses*, p. 5.
7. Ibid., p. 10.
8. Faulkner, *Selected Short Stories*, pp. 67, 69.
9. Ibid., p. 66.
10. Bertram Doyle, *The Etiquette of Race Relations in the South* (Chicago: University of Chicago Press, 1937), p. 7.
11. C. J. Jung, *Psychology of the Unconscious* (New York: Dodd, Mead and Co., 1931), p. 205.
12. James G. Frazer, *The Golden Bough* (London: Macmillan and Co., 1941), p. 3.
13. Ibid., p. 157.
14. Ibid., p. 576.
15. Ibid., p. 587.
16. Ibid., p. 73.
17. Doyle, *The Etiquette of Race Relations*, p. 25.
18. Ibid., p. 16.
19. Faulkner, *Go Down, Moses*, p. 13.
20. Faulkner, *Selected Short Stories*, pp. 62, 69, 71, 73.
21. Ibid., p. 67.
22. Ibid., p. 64.

NOTES TO CHAPTER 8

1. Saul Bellow, *Seize the Day* (New York: Viking Press, 1956). Subsequent references to this edition will appear in the text.
2. Otto Fenichel, *The Psychoanalytic Theory of Neurosis* (New York: W. W. Norton and Co., Inc., 1945), p. 9.
3. Sigmund Freud, "Psychopathic Characters on the Stage," *Psychoanalytic Quarterly* 11, 2 (1942):462.
4. Franz Kafka, "Letter to His Father," *Dearest Father*, trans. Ernst Kaiser (New York: Schocken Books, 1954), p. 163.
5. Kafka, "Letter to His Father," p. 173.
6. Ibid., p. 173.
7. Ibid., p. 158.
8. Fenichel, *The Psychoanalytic Theory*, p. 94.
9. Bernhard Berliner, "On Some Psychodynamics of Masochism," *Psychoanalytic Quarterly* 16, 4 (1947):460, 461–71 passim.
10. Ibid., p. 461.
11. Ibid., p. 462.
12. Ibid., pp. 463, 461.
13. Ibid., p. 464.
14. Ibid., p. 466.
15. Ibid., p. 467.
16. Ibid., p. 468.

17. Ibid., pp. 470, 471.

18. Fenichel, *The Psychoanalytic Theory*, p. 250.

19. Ibid., p. 528.

20. Karl Abraham, "Oral Eroticism and Character," *Selected Papers of Psychoanalysis*, trans. Douglas Bryan (New York: Basic Books, 1953), p. 400.

21. Freud, "Psychopathic Characters," p. 464.

22. William C. Menninger, "Characterological and Symptomatic Expressions Related to the Anal Phase of Psychosexual Development," *Psychoanalytic Quarterly* 12, 2 (1943):161–92 passim.

23. Fenichel, *The Psychoanalytic Theory*, p. 487.

24. Sigmund Freud, "Dostoevsky and Parricide," *Collected Papers*, trans. Joan Riviere (London: Hogarth Press, 1950), 5:222–42 passim.

25. Abraham, "Oral Eroticism and Character," p. 400.

26. Fenichel, *The Psychoanalytic Theory*, p. 317.

27. Ibid., pp. 312, 313, 316.

28. Abraham, "Transformations of Scoptophilia," *Selected Papers of Psychoanalysis*, trans. Douglas Bryan, p. 232.

NOTES TO CHAPTER 9

1. Sandor Ferenczi, "The Nosology of Male Homosexuality (Homo-eroticism)," *Sex in Psychoanalysis*, trans. Ernest Jones (New York: R. Brunner, 1950), p. 267.

2. Aldous Huxley, ed., *The Letters of D. H. Lawrence*, 1st ed., (New York: Viking Press, 1932), p. 458.

3. Ibid., p. 688.

4. Lawrence Durrell, *Balthazar* (New York: Dutton, 1958), p. 114.

5. Sylvan Keiser, "Body Ego during Orgasm," *Psychoanalytic Quarterly* 21 (April 1952):153–56.

6. Harry Thornton Moore, *The Intelligent Heart: The Story of D. H. Lawrence* (New York: Farrar, Straus & Young, 1954), p. 209.

7. D. H. Lawrence, *The Rainbow* (New York: Modern Library, n.d.), pp. 222–23.

8. Ibid., p. 452.

9. Ibid., p. 303. Suppressed bracketed quotation from Moore, *The Intelligent Heart*, p. 209.

10. Lawrence, *The Rainbow*, pp. 436–37.

11. Edward Nehls, ed., *A Composite Biography of D. H. Lawrence* (Madison: University of Wisconsin Press, 1958), 1:106.

12. D. H. Lawrence, *Women in Love* (New York: Modern Library, n.d.), p. 394.

13. D. H. Lawrence, *Aaron's Rod* (New York: Thomas Seltzer, 1922), p. 95.

14. Ibid., p. 31.

15. Ibid., p. 134.

16. Sandor Ferenczi, *Further Contributions to the Theory and Technique of Psychoanalysis*, trans. J. Suttie (London: International Psycho-analytic Library, 1926), p. 279.

17. D. H. Lawrence, *Lady Chatterley's Lover* (New York: Grove Press, 1959), p. 261.

18. D. H. Lawrence, *The Plumed Serpent* (New York: Alfred A. Knopf, 1926), pp. 451–52.

NOTES TO CHAPTER 10

1. William Butler Yeats, *Essays* (New York: Macmillan Co., 1924), p. 503.
2. Sigmund Freud, "Dostoevsky and Parricide," in *Collected Papers*, vol. 5, ed. James Strachey (London: Hogarth Press, 1953), p. 223.
3. Thomas Mann, *The Magic Mountain* (New York: Random House, 1953), p. 382.
4. Ibid., pp. 396, 404, 461.
5. Ibid., p. 464.
6. Ibid., p. 601.
7. Feodor Dostoevsky, *Diary of a Writer*, trans. Boris Bansol (Santa Barbara, Calif.: Peregrine Smith, 1979), p. 7.
8. Mann, *The Magic Mountain*, p. 466.
9. Feodor Dostoevsky, *The Brothers Karamazov*, trans. Constance Garnett (New York: New American Library, 1957), p. 224.
10. Feodor Dostoevsky, *Notes from the Underground*, trans. Constance Garnett (New York: Dell, 1960), p. 57.
11. Source of D. W.'s citation of Oscar Wilde not located by eds.

NOTES TO CHAPTER 11

1. William Phillips, ed., *Art and Psychoanalysis* (New York: Criterion Books, 1957).
2. Ella Freeman Sharpe, *Collected Papers on Psychoanalysis* (London: Hogarth Press, 1950), pp. 217–26.
3. Kenneth Burke, *Philosophy of Literary Form* (Baton Rouge: University of Louisiana Press, 1941), pp. 71–73.
4. Lionel Trilling, "Art and Neurosis," *The Liberal Imagination* (New York: Doubleday, 1950), p. 169.
5. T. S. Eliot, "Hamlet and His Problem," *Selected Essays* (New York: Harcourt-Brace and Co., 1932), p. 125.
6. Sigmund Freud, "An Obsessional Neurosis," in *The Standard Edition*, ed. and trans. James Strachey (London: Hogarth Press, 1955–61), 10:175–76.
7. Ernst Kris, "The Contributions and Limitations of Psychoanalysis," in *Art and Psychoanalysis*, ed. William Phillips, pp. 271–91.
8. Ernest Jones, *The Life and Works of Sigmund Freud* (New York: Basic Books, 1959), vol. 1, p. 13.
9. Sandor Ferenczi, *Sex in Psychoanalysis*, trans. Ernest Jones (New York: Dover Publications, 1956), pp. 234–35.
10. Frank O'Connor, "My Oedipus Complex," in *Stories by Frank O'Connor* (New York: Alfred A. Knopf, 1952), p. 262.
11. O'Connor, *Stories*, p. 164.
12. Havelock Ellis, *Studies in the Psychology of Sex* (Philadelphia: F. A. Davis, 1928), p. 382.

Index